Visible Hands

Taking Responsibility for Social Development

An UNRISD Report for Geneva 2000

Acknowledgements

EDITORIAL TEAM

- Peter Utting (Project co-ordinator)
- Cynthia Hewitt de Alcántara, Yusuf Bangura, Thandika Mkandawire, Shahra Razavi, Peter Utting and David Westendorff (Chapter co-ordinators)
- Peter Stalker and Cynthia Hewitt de Alcántara (Principal editors)
- Jenifer Freedman (Editor)
- Virginia Rodríguez, Toshihiro Nakamura and Matthias Rosenberg (Research assistants)
- Christine Vuilleumier (Secretarial assistant)
- Rosemary Max (Dissemination)
- Latitudesign, Geneva (Design and layout)

CONTRIBUTORS

The report draws on background papers by:

Bill Adams, Emmanuel Akwetey, Nadje Al-Ali, Adrian Atkinson, Solon Barraclough, Asef Bayat, Yusuf Bangura, David Barkin, Björn Beckman, Andrew Clayton, Andrea Cornwall, Nikki Craske, Bob Deacon, Yash Ghai, Cynthia Hewitt de Alcántara, John Foster, Joe Foweraker, Alan Fowler, Dan Gallin, Krishna Ghimire, Karl Gostern, Evelyne Huber, Yudit Kiss, Eddie Koch, Lars Lindström, Shail Mayaram, Thandika Mkandawire, Toshihiro Nakamura, Justine Nannyonjo, Andrew Nickson, Geoffrey Nkandimeng, Peter Oakley, Ruth Pearson, Rosalind Petchesky, Jules Pretty, Vithal Rajan, Shahra Razavi, Thimma Reddy, Charles Reilly, Virginia Rodríguez, Jorge Schvarzer, Ajit Singh, Georg Sørensen, Ramya Subrahmanian, John Stephens, Jon Taylor, Ole Therkildsen, Peter Utting, Edward Webster, and David Westendorff.

UNRISD would like to thank the United Nations Division for Social Policy and Development, and the governments of the Netherlands, Sweden and Switzerland for their financial contribution to this project. The Institute also acknowledges the support of these governments and those of Denmark, Finland, Mexico, Norway and the United Kingdom, which provide its core funding.

Printed in Switzerland
GE.00-01444 – May 2000 – 4,000
UNRISD / VH-E / 00 / 1

ISBN 92-9085-032-9

Preface

The World Summit for Social Development, held in Copenhagen in March 1995, marked a watershed in international thinking about development. Following years when international financial institutions and many government leaders had narrowly focused their attention on economic growth and stabilization, 117 heads of state or government committed themselves "to creating an economic, political, social, cultural and legal environment that will enable people to achieve social development" (Commitment 1 of the Copenhagen Declaration).

The Summit's Declaration and Programme of Action stressed the importance of equity, participation, empowerment and solidarity. Social development depended not only on economic growth and getting the so-called fundamentals of macroeconomic policy right, but also on social policy and better distribution of the benefits of growth. Effective institutions were also essential—and were seen to include a strengthened role for the state; a more efficient, transparent and accountable public sector; more supportive international agencies; partnerships with the private sector; and the active participation of civil society organizations in development interventions and policy making.

The task of getting the institutions right was to be accompanied by new approaches to financing social development and dealing with one of the major constraints on development for many countries in Africa and Latin America: the debt burden. The Social Summit also called for democracy and development to be more responsive to women's interests and concerns, and stressed the need to promote people-centred sustainable development.

But are the reforms that have been proposed really creating an enabling environment for social development? This report assesses what has been achieved in several key areas of policy and institutional reform, and identifies some of the major conditions and constraints that have impeded progress. The analysis is not restricted to initiatives directly associated with the Social Summit; it considers reforms that gained prominence in the 1990s, reflecting more generally the attempt to integrate social concerns into development strategies—a recognition reinforced not only by the Social Summit but also by other global summits, including those held in Rio, Cairo, Beijing and Istanbul.

Given the short time since the Social Summit, it is perhaps unrealistic to expect significant progress toward meeting the goals set out there. Furthermore, the absence of reliable data makes it extremely difficult to measure change. What we should expect, however, is progress in terms of policy changes and institutional reforms associated with the construction of an enabling environment that would facilitate progress.

What emerges is a fairly disturbing picture of initiatives that remain more at the level of agency rhetoric than effective implementation; and patterns of economic growth, liberalization and inequality that continue to obstruct rather than facilitate progress in the field of social development. Furthermore, the political momentum and pressures that are necessary for promoting social development appear relatively weak, as do the institutions that might mobilize and distribute resources more effectively.

This situation partly reflects the conditions

that prevailed just before and immediately after the Social Summit: the triumphalism of neoliberalism, the unprecedentedly high economic growth in Asian economies, the signs of recovery in Africa and Latin America. All these tended to obviate the need for drastic reform of the dominant model. The development experience of the latter half of the 1990s—in particular, the financial crisis that gripped Asia and again threatened Latin America, coupled with heightened poverty and inequality—revealed that several of the assumptions underpinning development strategy at the time of the Social Summit were seriously flawed or overly optimistic.

Since then there has been some reassessment of the role of the state, as well as some recognition of the limits of private capital flows as a panacea for development. There is greater social sensitivity in the discourse of public agencies and private corporations, and there appears to be a growing consensus regarding the types of institutional and policy reforms needed to facilitate social development, as shown by widespread support for initiatives or concepts associated with debt reduction, targeting, democratization, public sector reform, corporate social responsibility, partnerships, participation and empowerment.

But the role of social policy has been largely restricted to targeting specific social groups, or safety-net-type provisioning. Distributive justice and the role of social policies in facilitating sustained economic growth and development have been ignored. So too have basic issues related to the political economy of resource mobilization—that is, the political and institutional arrangements required to generate resources for social development and to ensure that they reach the needy. While the necessity for social protection has increased, resources allocated for this purpose are actually shrinking as a result of declining aid, cuts in government spending and tax avoidance.

The institutional crisis affecting social development is particularly evident in relation to the role of the state. Continuing pressures to downsize and control spending have imposed limits on a renewed role for the state in national development. The wave of democratization that held out much hope in the early 1990s has often failed to promote better citizen participation in public policy making, non-violent methods for resolving disputes and respect for human rights. Indeed, the increasingly technocratic style of decision making—where "experts" decide policy—undermines the accountability of state institutions and their responsiveness to citizens' demands.

Can actors other than the state play a key role in promoting social development, or even substitute for the state? In recent years, there have been some signs that big business is taking steps in this direction, projecting itself as socially and environmentally responsible. It should, however, be recognized that there are limits to the extent to which corporate social responsibility can be enhanced though voluntary initiatives and partnerships, as opposed to stronger forms of regulation and civil society pressure. Although most donors and multilateral agencies now stress the importance of working with and through civil society organizations, political and institutional constraints at international, national and local levels often limit the effectiveness of civil society both in advocacy and service delivery. International development and financial institutions have not fundamentally changed their governance structures to permit greater participation by civil society, while service delivery in the hands of NGOs often remains fragmented and unsustainable. Moreover, as NGOs become more aid-dependent and thus attempt to adapt to the priorities and procedures of donor agencies, there is a danger that their attributes of innovation and experimentation, and their flexible approach to local needs and conditions, are being undermined.

The insistence at the Social Summit that development interventions should be more responsive to people's priorities and concerns has been taken up particularly in relation to women's needs, and sustainable development. Women have certainly gained many hard-won rights, notably in relation to health, but translating these rights into effective policies and programmes has been constrained by public sector reform, cultural forces and women's limited participation in the formal political system. Not only is it difficult to make institutions more responsive to women's needs—those needs themselves are often increasing in contexts where economic liberalization has imposed additional burdens. So-called people-centred approaches are perhaps strongest in the fields of sustainable development and natural resource management. There is a considerable gap, however, between the rhetoric and experience of adjusting from top-down to participatory design and implementation.

The analysis in this report suggests that there has been increasing recognition of the need to rethink the roles and responsibilities of certain institutions—at both national and international levels—and to consider more closely the social effects of economic policies. However, there has been no major rethinking of economic policies themselves, nor any serious attempt to integrate social and economic policy. Social policy remains largely detached from economic policy, or is seen as an add-on intended to mitigate the social costs of economic liberalization and structural adjustment.

Nevertheless, there are signs that the ideological climate for rethinking development policy is more favourable than it has been for years. There is growing political opposition to the social blindness of structural adjustment, while academic inquiry has eroded the theoretical and empirical anchoring of the dominant neoliberal model. Some new perspectives are gaining force. Human rights and "rights-based" development—emphasizing the primacy of human rights law and people's ability to strengthen their claims on the state—are very much on the agenda.

The idea that development strategy is as much about politics as it is about growth and agency interventions to distribute limited public resources to the poor is to be welcomed, as is the idea that economic and trade rules should be linked to human rights considerations. What remains unclear is who will carry this agenda forward.

What is evident is that globalization faces a crisis of legitimacy—and even the dominant international finance and trade organizations are beginning to question their own prescriptions and models, and to consider some of the critical elements of the Social Summit agenda. This enabling ideological shift is one of the major gains of the latter half of the 1990s. As the Bretton Woods institutions themselves rethink their approach, there is a possibility that the more inclusive social agenda that was sown at Copenhagen will find a more fertile terrain.

A major point that emerges from this report—and is reflected in its title—is that development strategies must reassert human values, human priorities and human agency. The invisible hand of the market may be able to keep the global economy turning. But it takes the human hand to guide it in the most productive direction and to fashion a world that is socially inclusive, transparent and democratically anchored.

Thandika Mkandawire
Director
June 2000

Contents

ACKNOWLEDGEMENTS
PREFACE i
OVERVIEW viii

CHAPTER 1 – Globalization with a human mask 1
From development to adjustment 2
Equity sidelined
The positive East Asian example
The Social Summit 4
Globalization and economic growth 5
Growth and trade
Growth and financial flows
Liberalization and jobs
Unfavourable trends in employment 9
Poverty and inequality 11
The causes of failure 12
New views on growth and social development 14
Targeting the poor
Comprehensive development frameworks
Social services and world trade
Globalizing social standards
New architectures?
Globalization with a human mask 17

CHAPTER 2 – Who pays? Financing social development 19
Debt relief for the poorest countries 20
The HIPC initiative
Pressure for alternatives
Debt relief for middle-income countries 22
The debt crisis
The new bondage
Fresh departures for debt 25
New institutions for dealing with debt
Sovereign debt and bankruptcy
Conditionality
Development assistance 26
Donor fatigue
Reorienting development assistance
The 20/20 initiative
Alternatives to rigid targeting
Alternatives to aid
Tax reform 32
The eroding tax base
Taxing the consumer
International avoidance
Pension reform 35
Other issues in social protection
Mobilizing resources at the grassroots 38
Micro-finance
A balance sheet 40

CHAPTER 3 – Fragile democracies 41
The governing dilemma 42
Incomplete transitions 44
Latin America—military impunity
Overcoming opposition in Africa
The nomenklatura of Eastern Europe and Central Asia
The progress of political parties 46
President or parliament? 47
Industrialized countries
Developing and transition countries
Democracy as means or end? 48
The developmental state
The democratic alternative 50
The rise of the technocrats 51
The rise of the central bank
The rise of the technocratic finance minister
The new managerialism
Encouragement from Washington
Technocracy and democracy
Interest groups and social pacts
Ethnicity and democratization 55
The risk of secession

Electoral systems and ethnic diversity 59
Pluralistic parties and the alternative vote
Consociation and the party list
The merits of different systems

The democratic process 62

CHAPTER 4 – A new mission for the public sector 63

Pressures for reform 64

Fiscal stability 65
Public expenditure targets
Expenditure cuts in the social sector
The social effects of privatization

Managerial efficiency 68
The results of reform
Public accountability

Capacity building 71

The future of public sector reform 72

CHAPTER 5 – Calling corporations to account 75

From confrontation to partnership 78
Codes and verification

Corporate motivation 79

Piecemeal progress 82
Inflated claims

Alternatives to confrontation 85
Voluntary initiatives
Partnerships

From hard to soft 88

CHAPTER 6 – Civil societies 91

Civil society and service delivery 92
The changing character of NGDOs
NGDOs and the international aid system
State versus NGDO provisioning

Precarious partnerships 98
CSO-local government partnerships
Community and gender tensions

Civil society and international advocacy 101
CSOs and the UN
CSOs and the World Bank
CSOs and the Inter-American Development Bank
CSOs and the international treaty bodies
The future for international NGO mobilization

Intelligence, energy and rights 110

CHAPTER 7 – Getting development right for women 111

Women in democratization 112
Working within and against the state
Women in politics
The impact of women on government
Women's NGOs

Fulfilling women's rights 121

Reproductive health rights 122

Women's education rights 127
Why poor girls get less education
Donor-driven education reforms
Quality lags behind quantity

Women's economic rights 131
Work and empowerment
Strategies for achieving economic rights

A counter-alliance for women 136

CHAPTER 8 – Sustaining development 137

Sustainable cities 138
Local Agenda 21

Sustainable agriculture 141
Policies for sustainable agriculture

Sustainable water supplies 146
Damning the dams
New channels for irrigation

Forest conservation 151

Enduring realities 154

Continuity or change? 158

BIBLIOGRAPHICAL NOTE 160

BACKGROUND PAPERS 162

SELECTED BIBLIOGRAPHY 163

ACRONYMS 172

Tables

1.1 International economic activity, 1964–94 (average annual percentage changes) 6
1.2 Percentage annual economic growth, 1991–99 8
1.3 Poverty trends: People living on less than $1 (PPP) per day (millions) 11

2.1 OECD aid compared with military spending 27

3.1 A typology of ethnic structures 57

4.1 Public expenditure as a percentage of GDP 65
4.2 World Bank loan conditions, 1980–94 66

5.1 Corporate power 77

7.1 Women's representation—regional averages 117
7.2 Women in lower houses of parliament in selected countries 117
7.3 A feminist report card on the Cairo Programme of Action 125
7.4 Primary and secondary education by region 127

Figures

1.1 Aggregate net flows to developing countries, 1990–97 6
1.2 Regional distribution of private flows to developing countries, 1970–96 8
1.3 Gini coefficients, selected countries 12

2.1 Evolution of debt, 1985–97 20
2.2 Providing basic social services for all: Bilateral donors' fair share, 1995 30
2.3 Tax revenue and GDP 32
2.4 Sources of tax revenue, 1991–96 33
2.5 Population over 60, 1990–2050 35

3.1 Elections per state 1990–98 42
3.2 Alternations in power and disputed elections, 1990–99 44
3.3 Democracy and economic performance in developing countries 51
3.4 Armed conflicts by region, 1989–97 58
3.5 State creation in the twentieth century 58

4.1 Privatization revenues 67

7.1 The proportion of women in lower houses of parliament worldwide 116
7.2 Women's labour force participation, 1980s and 1990s 133

8.1 Millions of undernourished, 1995/97 141
8.2 Access to safe water by region, 1990–98 148
8.3 Change in forest cover, 1980–95 151

Boxes

1.1 Trade regimes threaten government services 15

2.1 Uganda's debt 22
2.2 Missing targets, the price of debt 24
2.3 Protests over social sector priorities 28
2.4 Salutary pension lessons from Chile 37

3.1 The United Nations promotes democracy 43
3.2 Human rights controversies 49
3.3 Social pacts in South Africa 56

4.1 Tax reforms in Peru 69
4.2 Public sector goals and reforms 73

5.1 Questioning corporate lingo 80
5.2 Jekyll, Inc. and Hyde Ltd. 84
5.3 The UN-business Global Compact 86
5.4 The watchdog on the Web 88
5.5 What makes a good voluntary initiative 89

6.1 A glossary of civil society terms 93
6.2 The need for intermediate organizations in Mumbai 99
6.3 Partnerships in Lima 100
6.4 Adjusting structural adjustment 105
6.5 Community development for peace in Guatemala 106

7.1 "Years of hardship, years of growth": Feminism in an Islamic Republic 113
7.2 Women in local government in India 119
7.3 The story of Futhi 123
7.4 Gender equality and gender equity 126

8.1 Can genetically modified (GM) crops feed the world? 142
8.2 Questioning the value of capital 143
8.3 Reviving land in the Sahel 144
8.4 Land reform, the forgotten issue 147
8.5 International protests against dams 149
8.6 Community forest management in the Philippines 152
8.7 Elusive communities in South Africa 153
8.8 Institutional change? 156

Overview

Globalization with a human mask

The Social Summit took place in Copenhagen in 1995 at a time when free-market enthusiasts were promising to deliver progress for all. But there was widespread discontent with the damage caused by neoliberal policies. Poverty and unemployment were growing rapidly in indebted Third World countries. The collapse of the Soviet Union exposed large numbers of people to the rigours of the market without making adequate provision for social protection. And the welfare state was under threat in OECD countries, where workers were subjected to levels of uncertainty unknown for decades.

Many Summit participants demanded change: a significant increase in economic opportunity, the creation of new and better jobs, a more equitable distribution of income, increased gender equality and inclusiveness. A chorus of well-informed protest also demanded economic policy reform, to reduce crippling instability in global markets and permit robust economic expansion.

In the five years since Copenhagen, events have confirmed the incapacity of the dominant macroeconomic model to meet these challenges. There has been relatively weak growth of global GDP, with unusually high or low growth in some countries or regions. This has been accompanied by falling real wages and the degradation of working conditions for large numbers of people.

The instability of the global financial system has deepened. The collapse of the Mexican economy, brought about by the uncontrolled flight of capital in late 1994, was followed during 1997 by a still larger economic crisis in some East and Southeast Asian countries. Macroeconomic statistics suggest that these nations have staged a rapid recovery, but millions of their people have not.

Unemployment and poverty

The most direct impact of crisis has been on jobs. Unemployment rates doubled in Asian countries where the depression of 1997–98 was worst. And in Latin America, unemployment stood in 1998 at its highest level in 15 years. Even those who do manage to find work are often obliged to accept temporary or part-time jobs. Or they are swelling the informal sector—which, in sub-Saharan Africa, for example, already contains at least two thirds of all jobs.

Wages in the current labour market are generally low. Intense competition for employment means that workers have little capacity to bargain in most countries. And in regions struggling to cope with long-term economic stagnation and indebtedness, the remuneration of workers is often inadequate. Real wages throughout much of Latin America and Africa have yet to return to levels considered normal 20 years ago. Even in China, which has experienced unprecedented growth during the past two decades, restructuring implies hardship. Millions of workers in state and collective enterprises are being placed on leave at half pay or less.

Failure to create sufficient employment has undermined the prospects for poverty reduction. The number of people living in income poverty fell in the mid-1990s but then started to rise again in almost all regions. This is not because the world as a whole has been getting poorer but because the benefits of growth are very unevenly spread. There has been a striking increase in inequality over the past decade.

The causes of failure

Faith in the ability of unregulated markets to provide the best possible environment for human development has gone too far. Too great a reliance on the "invisible hand" of the market is pushing the world toward unsustainable levels of inequality and deprivation. A new balance between public and private interests must be found.

Efficient markets, functioning in a way that

promotes widespread well-being, require the contributions of a well-run public sector. They require a healthy, well-educated and well-informed population. And they require the social stability that grows out of democratic governance and an acceptable level of social security.

In fact, the greater the degree of openness of a market economy—the greater its exposure to market forces—the more important is the role that must be played by national governments in the field of social policy. Yet the thrust of much of the neoliberal agenda has run directly counter to this dictum. For decades, the prevailing orthodoxy has counselled a reduction of state functions. And for decades, governments without the capacity to resist this pressure have been abandoning essential elements of public social provision.

The response of the international community

In response to obvious failures in the current development model, the international community has begun to move in various directions. There is little coherent orientation to this process. In fact, even within a single institution, it is usual to find initiatives that contradict each other—so that what may be accomplished through trying one new approach is largely offset by what may be lost through another.

A renewed emphasis on poverty alleviation is perhaps the most visible new departure. Although this is of vital importance, most agencies and governments are adopting a technocratic approach to a highly complex social problem. Their focus is narrowly remedial and is all too easily associated with an attack on the principle that public services should be extended to all citizens equally. Creating a dual structure of social services—one aimed at the poor and funded by the state, and one aimed at everyone else and provided by the private sector, is good neither for social integration nor for the quality of public services.

Public provision is under attack from other quarters as well. Both the aborted Multilateral Agreement on Investment and discussions in the WTO would convert basic public services into commodities—subject to the same competitive bidding as any other item in the general category of "trade in services".

To offset the divisive incursion of market forces into areas that are essential for social security and stability, there has been renewed support during the past five years for some form of global social standard-setting. When linked to trade sanctions, this has proved extremely controversial. Since increasing globalization requires the elaboration of shared social norms, it is necessary to find a way out of this impasse.

New architectures?

As the social and political nature of the market becomes obvious to a wider group of thinkers and policy makers, there is an incipient return to the kinds of integrated approaches to development that were in vogue in the 1960s and 1970s. The Comprehensive Development Framework of the World Bank, for example, tries to treat structural and social concerns in conjunction with aspects of the macroeconomy and finance.

At the same time, there is much talk of creating a new institutional setting at the international level, a new context for stimulating broadly based growth and reducing unacceptably high degrees of volatility and risk in the global economy. Useful as it may be, this discussion is concerned above all with ensuring the stability of the system. Movement toward alternative development models is not visible.

Moreover, there is complete silence on how to go about creating the social development architecture that would have to underpin the central vision of the Social Summit. This must allow for qualitatively new approaches to growth, based on a new understanding of the vital role of a healthy, literate and secure society in creating the conditions of economic progress. Yet social policy today remains largely detached from economics, or is seen as an add-on intended to remedy the ill effects of misconceived economic development. Until this changes, it is unlikely that the "society for all" envisioned by signatories of the Copenhagen Declaration will be within our grasp.

Who pays? Financing social development

More wealth has been generated over the past few decades than ever before. But far too little of it is being channelled into financing social development. In fact, while levels of social spending have generally been maintained in the advanced industrialized countries, they have plummeted in many highly indebted nations and in the Commonwealth of Independent States.

Debt relief

Since governments in many poor countries pay more in interest to foreign creditors than they allocate to basic social services, a resolution of the long-standing debt crisis is imperative. One apparently promising response to this challenge was the Heavily Indebted Poor Country (HIPC) initiative, launched by the IMF and the World Bank in 1996. In the event, the initiative has achieved little. Responding to pressure from international coalitions, notably Jubilee 2000, the Group of 7 industrialized countries promoted further debt write-offs in 1999, although these also fell short of expectations. The most effective steps have been taken by individual countries, some of which have announced plans to cancel all bilateral debt owed by the poorest nations.

HIPCs account for only about 10 per cent of total Third World debt. The rest is owed by less-poor or middle-income countries, where the debt crisis of the 1990s has evolved into long-term subjection to the international bond markets. The new debt bondage has serious implications for democratic control over social policy. Even to hint that the debt overhang is a constraint on social spending—or that social and economic policy must change—will flash warning signals to investors around the world. This will depress bond ratings, raise the level of interest that governments must pay to bondholders, and perhaps promote capital flight.

Continuing poverty and the likelihood of further crises demand not just urgent attention to immediate debt problems but also a fresh approach to future borrowing. This will require new institutions for dealing with debt, including the possibility of sovereign bankruptcy. A growing willingness to discuss this issue is one of the more positive developments of the past few years.

At the same time, it is important to confront the difficult issues posed by conditionality. If anything, the conditions imposed for potential debt relief grew more complex in the late 1990s. Now borrowers should not only carry out market reforms, but also target relief toward the reduction of poverty. While this is understandable, it is not likely to be effective. It is probably more useful simply to insist that each debtor government take its budget decisions in an open and democratic fashion.

Development assistance

To strengthen the economies of the poorest countries, debt relief is not enough. An increase in development assistance is also essential. Although this was promised at Copenhagen, it has not been forthcoming. By 1998, development assistance was down to 0.23 per cent of donor countries' GNP.

This decline is partly a result of "donor fatigue"—disenchantment with inefficiency and corruption in recipient countries. But problems with aid are not entirely due to the weakness of Third World institutions. In recent years, development assistance has had to operate in such a generally hostile global economic climate that its limited success is hardly surprising. Not only has a considerable proportion of all aid been channelled toward debt repayment, but it has also been used to finance donor-mandated policy reforms that have produced meagre results.

As donors increasingly recognize the pitfalls associated with conditionality, some are changing tactics. Instead of being selective within countries—indicating areas of priority action—they are being more selective among countries. They are choosing partners with records of good governance and economic reform and allowing them greater control over the use of funds. This is progressively reducing the number of countries to which bilateral donors provide assistance.

A way to avoid the dilemmas associated with foreign aid is simply to replace it—perhaps with a new international development fund that would automatically transfer money from rich countries to poor ones. Proposals of this kind, which frame the challenge of poverty eradication in terms of human rights, rather than discretionary giving, are often linked to demands for new forms of international taxation.

The need for tax reform

Even if there were to be less debt and more aid, developing countries attempting to meet the most pressing social needs of their people must generate more of their own resources through taxation. But their already precarious tax base has been further weakened by recent free-market reforms. Much of their public revenue comes from taxation on trade—a source that diminishes brusquely as tariffs fall. A further problem—for all countries—is the prospect of tax competition. Governments are wary of raising taxes on foreign, or even national, businesses, because they might relocate elsewhere. A growing informal sector also shrinks the number of taxpayers.

The trend virtually everywhere has been to make up for growing shortfalls by increasing consumption taxes—and particularly the value added tax. This may raise revenue, but it is essentially regressive—taking a larger proportion out of the incomes of the poor.

There are more progressive options. One would be to remove tax benefits for offshore accounts. An IMF study has calculated that if these $8 trillion-worth of deposits earned income of around 5 per cent per year, and this were taxed at 40 per cent, some $160 billion would be raised annually—almost double what it would take for all countries to guarantee basic social services.

In the last analysis, only co-ordinated international action can protect the revenue base of governments. New information technologies and financial liberalization give individuals and businesses increasingly sophisticated options for moving their funds internationally, in ways that elude taxation. As awareness of this threat becomes more widespread, there are growing efforts to counter cross-border avoidance. Proposals to establish a World Tax Organization are also gaining considerable attention.

Pension reform

Pension schemes all over the world have come under pressure from a combination of shrinking government resources and aging populations. Advanced industrialized countries have remodelled their public pensions schemes without abandoning them. But many developing countries have been encouraged by the World Bank and the IMF to attempt a radical privatization of pension programmes.

Both the theoretical and practical bases for this experiment have been questioned. In late 1999, the World Bank itself prepared a thoroughgoing critique of the economic and actuarial justification for privatization. And recent evaluation of the Chilean experience suggests weak performance in terms of efficiency, yield, coverage and gender equity.

It is time to introduce a note of caution and realism into what has often been a highly ideological debate. The most creative attempts to provide security for the aged have involved innovative combinations of public and private schemes.

Mobilizing resources at the grassroots

When facing high debt payments, declining development assistance and falling tax revenues, governments must make a special effort to use scarce resources efficiently. In this regard, the international development community has strongly recommended such measures as decentralizing and targeting services, and introducing user fees in basic education and health. These are not panaceas. In some cases, they are useful. In others, they simply shift the burden for financing social development downward, away from those who have most toward those who have least.

Providing micro-credit has become one of the most popular forms of assistance at the local level. These small loans alleviate immediate problems, but they do not usually lift people out of poverty. It is remittances—income sent back home by migrant workers in foreign countries—that play by far the largest role in improving the level of living of low-income groups in developing countries. Between 1970 and 1995, global flows of remittances are estimated to have grown from $2 billion to around $70 billion. Providing a broader range of financial services at the local level could enhance the usefulness of these resources.

Fragile democracies

As participants in the Social Summit affirmed, promoting social development requires vigorous democratic institutions. And in fact, the vast majority of countries now have formally democratic systems of government—many of the newer ones with strong support from the United Nations. But the creation of the full range of institutions required to support democratic deepening is a long and difficult process. A number of countries are only setting out on this road, or appear to have stopped along it at an early stage.

Incomplete transitions produce illiberal democracies, lacking such essential democratic institutions as an independent judiciary and a free press. These incomplete democracies continue to shelter powerful groups, who are accustomed to operating outside the democratic arena. Thus in Latin America, governments still unable to complete the transition to democracy provide continued protection to former military leaders. In Africa, they allow autocrats a continued hold on power. And in a number of countries in Eastern Europe and Central Asia, they permit old party bosses to rule behind the façade of elections. Such countries also tend to have weak administrations, with poorly paid and ill-trained civil servants who are vulnerable to corruption.

Even countries that have made considerable progress in the construction of democracy confront dangers that should be recognized. The first of these is voter disillusionment, when elected governments confront difficulties in ensuring stability and economic development. People may prefer authority to uncertainty. Thus there is always a risk that underperforming democracies will harden into autocracies.

Ethnicity and democratization

Democratic regimes are also vulnerable to the centrifugal forces of ethnic conflict—and in fact, some governments are tempted by autocracy as a means of holding multi-ethnic states together. Ethnic diversity is not a problem in itself. The problems arise only when ethnic identity is politicized—at which point it can be used to provoke behaviour that is insular, xenophobic and destructive. The civil wars of the 1990s may not have started as ethnic conflicts—but ethnic identity certainly came to the fore once they were under way.

There are many ways of accommodating the interests of ethnic groups, to coincide with the needs of different political systems and societies. For example, federal structures can devolve considerable authority to state or provincial assemblies. Governments can also choose electoral systems that encourage parties to appeal to voters across ethnic lines. Or they can accept the fact that citizens will vote along ethnic lines, and design a system that obliges ethnically based parties to share power.

Reforms should aim to weaken polarity and promote moderation. They should also strengthen institutions constructed in non-ethnic ways—such as trade unions, professional associations and other civic organizations. Governments must try to avoid freezing existing ethnic cleavages, and they must leave citizens the room to change their affiliation or express multiple identities.

THE RISE OF TECHNOCRACY

Finally, contemporary democracies—whether new or old—are increasingly vulnerable to takeover by technocrats. As globalization and financial liberalization subject national economies to the dictates of international financial markets, power is being drained away from elected representatives toward officials who operate beyond democratic oversight. Governments anxious to maintain their credibility try to lift macroeconomic decisions out of the day-to-day political fray and into the more esoteric realm of highly trained finance ministers and central banks, as such moves are likely to generate confidence among international investors.

Technocratic decision making has also been spurred by the growing ascendance of the new managerialism, in which governments are supposed to operate more like businesses. This way of thinking has had greatest impact in the OECD countries, but developing countries have also been affected by it.

Citizens may not worry about technocratic government if it delivers economic stability and development. But isolating policy makers from popular sentiment can alienate citizens and block the way to future progress. It can also weaken democratic institutions. Therefore parliamentary oversight of key economic policy decisions must be improved.

Democracy is not a static condition. It is a constantly evolving process. The best way to achieve durable support is through participation, dialogue and compromise. Without these, democracies can mutate in unpredictable and unsettling directions.

A new mission for the public sector

Between 1945 and 1980, the public sector enjoyed unprecedented expansion. Most people wanted their governments to play a central part in national development. During the 1980s and 1990s, however, some states disintegrated and many were affected by free-market reforms.

The most pervasive and far-reaching reforms have been those that aim for fiscal stability—concentrating particularly on cutting public expenditure. It is significant that in the advanced industrialized democracies, states did not succeed in cutting expenditures by much. They faced stiff resistance from citizens who defended existing social services and entitlements.

Developing countries faced less well-organized civic opposition and cut expenditures much more sharply. Their resolve was stiffened by pressure from international financial institutions. In fact, budgetary reforms have been the single most important condition imposed in conjunction with structural adjustment loans over the past two decades.

Between 1990 and 1997, public expenditure as a proportion of GDP fell from 26 to 22 per cent in sub-Saharan Africa. Meanwhile, in the OECD countries it rose from 45 to 47 per cent. The privatization of public enterprises was another strategy employed to reduce budget deficits. Developing and transition countries privatized public enterprises worth $155 billion between 1990 and 1996. Governments in Latin America led the way—accounting for more than half these sales.

With the encouragement of the World Bank and the IMF, governments have also aimed to increase the efficiency of the public sector. In this, they have been guided by theories of new public management, which apply principles of economics to political and bureaucratic processes. Generally, this means breaking activities into more manageable parts—creating new agencies and quasi-markets within the administration, as well as contracting services out.

Such systems can only work if there is effective monitoring based on sound budgeting and regular flows of accurate information—areas in which many governments of developing countries are weak. In these circumstances, the new systems may create little more than an empty managerial shell.

Effective public sector reform requires a skilled cadre of people who are well educated and well paid. Yet public servants in the majority of developing countries have seen their real wages fall steeply, and systems of higher education in poorer countries are often in crisis. University buildings are decaying, equipment is non-existent and teachers are joining the private sector, taking on extra jobs or migrating abroad. This is in part an outcome of forcing a trade-off between improving "basic education" and supporting secondary and university instruction.

Reforms of the public sector should be firmly grounded in what citizens see as the mission for their state. In the last analysis, these missions are not managerial; they are social. People want to move toward societies that are more prosperous, equitable and harmonious. Having ambitious managerial targets may be a part of this—but only a small part. Indeed, focusing too rigidly on market-driven reforms, without building broad political consensus for change, is likely to perpetuate the incidence of failed states, civil wars and developmental stagnation.

Calling corporations to account

In the past, transnational corporations were rarely called upon to have explicit social policies. But that is changing. Today, TNCs find themselves embroiled in many of the most vexed social issues, from global warming to child labour to genetically modified food.

There are a number of reasons for this. One is the sheer scale of transnational operations: some 60,000 corporations now account for one third of world exports. This inevitably gives them a higher public profile. But corporations have also come under much closer scrutiny from non-governmental organizations, particularly those concerned with the environment and human rights.

In response, TNCs have developed a series of voluntary initiatives—including codes of conduct, environmental and social certification and auditing systems, and compliance with various international standards. They have also started to work in partnership with their critics, as well as with agencies of the United Nations.

This may occur because corporations believe it is their duty. More likely, it is a strategy of reputation management, deployed either to gain a competitive advantage through a cleaner, greener, image or to avoid negative publicity and the risk of consumer boycotts. Although only a few consumers will go out of their way to buy ethical goods, many more will shun companies that have been accused of environmental destruction or of employing child labour.

Many companies have mastered socially

responsible rhetoric, but few have taken comprehensive action. Only a small proportion of companies have introduced codes of conduct. These tend to be narrow in scope and are often not independently verified. Some of the most inflated claims come from corporations that say they are contributing to sustainable development—which generally means merely that they are making some efforts to achieve eco-efficiency.

Corporations want to avoid "hard" regulation and would prefer "soft" approaches through voluntary initiatives and partnerships. But left to their own devices, TNCs are likely to fulfil their responsibilities in a minimalist and fragmented fashion. Ultimately, most corporations will only respond to stronger regulation, and to close monitoring by NGOs, trade unions and consumer groups.

Civil societies

The Social Summit, like many other international gatherings before and since, placed a lot of trust in civil society—all the myriad groups that belong neither to government nor to the profit-making private sector. Civil society organizations (CSOs) have certainly been proliferating in recent years, partly as an outcome of increasing democratization, but also in response to the availability of donor funds seeking civil-society partners.

CSOs and service delivery

Non-governmental development organizations—NGDOs—are an important subset of civil society. For decades they have made important contributions to key issues of development policy. What is different today—particularly in developing countries—is the extent to which governments and aid agencies expect them to provide social services, either independently or in collaboration with the state. This is part of the more general trend toward reducing the obligations of governments and shifting responsibility for social provision to the profit-making private sector and non-profit organizations. By the mid-1990s, NGDOs disbursed approximately 15 per cent of total public development aid.

Donors assume that NGDOs are more efficient at providing services than governments, but there is little evidence to support this. In fact, NGDOs tend to have an uneven reach, to offer services of inconsistent quality and, often, to provide sporadic coverage. Their advantage usually lies in their ability to experiment with new approaches and adapt projects to local circumstances.

Donors would like the NGDO ethos of independence and creativity to pervade official aid programmes. Unfortunately, the reverse appears to be happening: NGDOs are becoming dependent on foreign donors and tend not to challenge donor policies and procedures. Today, far fewer NGDOs than in the past would consider themselves campaigning advocates for the poor. As contract-based service providers, many do as they are told.

Perhaps the most serious danger in delivering services through NGDOs is that of confusing lines of accountability. Even when services are subcontracted, ultimate responsibility for their quality must lie with the state. Yet as governments withdraw from certain areas, their capacity to formulate effective strategies, or to monitor or evaluate sub-contractors, may be reduced.

International advocacy

International advocacy is another area in which CSOs have achieved greater prominence during the past few years, particularly at the United Nations. CSOs do not generally participate in formal UN decision making, but they do affect the terms of the debate—particularly in areas such as human rights, which are politically controversial.

CSOs were prominent in the series of UN

conferences held during the 1990s. By the time of the Social Summit, CSOs had debated and provided alternatives to every key phrase in the draft documents. In addition, 1,500 CSOs now have official accreditation to the United Nations Economic and Social Council—ECOSOC—and there have been attempts to accord them a formal status in the General Assembly as well.

The international agency that has received the most sustained criticism from CSOs is the World Bank. Opposition to World Bank programmes intensified in the 1990s, with blanket denunciations of its development policy (expressed through the "Fifty Years Is Enough" campaign), as well as mobilization against high-profile dam and resettlement programmes. This finally forced the Bank to abandon some projects and to establish improved mechanisms for internal review.

The women's movement has also made effective criticisms of Bank programmes, prompting establishment of a Gender Analysis and Policy Group. But although CSOs have had an impact in certain areas of the World Bank's work, it remains to be seen whether these changes affect the Bank's core activities. They have not yet shifted the economic rationale for project decisions—and they do not yet seem to be incorporated into the day-to-day operation of the institution.

At least, the World Bank has become more willing to co-operate with CSOs. This represents progress, but it also enhances the risk that members of civil society organizations will be offered pseudo-influence. Some of their members, incorporated into Bank activities, may be able to promote incremental reforms. But more fundamental change will probably only come from persistent, objective external criticism.

In terms of achieving policy change, one of the most significant achievements of international civil society in the 1990s was the sinking, or at least the temporary submersion, of the Multilateral Agreement on Investment in 1998. The anti-MAI campaign probably signalled the coming of age of the Internet for the hundreds of pressure groups that used e-mail and Web sites to co-ordinate their strategies. This experience was used to good effect in other international campaigns, like the Jubilee 2000 coalition against debt, the mobilization against land mines and protests against genetically modified food. It also served as background for massive protest surrounding the World Trade Organization meeting in Seattle in November 1999, which underscored growing public unease with the nature of negotiations on free trade.

Increasing international activism is sometimes taken as proof that a new global civil society has been born. This probably overstates the case. What has emerged is a raucous and intelligent combination of research, idealism and cheap technology—now armed with human rights law. Governments, corporations and international institutions ignore these voices at their peril.

Getting development right for women

Women's groups and coalitions played a prominent part in the international conferences of the 1990s. But despite such visibility, many political and cultural barriers to gender equity remain stubbornly in place. And women often bear much of the burden of the social dislocation that has accompanied economic liberalization during the past two decades.

Democracy and gender equity

Recent transitions to democracy owe a great deal to pressure from women's movements—with feminists and popular women's groups working together to bring about changes in government. But the heterogeneity of these groups often makes it difficult for them to forge coalitions in subsequent democratic regimes—and thus to improve the institutional context for gender equity.

Democratic institutions are not automatically gender equitable. In fact, the low level of participation by women in formal democratic politics remains a problem in the large majority of countries around the world. On average, only 13 per cent of all members of parliament in the world are women. The cultural construction of political office as masculine plays a significant role in maintaining this imbalance. And to overcome it, some governments and political parties are engaging in electoral engineering—requiring that a certain proportion of all candidates be women, or specifically reserving a certain number of seats in parliament for them.

Unfortunately there is no guarantee that women who are elected to office will stand up for women's interests. Many successful women politicians have not been feminists. And those who have achieved representation through quotas or reserved seats may be reluctant to voice dissent. Still, women parliamentarians in many countries have come together to push for progressive legislation on such issues as divorce, domestic violence and reproductive rights.

Women and social policy

Women in parliament have been less successful in influencing decisions on social policy and public expenditure that have crucial implications for women. For example, the kind of health sector reform introduced in many developing countries during the 1990s has frequently been disastrous for poor women. Aimed at improving cost-effectiveness, these reforms have introduced user charges and greatly restricted the kinds of services available in public clinics. They have also raised difficult questions for the women's NGOs that are being drawn into them as service providers and monitors.

Economic crises and structural adjustment programmes have obviously affected educational opportunities as well. There is a new emphasis on expanding primary school enrolment, and this has been increasing in recent years. But drop-out rates remain high, and many poor families have to choose which of their children they can afford to have educated. For economic or cultural reasons, they frequently choose to keep girls at home.

Moreover, the reduced coverage and quality of secondary education is emerging as a major concern. The cultural constraints on female education tend to become particularly acute at the secondary level. Thus as the quality and coverage of secondary education declines, girls in particular may lose out. And, ironically, many studies have shown that the much-publicized benefits from female education tend to be greatest at higher levels of schooling.

Education should also enhance women's economic entitlements. Certainly, more women are working outside the household than ever before, for a variety of reasons. First, more women now need to work to ensure family survival. Second, there are now more women-supported households. Third, there has been a rapid growth in the industries that employ a high proportion of women.

This offers women more opportunities but also exposes them to new risks. Many industries that employ women offer poor wages and working conditions. While there is some evidence that men's and women's wages may be converging, it seems that this is often because men's wages have been falling—not because women's have necessarily been rising.

Fulfilling women's rights

Improving the condition of women will mean not simply meeting their needs, but fulfilling their rights. Some of these, like freedom from repressive traditional codes of behaviour, and freedom from domestic violence and forced pregnancy, are basic civil and political rights. Others are social and economic rights, like access to high-quality public services in the field of family care. In a world where much of the responsibility for social services is being pushed off on communities and families, the societal value of women's work as care-givers must be recognized. Decent "care conditions" are at least as much an entitlement of citizens as decent conditions of work.

Sustaining development

Development agencies now claim to be pursuing people-centred sustainable development. This should imply working in a more integrated fashion—taking a serious look at the sustainability of existing patterns of production and consumption, and co-operating closely with local communities in setting priorities for action.

Sustainable cities

If these principles are to have any lasting value, they will have to work in cities—which now house almost half the world's population. In fact, the Earth Summit considered ways to achieve sustainable development in cities, and spelled out priorities as Local Agenda 21.

A number of campaigns are under way, but their impact has been limited. The impetus for change has often come from middle-class communities, who are more interested in dealing with specific environmental problems than with altering unsustainable patterns of consumption, or inequality. Meanwhile, many poor communities are involved in self-help initiatives, but they rarely take part in wider urban planning or politics.

Achieving sustainable cities demands strong civic cultures and a new politics of cohesion and collaboration. These take time to build—longer certainly than most development agencies customarily contemplate.

Sustainable agriculture

The world has proved remarkably successful at food production—though less effective at distributing the output so that no one goes hungry. Many people argue that, with new technologies, production will continue to keep pace with population. But many aspects of modern agriculture are unsustainable—absorbing ever-increasing quantities of energy and degrading the environment.

Some international agencies and governments are paying more attention to forms of agriculture that replenish—rather than exhaust or degrade—natural, human and social capital. This would mean making better use of natural processes such as nutrient cycling, nitrogen fixation, soil regeneration or natural pest control—and fuller use of the special knowledge and skills of farmers.

But this experience is likely to remain localized unless some major constraints are overcome. Most attempts to promote sustainable agriculture have had to struggle against existing national policies that heavily subsidize energy-intensive agriculture and promote patterns of structural adjustment that weaken farming communities. There has also been far too little co-operation with farmers to explore what works best under local conditions. Sustainable agriculture is not a concretely defined set of technologies; it is a process of social learning.

Sustainable water supplies

There is increasing pressure on global water supplies. In the past it was assumed that the solution was large-scale state provision. Now many governments believe that the private sector and communities should take greater responsibility, and that activities should be on a smaller scale. Some of this change has grown out of public opposition to the construction of large dams that have caused serious environmental damage and social dislocation. And it is clear that many large-scale irrigation systems have also been ineffective and expensive.

One of the most common solutions to water supply problems is to make associations of farmers responsible for running smaller-scale irrigation schemes. This is not an easy option.

It assumes that the irrigation system is actually working. It also assumes that farmers see some economic benefit in taking on this commitment. In practice, achieving efficiency, sustainability and equity can be very difficult. But it is at least clear that water resources planning needs to be taken out of offices and into villages and town squares. Only then can it identify real bottlenecks and propose manageable solutions.

Forest conservation

World development has frequently been at the cost of the world's forests. And the process of degradation appears to be continuing. Poor communities have always struggled to protect their own environments, but have often been overcome by economic or climatic pressures, or overwhelmed by outside forces. Halting this process will mean moving toward more participatory conservation that takes into account the rights and needs of local communities. In particular, it will mean promoting more diverse forms of income generation, so people can earn their living while conserving their environment.

Continuity or change?

The term people-centred sustainable development has reminded the international community that development demands more than economic growth; that some features of modernization have unacceptable social and environmental costs; and that this requires different economic policies and approaches to project implementation. But few governments and international agencies have made significant changes. Most have simply applied new terminology to what they were already doing—perhaps with a few extra elements bolted on.

Governments and international finance and trade institutions need to be far more sensitive to the social and environmental costs of their policies, and to make their decision-making processes more democratic. Popular mobilizations that got sustainable development on the agenda in the first place still have much to do if they want to see new ideas implemented.

In the last analysis, action depends on people's interpretation of what is possible and right. Thus the longer-term nature of mobilization for sustainable development depends not only on activism, but on dominant views about where the world could—and should—be going. If those views support high-consumption lifestyles, then many hard questions about environmental sustainability will not be seriously addressed. And if they sanction unlimited individual gain, it is obvious that institutions designed to promote the common good will suffer.

Five years after Copenhagen, there is little indication that the fundamental goals and values orienting world development are moving toward greater social responsibility. Incentive structures in everything from education to investment decisions have been reoriented toward improving the options of the profit-maximizing individual. The investor has become much more important than the worker. And the consumer has gained higher status than the citizen.

Questioning extreme individualism and the unbridled power of money—reasserting the value of equity and social solidarity, and reinstating the citizen at the centre of public life—is a major challenge of our time. The "invisible hand" of the market has no capacity to imagine a decent society for all people, or to work in a consistent fashion to attain it. Only human beings with a strong sense of the public good can do that.

Globalization with a human mask

Eric Draper, Associated Press AP

World trade protest.
Seattle, Washington, United States

Globalization is splintering many societies and doing little to eradicate poverty. Grudgingly, the international financial institutions have conceded that the neoliberal model has harmful consequences. But they prefer to mask the damage rather than shift to more humane—and more productive—forms of development.

Globalization has had the aura of an irresistible force of nature—a tidal wave of free trade, open markets, capital flows and high technology, and a deluge of information, that will eventually deliver progress for all.

This triumphalist tone can still be heard—but less often. Integration has certainly proceeded apace, and communications technology and the Internet sweep onward, while the trading environment becomes ever more liberal. But now there is less certainty that these developments are really improving people's lives.

From development to adjustment

Conventional wisdom on development has shifted over the years. Often this has been a response to new circumstances—as countries have moved through different periods in their development. But sometimes the changes merely represent shifts in fashion.

From the 1950s onward, many governments drew up development plans in conjunction with visiting experts from the World Bank and elsewhere. They planned to accelerate economic growth, while simultaneously improving standards of health and education and promoting community development. Many had considerable success.

Over the period 1960–85, countries defined by the World Bank as low- and middle-income grew on average by 5.9 per cent annually. Of course some regions grew faster than others, and progress was uneven. Thus East Asia and the Pacific grew at 7.3 per cent, while sub-Saharan Africa managed only 4.2 per cent and South Asia only 3.6 per cent. Latin America seemed to be doing reasonably well over this period, growing at 6.0 per cent annually—indeed some of the faster-growing Latin American countries, such as Mexico and Brazil, seemed to be pressing on just as rapidly as newly industrializing economies in Asia.

Although such growth rates contributed to increases in per capita income, it became clear that benefits were not trickling down to the poor. This led in the 1970s to a shift in emphasis toward redistribution with growth. Governments hoped that the benefits of additional growth could be directed toward the poor, while not demanding too many sacrifices from the rich. Adoption of the basic needs approach and promotion of strategies for integrated rural development were associated with this stage in development thinking.

But any prospect of growth with equity was soon undermined: the oil shocks of the 1970s, the decline in commodity prices, and the escalating debt burden all slammed the brakes on economic expansion and plunged many poor countries into economic crisis.

The 1980s marked the emergence of a great continental divide. Asian countries continued to prosper: over the period 1980–89, East Asia and the Pacific grew by 7.9 per cent annually, and South Asia by 5.5 per cent. But Latin America and sub-Saharan Africa saw growth collapse to an annual rate of 1.7 per cent.

The causes of this striking bifurcation have been a subject of continuing debate. The orthodox view, held by the IMF, the World Bank and others, was that governments in Latin America and sub-Saharan Africa were paying the price of policy errors: allowing their economies to be dominated by the state and protecting them from many aspects of international competition. Others had a different explanation. They argued that these regions were simply victims of a series of shocks beyond their control—particularly the debt crisis, which had little effect on most Asian countries.

In the event, the view that prevailed was the orthodox one, not least because its proponents held the purse strings. Latin American countries adopted the policies of the Washington consensus—shrinking their states and opening their markets. This certainly brought them benefits—attracting huge flows of foreign capital that helped revive economic growth, bring inflation under control and achieve macroeconomic stability—even if at the cost of regular crises. Over the period 1990–96, Latin America achieved average annual growth of 3.2 per cent. This was considerably lower than during its state-driven period; but at least growth was positive.

Sub-Saharan Africa's experience was far worse. Although African countries subjected themselves to the same purgative structural adjustment programmes prescribed by the Bretton Woods institutions, they gained very little foreign investment and languished at lower levels of employment and income.

EQUITY SIDELINED

In the adjustment era, considerations of equity and poverty reduction went into abeyance as the Bretton Woods institutions tried to help developing countries cope with these new circumstances. At first, international financial institutions required governments to achieve stabilization, which usually meant cutting public expenditure and raising interest rates. These temporary measures soon gave way, however, to full-blown programmes of structural adjustment. In future, governments requesting outside assistance would have to reform their economies according to free-market ideologies—reducing the reach of the state, privatizing industries and liberalizing trade and finance. They would have to postpone poverty reduction, in the hope that stability and growth would eventually benefit everyone.

It rapidly became clear, however, that most structural adjustment programmes were working only slowly—if at all. And the poor were not just having to make temporary sacrifices; they were suffering long-term damage. Structural adjustment even harmed groups among the poor who were supposed to benefit from neoliberal reforms. Thus liberalization promised to help rural producers by removing the market distortions that kept food prices low. But since it also resulted in more expensive credit and higher prices for agricultural inputs, many farmers found themselves worse off.

Numerous NGOs, churches and international agencies called on the BWIs to pay more attention to social concerns—in the words of UNICEF, to achieve "adjustment with a human face". In 1990, UNDP incorporated many of these ideas into its proposals for human development, which placed people, their needs, their aspirations and their capabilities back at the centre of development efforts.

In the same year, the World Bank responded to this criticism to some extent—relaxing its excessive focus on debt management and adjustment, and putting more emphasis on poverty. The Bank still believed that structural adjustment would provide an enabling environment conducive to "efficient labour-intensive growth". But it now said that this could be supplemented with deliberate anti-poverty measures, particularly greater investment in health and education. Later the World Bank added a third element: social safety nets to provide the very poorest with food, for example, or basic incomes.

THE POSITIVE EAST ASIAN EXAMPLE

Meanwhile, Asia powered on. Most attention at the time was focused on the so-called tiger economies, like the Republic of Korea. But the experience of Asia's—and the world's—two most populous countries was in many respects even more remarkable. Over more than two decades, China, a country with more than one billion people, achieved double-digit economic growth. India also stepped up economic growth in the 1990s.

Throughout the past decade, much of the development debate has been influenced by the dramatic progress made in East and Southeast Asia—although different people have drawn different lessons from it. Many have agreed that these countries prospered because of a relatively more equitable distribution of assets following reforms of the 1950s, and because they subsequently pursued employment-intensive growth.

But there has been less agreement about the influence of the state. The BWIs initially asserted that the Asian NICs have succeeded largely because governments intervened very little in the economy and maintained a market-friendly environment. Critics pointed out, however, that governments in these states have actually been very proactive—giving incentives and priority to specific national industries. In 1993, the World Bank admitted that there has been state intervention—but essentially argued that these countries have succeeded not because of state intervention, but despite it. The Bank conceded, however, that some Asian institutions for co-ordinating investment decisions between government and private businesses have been effective tools for stimulating growth.

There have also been differing interpretations of the role of trade liberalization in the "Asian miracle". The BWIs saw the Asian experience as a vindication of open markets. Again there were objections. Certainly these countries were export oriented. But in fact they maintained extensive import controls. They integrated into the world economy in a strategic fashion—opening their economies only as far as was useful.

A third area of debate has focused on welfare policies. Asian countries have been praised by the supporters of open markets for spending very little on social security and social welfare. Such responsibilities have been left largely to families, communities and companies. This has the advantage not only of discouraging dependence on the state and providing positive incentives for work, but also of keeping taxes low and conserving public spending for directly productive uses.

An argument of this kind implies that other countries—those with comprehensive social programmes—are on the wrong track. Instead of spending on social services, they should be pursuing growth and employment. But commentators have pointed out that even if the NICs did not have high public investment in social services, they did nevertheless exert a strong influence on welfare by offering incentives to both families and enterprises to provide many essential elements of social protection.

The Social Summit

The Social Summit marked both the high point of neoliberal influence and the beginning of its decline. Emboldened by the collapse of the Soviet Union, the Washington consensus maintained that transition and developing countries had no alternative to free-market restructuring. If they were to make progress, they had to subject themselves to structural adjustment—opening their markets and aligning their societies with the force fields of globalization. They cited Asia's miracle economies as further evidence of these claims. And they could also point to Latin America, and even Africa, where there were signs in some countries that liberalization had led to economic recovery.

Yet the fact that the Social Summit was held at all reflected widespread and growing discontent with the damage caused by unregulated globalization. By 1995 there was serious social crisis in many parts of the world, expressed most visibly in cruel civil wars and an increase in violent crime. This prompted talk of social disintegration and the need to reverse it. Poverty and unemployment were growing rapidly in indebted Third World countries—and, indeed, in a number of industrialized countries as well. The collapse of the Soviet Union exposed most people to the rigours of the market without making adequate provision for social protection. The welfare state was said to be in crisis even in OECD countries, where workers were subjected to levels of uncertainty unknown for decades. Participants in the Social Summit were angry about this state of affairs and convinced of the need to search for alternatives.

They pointed out the fragility of economic recovery under neoliberal programmes—the constant vulnerability of nations and people to shocks and crises. Much-touted economic recovery could simply be the result of better weather or improving commodity prices or a sudden influx of short-term foreign investment—all of which were easily reversed. Figures for GNP growth went up and down, but adjustment itself was continuing to make matters worse for the majority of people in many parts of the world.

Moreover, models informed by this orthodoxy were inadequate as a basis for long-term development. The "fundamentals" to which SAPs were tethered were designed to promote stabilization, not growth and development. A chorus of well-informed protest demanded a reorientation of development policy and practice.

Globalization and economic growth

What was needed, in order to deal with growing poverty, unemployment and social disintegration, was a widespread increase in economic opportunity. This depended on an appreciable increase in growth. Without robust economic expansion—on the order of at least 5 to 6 per cent annually—there could not be steady improvement in the levels of living of low-income groups. There was nothing outlandish about this target, since many countries had achieved similar growth rates in the 1960s and 1970s.

But high economic growth is not in itself sufficient to achieve the goals set by the Social Summit. What matters—if benefits are to flow beyond a very limited circle—is the quality of growth: whether it entails a more equitable distribution of income, more and better jobs, rising wages, more gender equality and inclusiveness.

The relevant question, both at the time of the Social Summit and in the five years following it, is whether global liberalism creates an environment in which high-quality growth can be attained. Are free flows of capital and an ever more open trading system essential for economic growth and equitable development?

Growth and trade

Table 1.1 casts doubt on the claim that further liberalization of trade and finance is a necessary element in stimulating economic growth. It summarizes the extent of economic integration during the past four decades and shows that the world economy was already integrating rapidly, long before the era of liberalization and globalization. Indeed, the period 1964–73 saw world exports and GDP expanding far more rapidly than they have subsequently—and this was a period when trade barriers were still quite high. In Latin America and East Asia, tariff and non-tariff barriers were around twice as high as they were in the early 1990s. Thus it seems likely that faster growth led to more trade, rather than the other way round. And in this case, the current orthodoxy offers no convincing claim to superiority.

One of the main advantages of more open trade—often cited by its supporters—is that it should promote greater convergence in incomes, both within countries and among them. But the evidence for this, too, is weak. Indeed, one study suggests that free trade actually tends to promote divergence in income. While it is true that the distance between levels of GNP per capita in fast-growing Asian countries and the industrialized countries shrank over the past decades, as they became more integrated in global markets, this situation has deteriorated under the impact of recent economic crisis. Furthermore, there is no question that income polarization in these countries—and in global society in general—has grown sharply during the period since 1980.

Table 1.1 – International economic activity, 1964–94 (average annual percentage changes)

Period	World export volume	World FDI flows	International bank loans	World real GDP
1964-73	9.2	..	34.0	4.6
1973-80	4.6	14.8	26.7	3.6
1980-85	2.4	4.9	12.0	2.6
1985-94	6.7	14.3	12.0	3.2

Source: Perraton et al., 1997

Finally, in neo-orthodox theories, it is assumed that the gains from trade are best ensured by open trading systems and non-intervention by governments in labour markets. One policy implication of this view has been to associate better performance in trade with reduced public sector activity in the field of social protection. Such a view goes against the historical record, which shows that some of the most successful open economies or trading nations—including the Nordic countries and the Netherlands—have had comprehensive social policies. Such policies have not only facilitated the creation of human capital through education (or retraining) and better health, but have also made the costs of greater openness—including the heightened vulnerability of certain groups—more politically acceptable. Citizens have been willing to support economic openness because they have been confident that their own social security would not be threatened by such changes.

Growth and financial flows

What evidence is there for strong links between growth and a second critical element of globalization—increasingly unregulated financial flows? The Social Summit took place during a marked upswing of private financial flows to developing countries. Figure 1.1 shows that private flows rapidly overtook development assistance as the main source of foreign capital available to these countries during the 1990s.

In fact, the prospects for financing development through private capital may have contributed to the relaxation of pressures on the industrialized countries to increase their foreign aid. Even within the United Nations, there was a growing view that partnerships with the private sector would mobilize the necessary resources for addressing a wide range of issues related to development. In addition, it was hoped that these capital flows could be taxed (through the proposed Tobin Tax, for

Figure 1.1 – Aggregate net flows to developing countries, 1990–97

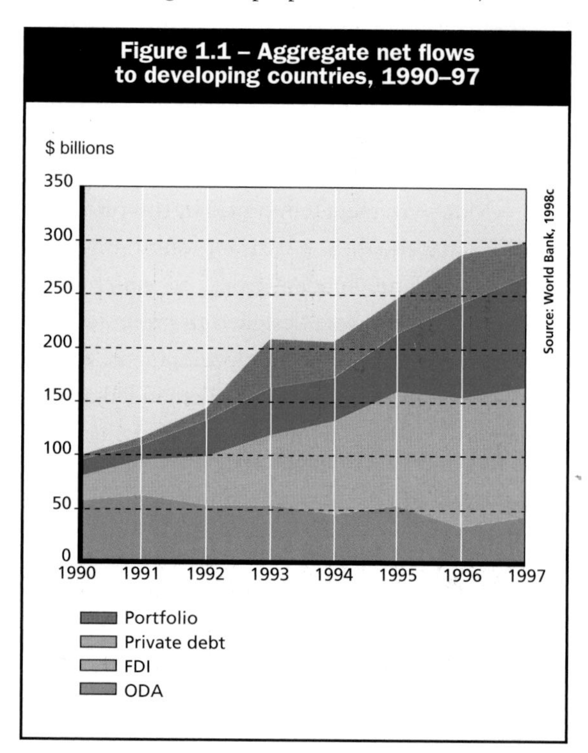

example), not only in order to stabilize financial markets but also to finance development programmes and poverty alleviation. Ideally, taxes on private capital flows could also solve some of the fiscal problems faced by national governments—faced with increased tax avoidance by transnational corporations—and enhance the policy autonomy of national governments.

As this figure indicates, however, an increasing proportion of all capital entering developing countries from abroad has taken the form of private debt and portfolio investment. These tend to be quite volatile and, as the Mexican crisis of 1994 and the more recent Asian financial crisis have demonstrated, can be rapidly withdrawn. Figure 1.2 serves as a reminder that increases in private flows to developing countries during the 1990s are not a new phenomenon, but the continuation of an earlier trend that was interrupted in the 1980s. Compared to the period prior to the debt crisis of the 1980s, there was little increase in net capital inflows to most developing countries during the past decade, if this is considered as a share of recipient countries' GNP. Furthermore, most of the new money has gone to only a small number of countries in Latin America, East Asia and the Pacific.

Have these flows of finance helped improve the environment for strong economic growth? There is cause for doubt. For example, one study of 100 developing countries for the period 1975–89 found no relationship between the openness of the capital account regimes and the growth of GDP. And despite the fact that industrialized countries have effectively had free trade and free capital movements since the early 1980s, their growth performance has scarcely improved. Out of the 22 OECD countries, 21 had lower GDP growth in the 1980s and 1990s than they did in the much less liberal 1950s and 1960s. They have also seen little improvement in productivity: the corresponding growth rate is now less than half what it was in the 1950s and 1960s.

Even more disturbing is the extreme fragility of growth based on the largely unregulated flow of private capital around the world. The Mexican experience provides a case in point. By the time of the Social Summit, Mexicans were suffering through one of the most devastating economic crises in their history, triggered when speculators launched an attack on the peso. Foreign money, flowing massively into the country following implementation of the North American Free Trade Agreement in early 1994, reversed course at the end of the year. Uncontrolled capital flight led to devaluation of the currency—and to a collapse of the economy that could only be halted through a $50-billion rescue package led by the United States.

The "tequila crisis" was to prove short-lived for investors. But it has had far-reaching effects on the Mexican banking system, interest rates and prospects for longer-term economic recovery. And the crisis of confidence unleashed by the Mexican collapse of 1995 meant increased vulnerability and slow (or negative) growth in a number of other Latin American economies that have become extremely dependent on short-term foreign investment.

The experience of Mexico was repeated on a still larger scale in 1997, when another round of failing investor confidence, devaluation and capital flight caused immense damage in a number of East and Southeast Asian countries. The worst-affected among them sustained huge losses: in 1998, Indonesia's GDP fell by 9 per cent, Thailand's by 8 per cent, and the Republic of Korea's by 6 per cent. Significantly, China and India—countries that despite some liberalization had maintained extensive capital controls—escaped the worst of the financial crisis. And India's economic fundamentals were much weaker than those of the crisis-affected countries.

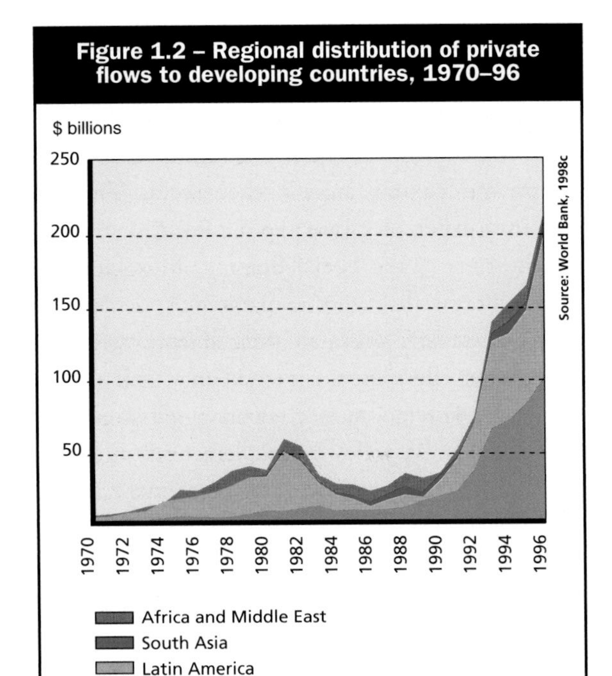

Figure 1.2 – Regional distribution of private flows to developing countries, 1970–96

Even so, some Asian economies staged a rapid recovery. By 1999, the Republic of Korea was growing again, by 6 per cent, and Thailand by 4 per cent. Asia as a whole was expected to grow 4.7 per cent in 1999. And Indonesia is expected to have positive growth in 2000. In the meantime, prospects for Latin America are less good. Latin American countries have been affected not just by Asia's problems but also by Russia's financial crisis. Overall growth fell to 2.3 per cent in 1998 and was negative in 1999.

Even when macroeconomic statistics suggest that countries have bounced back from financial crises, it is important to remember that millions of their people have not. Successive crises have ripped the social fabric and plunged many more people into poverty.

Liberalization and jobs

The most direct effect of economic collapse was on jobs. But the problem of unemployment has been growing almost everywhere, even when countries have avoided direct involvement in some of the major economic crises of the past two decades. In the European Union, for example, average unemployment stood at over 10 per cent in 1999. Forty years earlier, governments of these countries would have worried if the figure rose much above 3 per cent.

Neoliberal orthodoxy holds that the root of the problem is excessive state interference in labour markets, associated with excessive labour costs. In this view, the best way to maximize employment is to keep labour markets flexible, so that workers will move more easily from one job to another and be prepared or obliged to accept low-wage jobs. This, in turn, supposedly keeps inflation low, and encourages investment and growth.

Table 1.2 – Percentage annual economic growth, 1991–99

	1991	1992	1993	1994	1995	1996	1997	1998	1999
World	1.8	2.7	2.7	4.0	3.7	4.3	4.2	2.5	2.3
Advanced economies	1.2	1.9	1.2	3.2	2.6	3.2	3.2	2.2	2.0
Developing countries	4.9	6.7	6.5	6.8	6.1	6.5	5.7	3.3	3.1
Africa	1.8	0.2	0.7	2.2	3.1	5.8	3.1	3.4	3.2
Asia	6.6	9.5	9.3	9.6	9.1	8.2	6.6	3.8	4.7
Middle East and Europe	2.7	7.0	4.0	0.6	3.7	4.7	4.4	2.9	2.0
Western hemisphere	3.9	3.3	3.9	5.2	1.3	3.6	5.2	2.3	-0.5
Transition countries	-7.4	-11.7	-6.4	-7.5	-1.1	-0.3	2.2	-0.2	-0.9

Source: IMF, 1999

Supporters of this prescription commonly contrast the United States with Europe. They say that the United States currently has lower unemployment than Europe because US labour markets are more flexible. But this explanation is not adequate, since it does not account for the employment pattern in earlier periods. In 1964–73, for example, Germany's labour market was even more rigid than it is today, yet unemployment averaged only 1.1 per cent—compared with 4 per cent in the United States.

Although neoliberal economic theory has a prescription for promoting employment, it is not oriented toward the goal of full employment. This goal, enshrined in government plans of the postwar period—and in the Copenhagen Declaration—is considered dangerous by the orthodox economists of the 1980s and 1990s, because pressure in a tight labour market raises wages and threatens to provoke inflation. And inflation is not good for growth. In other words, they argue, a certain minimum level of unemployment is essential for ensuring growth.

Yet the historical record of inflation is not congruent with such an interpretation. During the 1950s and 1960s, Western Europe enjoyed virtually full employment, yet achieved this with low inflation. There is also more recent contradictory evidence from the United States, which has managed to sustain comparatively low unemployment with low inflation, while the US GDP has continued to grow steadily. Some people suggest that this is an anomaly and that inflation is lurking in the wings. But it does at least suggest that governments can achieve high levels of employment together with price stability and growth.

A dogmatic insistence on the role of labour flexibility and low wages in promoting employment and growth seems particularly misplaced in the developing world. The poorer countries already have very flexible labour markets. A high proportion of people work in the informal sector. With little prospect of unemployment benefits, they are forced to take or create whatever jobs they can—however unproductive or badly paid—picking garbage, shining shoes, pedalling rickshaws. So most people are working even if they do not appear to produce much.

As a result, little can be read into unemployment statistics for many parts of the world. In Bangladesh, for example, official unemployment is usually cited at around 5 per cent in urban areas and 2 per cent in rural areas. However, many more people are underemployed. One estimate suggests that, at any given time, around one quarter of the workforce is effectively unemployed. Even those fortunate enough to have jobs in the formal sector are often working for very low wages. Women in Dhaka's garment factories, for example, may earn little more than $20 per month.

To improve the lives of most people in developing countries, the quality of work and the level of wages must rise. And the experience of fast-growing Asian economies in the 1980s and 1990s shows that—contrary to the orthodox view on employment—there is no hard-and-fast reason why rising wages cannot be compatible with increasing employment and fast growth. During those decades, employment and real wages in fast-growing Asian countries increased by almost 5 per cent per year. At the same time, their formal sectors expanded while their informal sectors shrank. Indeed, many of these countries became significant net importers of labour. Thailand, for example, shortly before the financial crisis had around 600,000 immigrant workers.

Unfavourable trends in employment

But this is not the situation that prevails in most of the world five years after Copenhagen. As table 1.2 shows, the dominant macroeconomic model is underwriting a pattern of relatively weak growth of global GDP—with exceptionally high, or dramatically low, growth in some countries or regions. This is accompanied by falling real wages and the degradation of working conditions for large numbers of people.

Although important exceptions can be cited—North America, Australia and New Zealand, India and China—the employment situation is worsening in the majority of countries. Following the Asian crisis, for example, unemployment rates doubled in the most affected economies of the region. In Indonesia, the ILO has estimated that between 3.8 and 5.4 million workers lost their jobs. In Thailand, the rate of open unemployment increased from 2.2 to 4.8 per cent between 1997 and 1998. Japanese figures show an increase from 2.5 per cent in 1993 to 4.1 per cent in 1998. Meanwhile, in Latin America, unemployment in 1998 stood at its highest level in 15 years. And steadily rising rates of open unemployment in North Africa reached 11 per cent in Egypt, 18 per cent in Morocco, 15 per cent in Tunisia and 26 per cent in Algeria.

With falling or stagnant growth, people move out of the formal sector into the informal sector, where conditions of work are often worse. This occurred in Latin America, where the percentage of the workforce engaged in informal activities rose from 40 to 55 per cent between 1980 and 1995. It has also been the experience of transition countries in Eastern and Central Europe. In Bulgaria and the former Yugoslav Republic of Macedonia, for example, around one third of the work force is to be found in the shadow economy, and in the Ukraine, the proportion is around one fifth. In sub-Saharan Africa, people continue to stream into an informal economy that already accounts for at least two thirds of all jobs.

Even those who do find work in the formal sector are often having to accept temporary or part-time jobs, despite their need for full-time employment. Emphasis on flexible labour markets promotes this outcome. In Latin America, eight out of 10 new jobs are part-time or temporary. And even in Western Europe, 18 per cent of employees were working part-time in 1997, while nearly one quarter of them would have preferred full-time work.

Wages in the current labour market are relatively low. Intense competition for employment means that workers have little capacity to bargain in most countries. Thus even in unionized enterprises, there is a tendency for wage increases to lag behind any growth in productivity. And in regions struggling to cope with long-term economic stagnation and indebtedness, the remuneration of workers is often shamefully inadequate. Real wages throughout much of Latin America and Africa have yet to return to levels considered normal 20 years ago.

The situation in transition countries has been particularly dramatic. Large-scale restructuring has implied hardship for many people. In China, for example, where overall employment figures are positive, millions of workers in state and collective enterprises are being placed on leave at half pay or less. In Russia, with an official unemployment rate of 10 per cent, it is estimated that an additional 11 per cent of the labour force is kept on the payroll at minimal rates or pushed into taking "holidays" that are ill-disguised forms of job loss. Real wages in Russia fell annually by 8.3 per cent over the period 1989–96, and they often were not paid on time.

One other negative aspect of current trends in labour markets is the widening of wage differentials within countries and industries. In most parts of the world, the pattern of growth has favoured skilled over unskilled labour, raising demand for highly trained workers and increasing their remuneration. International wage differentials have also grown wider—a trend that encourages migration of the best-prepared people in developing countries to Asia, North America or Europe.

Poverty and inequality

Given the growing dearth of decent employment, it is hardly surprising that the world has made little progress in reducing poverty—both income poverty, which refers to basic consumption, and human poverty, which refers to a lack of essential human capabilities such as being literate or adequately nourished.

The measure of income poverty used by most international agencies is the proportion of the population with a purchasing power equivalent to less than $1 per day. This is probably an indefensibly low figure: in fact, in some parts of the world, no one could live on this amount. Thus it is a measure that seriously underestimates the gravity of the problem. Even so, estimates relying on this standard suggest a dismal picture. At least 1.2 billion people—one fifth of humankind—were living in absolute poverty in 1998, roughly the same situation as a decade earlier. Figures provided in table 1.3 suggest that this number fell between 1993 and 1996, primarily because there were falling numbers of the very poorest in China. Then it started to rise again—largely as a result of the global financial crisis. Almost all regions saw a rise in the number of people living in absolute income poverty during 1996–98.

For human poverty, there are a number of possible indicators. One of the broadest is life expectancy. The world as a whole has seen an increase in life expectancy over the past three decades. But there have been some notable setbacks. The transition countries of Eastern and Central Europe saw a remarkable dip in life expectancy in the immediate aftermath of the fall of communism. In Russia between 1980 and 1995, male life expectancy fell by four years, to only 58—10 years less than in China. Since then, however, there seems to have been a recovery. The other region where life expectancy has fallen is sub-Saharan Africa, due partly to the effects of war and civil unrest, but largely to the ravages of HIV/AIDS. In this case, however, the situation will get worse. Nine countries in Africa are expected to see life expectancy fall to 47 years by 2010—the level of the 1960s.

Table 1.3 – Poverty trends: People living on less than $1 (PPP) per day (millions)

	1987	1990	1993	1996	1998
East Asia and the Pacific	**415.1**	**452.4**	**431.9**	**265.0**	**278.3**
(excluding China)	***109.2***	***76.0***	***66.0***	***45.2***	***55.6***
Eastern Europe and Central Asia	**1.1**	**7.1**	**18.3**	**23.8**	**24.0**
Latin America and the Caribbean	**63.7**	**73.8**	**70.8**	**76.0**	**78.2**
Middle East and North Africa	**25.0**	**22.0**	**21.5**	**21.3**	**20.9**
South Asia	**474.4**	**495.1**	**505.1**	**504.7**	**522.0**
Sub-Saharan Africa	**217.2**	**242.3**	**273.3**	**289.0**	**290.9**
Total	**1,196.5**	**1,292.7**	**1,320.9**	**1,179.9**	**1,214.2**
(excluding China)	***890.6***	***916.3***	***955***	***960.1***	***991.5***

Source: World Bank, 1999a

The incidence of poverty has increased in the past few years not because the world as a whole is getting poorer, but because the benefits of growth have been unevenly spread. There has been a striking increase in inequality. UNDP has estimated that the distance between the richest and poorest countries, which was 44 to 1 in 1973, rose to 72 to 1 by 1992.

Within nations, rising disparities are evident even in the industrialized world. In the

Figure 1.3 – Gini coefficients, selected countries

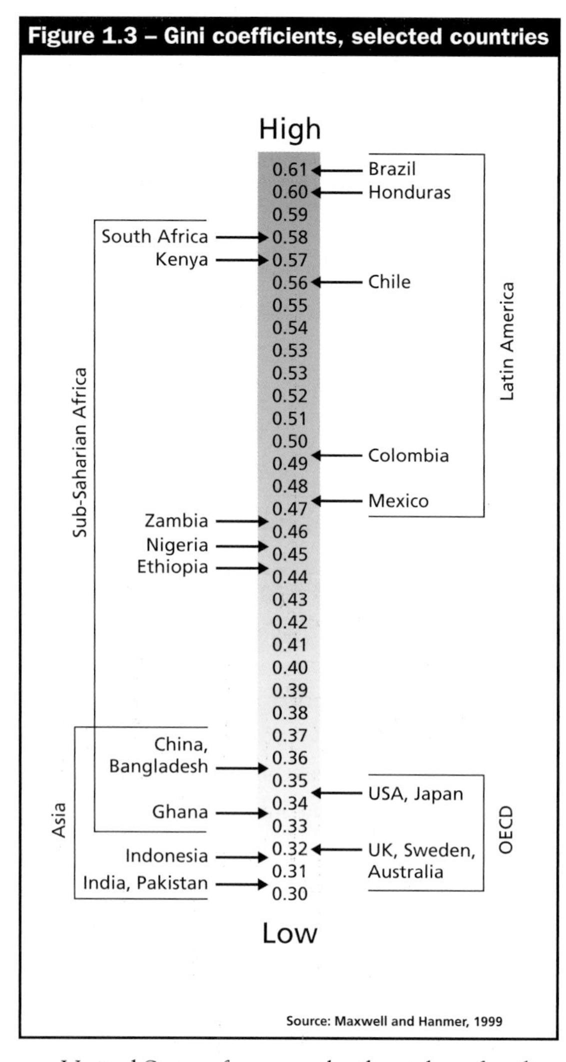

Source: Maxwell and Hanmer, 1999

United States, for example, the richest families saw their average income rise by 15 per cent during the 1990s, while the poorest families saw no increase at all. But the widest income disparities are to be found in some African and Latin American countries. This is evident from calculation of the Gini coefficient, a measure which for any country varies from 0 (absolute equality in distribution) to 1 (one person gets everything). The range of situations is indicated in figure 1.3, which identifies Brazil as one of the most unequal societies in the world. Although the Gini coefficient is usually slow to change, this is not always the case. In Bulgaria, for example, it increased from 0.23 to 0.38 between 1987–88 and 1993.

The causes of failure

The evolution of growth, employment and income over the past few decades suggests a world edging ever closer to unsustainable levels of inequality and deprivation. The kind of economic expansion that has occurred has been erratic, unstable and regressive in its distributional impact. Thus prospects for achieving the aims of the Copenhagen Declaration are not at all promising if the present tide of global liberalization continues.

Why has the liberal economy not delivered? Some would say that the extreme forms of market-driven restructuring that began several decades ago were never intended to promote enhanced equality and social welfare—the principal concerns of the Social Summit. There is a strain of Social Darwinism in dogmatic neoliberalism that is not uncomfortable with the idea of "survival of the fittest". Leaving aside this argument, however, excessive reliance on market forces rests on an unrealistic view of economies and societies. Markets are assumed to perform like well-oiled machines—adjusting in a relatively automatic fashion, so that changes take place smoothly and with an optimal outcome.

But markets are social and political institutions, composed of people with varying degrees of power and influence—and an imperfect capacity to obtain the information they need. There are always major problems of co-ordination. As John Maynard Keynes warned, "...to suppose that there exists some smoothly functioning automatic mechanism of adjustment which preserves equilibrium only if we trust to matters of *laissez-faire* is a doctrinaire delusion...".

These discontinuities are evident in production and trade, but they are even more marked when it comes to finance. Here the orthodox model assumes that prices are based on rational expectations and are fundamentally correct. This ignores the impact of speculation, day trading, and other issues that have more to do with psychology than with economic fundamentals. In practice, financial flows are often far from rational. They are based to a significant extent on an elusive notion of confidence that responds to instinct and herd behaviour.

Rational capital should, for example, move from surplus countries to deficit countries. But it seldom does. Prior to the Asian crisis, many investors poured money into Southeast Asia despite the fact that these countries did not really need it. They already had massive savings: from 1990 to 1997 gross domestic savings in East Asia and the Pacific were 36 per cent of GDP. In Latin America and the Caribbean, by contrast, they were 20 per cent and in sub-Saharan Africa, 17 per cent. Yet investors continued to lavish funds on Asia. Unsurprisingly, many of the extra funds were squandered on dubious projects. In Indonesia, for example, around one quarter of the funds borrowed from commercial banks went into real estate. A panic and crash were not far behind.

Too much confidence in the rationality of the "invisible hand" has been matched, over the past two decades, by too little understanding of the necessary relation between public policy and the market. Efficient markets require the contributions of a well-run public sector. They require a healthy, well-educated and well-informed population. And they require the social stability that grows out of democratic governance and an acceptable level of public provision.

In fact, the greater the degree of openness of a market economy—the greater its exposure to global market forces—the more important is the role that must be played by national governments in the field of social policy. Yet the thrust of much of the neoliberal agenda has run directly counter to this dictum. For decades, the prevailing orthodoxy has counselled a reduction of state functions. And for decades, governments without the capacity to resist international pressure have been abandoning essential elements of public social provision. Perhaps graver still, a combination of economic instability, indebtedness and external pressure to conform with dominant ideology has significantly weakened the overall administrative capacity of many states, as well as the role of democratic institutions in

Charles Dharapak, Associated Press AP

Crisis in Asia: Protest against rising food prices. Jakarta, Indonesia economic policy making. This is not an environment in which either equity or growth is likely to thrive.

New views on growth and social development

As the unsustainability of the present development model becomes obvious, the international community has begun to move in various directions. There is little coherence to this process. In fact, even within a single institution, it is usual to find initiatives that contradict each other—so that what may be accomplished through trying one new approach is largely offset by what may be lost through another.

TARGETING THE POOR

A renewed emphasis on poverty alleviation is perhaps the most visible new departure of the past few years. The sheer scale of growing deprivation has once again placed this problem at the centre of the development agenda. But the approach adopted by most agencies and governments is narrowly remedial. People living in poverty are being assisted through very specific forms of targeting and social safety nets —oriented, in principle, toward identifying and assisting only those in greatest need.

This is a technocratic approach to a highly complex social problem. It can be partially successful, but often at the cost of isolating and stigmatizing beneficiaries—and making them dependent on the individuals and institutions providing assistance. A narrow focus on poverty reduction is also likely to obscure issues of income distribution and social equity.

In the absence of serious parallel attention to these issues, poverty reduction can be converted into a zero-sum game: providing public services and support to the poorest implies reducing the access of other groups in society to the same benefits. This leads to creation of a dual structure of social services—one aimed at the poor and funded by the state, and one aimed at everyone else and provided by the private sector.

This decision to discard any pretension to universalism is based on the argument that, given limited public resources, these should not be captured by citizens who have the capacity to pay. But such an approach—which the World Bank has championed—is designed from the vantage point of an external funder, not from that of a national society. In its concern with the efficient disbursal of scarce external resources, it fails to consider the equally serious question of how to create an enabling environment for the generation and disbursal of domestic resources.

Withdrawing access to public services from all but the poorest—or seriously limiting the quality of services that can be obtained by ordinary citizens from public institutions—is guaranteed to weaken public willingness to pay taxes. A downward spiral of dwindling domestic resources is entirely predictable. In contrast, the experience in developed and middle-income countries is that providing universal access is one of the most effective ways to ensure middle class support for quality public services, as well as the mobilization of sufficient revenue to maintain them.

Growing dualism in social services is also not good for the poor. It is likely to be accompanied by the movement of well-qualified people from the public to the private sector and, as this occurs, by a decline in the quality of attention available to people living in poverty.

COMPREHENSIVE DEVELOPMENT FRAMEWORKS

A second approach to present social and economic dilemmas is much broader and more socially conscious. As the social and political nature of the market becomes obvious to a wider array of thinkers and practitioners, there is now an incipient return to the kinds of integrated approaches to development in vogue in the 1960s and 1970s. Indeed, the World Bank has gone so far as to propose a Comprehensive Development Framework in which structural and social concerns will be treated in conjunction with aspects of the macroeconomy and finance.

There is nothing new in such an approach. In fact, the case for development planning in pre-adjustment years was argued along the same lines, and so was the insistence on balanced growth. But in the interim, the world has passed through a devastating attack on state capacity and legitimacy. Thus there is a danger that the new agenda will overburden the much-weakened public sectors in a large number of developing countries. In the absence of strong and well-funded national planning institutions, the temptation to draw up Comprehensive Development Frameworks in donor countries—or the World Bank—will be enormous.

Social services and world trade

If insights from a Comprehensive Development Framework were applied to the Bank's divisive recommendations on targeting public social services toward the poor, this might well provoke a serious reassessment of policy. In the meantime, prospects for protecting universal public services are under attack from other quarters as well. The proposed Multilateral Agreement on Investment, first discussed in the OECD in 1995, would have opened an assortment of essential social services to foreign investment by including them in the general category of trade in services. Among other things, it would have undermined the ability of governments to subsidize local health care (box 1.1).

Discussions on liberalizing trade in services (including education and health) are also on the agenda of the World Trade Organization, where they have raised the spectre of "most favoured nation" clauses in basic public ser-

Box 1.1 – Trade regimes threaten government services

The proposed Multilateral Agreement on Investment (MAI) would have allowed foreign private providers to challenge national government prerogatives to provide free services or to subsidize national non-profit providers. The scheme would have embraced the full range of health and social services, including childcare centres, hospitals and community clinics, as well as private labs and independent physicians. Although the MAI was defeated, this issue will continue to resurface in the World Trade Organization (WTO).

A working paper by the Secretariat of the WTO Council for Trade in Services confirms that the next round of world trade negotiations "offers members the opportunity to reconsider the breadth and depth of their commitments on health and social services, which are currently trailing behind other large sectors". It notes with approval signs of increased global trade in health care from developing to developed countries, "with better-off people seeking rapid access to high-quality services abroad". The parallel paper on education is a little more restrained in its ambitions for increased trade, limiting its comments to higher education. Even so, regulating the content of educational material and providing student grants to citizens could both be deemed unfair practices or "barriers to free trade in education".

vices—clauses that could convert these areas of national life into markets, as open to competition from international firms as any other service sector in the local economy.

GLOBALIZING SOCIAL STANDARDS

The incursion of unbridled market forces into all corners of public and private life has prompted calls for some form of global social standard-setting. As workers in countries around the world are forced to compete with each other in global markets, there is a growing danger that wages will be standardized downward. And if transnational corporations become the arbiters of global policy, some fear that they will gravitate not only toward countries where wages are lowest, but also where taxes are lowest. Governments with lower tax revenues will have less to spend on social services. This race to the bottom would be extremely damaging.

If there is to be some countervailing force to the disruptive reign of markets, where will it come from? In many respects, governments probably have more freedom of action than they realize. In the case of wages, for example, it has been assumed that—in the current global economy—establishing or defending minimum wages will price people out of jobs. Whatever the economic rationale for this, it does not necessarily happen in practice. The United Kingdom, for example, during years of Conservative rule resisted the principle of a minimum wage. Yet when it was introduced by a Labour government in 1998, it not only gave 2 million people a 20 per cent wage increase on average, but it also appears to have increased employment in most of the sectors where these people worked. No reputable enterprises went out of business; indeed, most were relieved that they were less likely to be undercut by rogue companies paying starvation wages.

Nevertheless, free trade imposes limits on national decision making. While some low-paid work, from haircutting to burger-flipping, cannot be traded internationally, an increasing proportion of service activities can—notably those with the potential to be delivered electronically. Telephone support workers in call-centres in Ireland and Sweden will increasingly find themselves competing with people in India or the Philippines.

It is this kind of worry that has increased pressure for the implementation of minimum standards globally. In fact, these already exist to some extent in the form of ILO conventions. There is general agreement and support for what are considered core standards, such as those on forced labour, child labour and non-discrimination. But there is less support for extending international standards into other areas.

Part of the problem is that developing country governments interpret such moves as a ploy on the part of industrialized countries to reduce the competitive threat from poorer countries. This perception bedevilled efforts in 1996 to introduce social clauses into world trade agreements. There are also understandable fears that such clauses will be added to the list of conditionalities that have accompanied aid during the past two decades.

It should be admitted that some of these arguments come from governments with poor human rights records, for whom social clauses would entail radical shifts in domestic social policies and priorities. However, they are supplied with a convenient defence when hectored by moralizing Northern governments. They argue, with some justification, that rich governments hypocritically want them to meet international standards while systematically denying them the means—via trade or aid—that would enable them to fulfil their obligations.

Since increasing globalization requires the elaboration of shared social norms, it is necessary to find a way out of this impasse. Developing countries must not place themselves in a purely reactive position that has the potential of leading them into a moral and ideological cul-de-sac. On the contrary, they must play a proactive role in devising standards that are in line with international conventions and the social goals they are already pursuing. Then the issue will be how to devise, at national and global levels, trade regimes that are supportive of, and compatible with, these social norms and goals.

NEW ARCHITECTURES?

In the current search for new approaches to social and economic progress, there is much talk of creating a new institutional setting at the international level, a new context for stimulating broadly based growth and reducing unacceptably high degrees of volatility and risk in the global economy. Since the Social Summit in 1995, there have been important new initiatives in the field of debt relief and growing pressure for reform of the principal international financial institutions. There are new proposals on how to deal with financial crises and panics. There is also progress in discussions on co-ordinating national policies in fields like taxation and corporate regulation. A number of these initiatives are analysed in the following chapters.

Useful as it may be, the current discussion of new institutional frameworks for a fragile global economy is concerned above all with ensuring the stability of the system. Movement toward alternative development models—which would probably require a co-ordinated effort to reintroduce appropriate capital controls, and to provide special and differential treatment for developing countries in the world trade regime—is not visible. Neither is there a wide-ranging commitment by industrialized countries to generate the kind of sustained economic expansion, based on labour support and concomitant wage restraint, that could generate full employment and rising wages in both the developed and developing world.

Moreover, there is complete silence on how to go about creating the social development architecture that would have to underpin the central vision of the Social Summit. This must allow for qualitatively new approaches to growth, based on a new understanding of the vital role of a healthy, literate and secure society in creating the conditions of economic progress. Yet social policy today remains largely detached from economics, or is seen as an add-on intended to remedy the ill effects of misconceived economic development. Until this changes, it is unlikely that the "society for all" envisioned by signatories of the Copenhagen Declaration will be within our grasp.

Globalization with a human mask

Today, there is a growing clamor for thoroughgoing reform that reinforces human values in political and economic processes. But, on present trends, changes are likely to be far more superficial. In fact, what we are more likely to see is globalization with a human mask. Human values are not being placed at the centre of policy making, but scattered to the periphery and painted onto the surface.

This minimalist view is evident across the whole spectrum of social policy. Current wisdom urges governments to confine themselves to damage control, providing safety nets for the poor and destitute, while targeting other social services at those who can demonstrate the greatest need. For everyone else, social services—be they education, health, or care for the aged—should be fragmented and dispersed among NGOs and private providers. If current trends continue, governments may also have to stand back from social provision and clear the field for the arrival of any corporation that wants to sell its services.

This has the superficial logic of economic efficiency, but it is blind to essential social processes. The experience of the second half of the twentieth century shows that the greatest advances in social welfare have grown from widely shared experience, shared values, and above all shared interests. This has been inherent in nation building—in creating spaces for common identities and the public institutions that uphold solidarity among citizens.

Neoliberal globalization works in the other direction—it further polarizes and splinters. If this trend is to be halted, the "visible hands" of governments and citizens must intervene to reassert the value of equity and social cohesion. And there must be strong renewed commitment to the public good.

Who pays?
Financing social development

Efrem Lukatsky, Associated Press AP

Pensioner in a supermarket. Kiev, Ukraine

If governments are to achieve more equitable development, they will have to resolve the debt crisis and reorient development assistance. They will also need to adopt new approaches to taxation and pensions and find ways of generating more resources locally.

More wealth has been generated over thepast few decades than ever before. But the world does not yet have ways to channel enough of this into social development. Five years after Copenhagen, there is an even greater contrast between available resources and manifest need.

Most of the damage has been concentrated in developing and transition countries. There is less of a problem in the industrialized countries whose governments have generally sustained their social spending. The United States has been able to do this because its economy has been growing strongly. And the governments of Western Europe and Japan have given priority to social programmes. This contrast between resources available for social provision in industrial and developing countries threatens to widen disparities between rich and poor still further. An important goal for the years ahead must be to reverse this destructive trend.

Debt relief for the poorest countries

At the time of the Social Summit, the debt of the Third World and the former Soviet Union had reached $2.2 trillion and was climbing steadily, both through the inexorable magic of compound interest and the need to borrow yet more money to meet the most pressing demands for payment (figure 2.1). By 1994, annual debt service payments for a number of African countries were already equivalent to more than 40 per cent of their total exports of goods and services; and governments were often paying more in interest to foreign creditors than they were allocating to basic social services such as health and education, whose quality was declining markedly.

Many delegates at the Social Summit highlighted the seriousness of the problem and argued that it would be impossible to improve the living standards of millions of poor people when their governments were saddled with such an enormous burden of debt. This concern was reflected in the Copenhagen Declaration, which committed all signatories to "ensure the urgent implementation of existing debt relief agreements and negotiate further initiatives to alleviate the debts of the poorest and heavily indebted low-income countries at an early date".

The HIPC initiative

The most elaborate response to these concerns emerged in 1996, when the IMF and the World Bank launched the Heavily Indebted Poor Country (HIPC) initiative. This was promising for a number of reasons. First, it raised the prospect of cancelling debt owed to the multilateral institutions; previous debt relief

Figure 2.1 – Evolution of debt, 1985–97

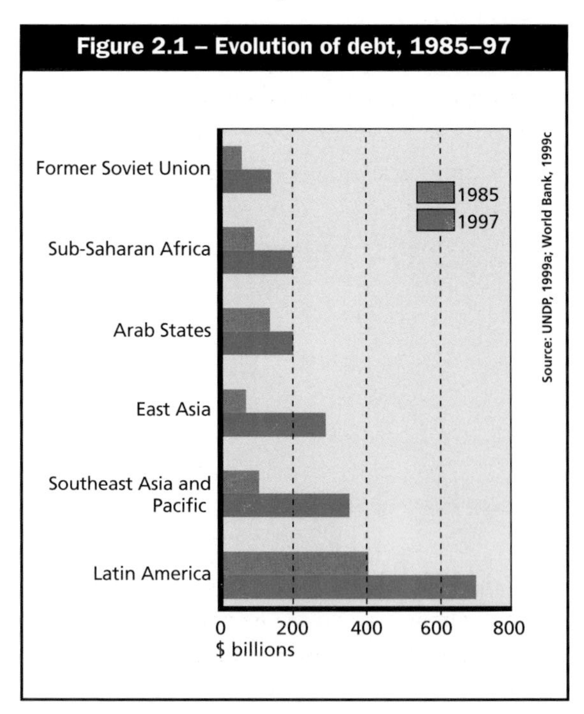

schemes had been concerned only with bilateral or private debt. Second, it established a different criterion for debt forgiveness—based not on the magnanimity of the creditor but on the debtor's real capacity to pay. The aim was to reduce the debts of the poorest countries to levels that were "sustainable"—repayable out of export revenues over a reasonable period. On this criterion, 41 countries were classified as HIPCs—whose debt was judged too high a multiple of their likely exports of goods and services—and who should thus be considered for debt relief.

In the event, the HIPC initiative has achieved little. It places such onerous conditions and requires so many different levels of certification that few of the 41 countries have so far qualified for relief. First, the country has needed to prove that, after all other avenues of debt relief have been exhausted, the net present value of public and publicly guaranteed debt would still be 200 to 250 per cent greater than the value of exports of goods and services. For most countries this is an unreasonably high threshold. Second, the country has to prove its commitment to neoliberal policy prescriptions. It must demonstrate a six-year track record of structural adjustment and submit to close inspection of its economic management. Finally, following a series of debt reductions by bilateral donors and commercial creditors, the multilateral agencies may step in to provide additional relief.

Unsurprisingly, only a few countries have survived the course. Within the first two years—1996–98—only Bolivia and Uganda managed to meet the criteria. Burkina Faso, Côte d'Ivoire, Guyana, Mali and Mozambique are scheduled to follow shortly. But the relief they can expect to receive is hardly generous. As a result of the HIPC initiative, Mozambique, for example, would see its annual debt service payments fall by only $13 million—from $113 million to $100 million. Uganda's experience, too, suggests that the HIPC initiative is unlikely to produce lasting benefits (box 2.1).

Pressure for alternatives

By 1998, criticisms of the HIPC initiative were mounting. Many people, particularly in the NGO community, were outraged at the lack of progress—especially during a period of booming global financial markets. Between 1996 and 1999 the rich countries saw their total stock market wealth increase by over $5 trillion, yet they seemed unwilling to deal with the HIPC debt of only $245 billion.

This groundswell of opinion took its most effective form in Jubilee 2000, which has proved one of the largest and most influential international NGO coalitions. With activists in over 40 countries, it called for "a debt-free start to the millennium for a billion people".

Responding to pressure from Jubilee 2000, and others, the Group of 7 industrialized countries announced that their June 1999 meeting in Cologne would include a comprehensive debt relief package. To concentrate their minds on this issue, thousands of activists also converged on Cologne for an alternative economic summit—bringing with them a petition signed by 17 million people.

At the end of their meeting, the G-7 members presented the Cologne Debt Initiative, which included limited debt write-offs: up to $90 billion for the poorest and most indebted countries. They also called on individual countries to cancel debts and requested the international financial institutions to provide faster, deeper relief. In addition, they changed existing HIPC rules, modifying the definition of debtors in distress to those with a ratio of debt to exports of 150 per cent or more.

But, overall, the response was disappointing. The G-7 countries avoided any large-scale debt cancellation and, if anything, they added to the conditions for debt relief. Administration of the initiative was placed in the hands of the

Box 2.1 – Uganda's debt

Between 1980 and 1996, Uganda's total debt rose from $0.7 billion to $3.6 billion. This was despite a sequence of debt-relief efforts, mostly arranged through the Paris Club—a group of bilateral creditors who have provided relief on increasingly concessional terms. By 1996, the country's debt was equivalent to 61 per cent of GNP. Sixty-two per cent of the total was owed to multilateral creditors.

Uganda could point to a long and satisfactory record of structural adjustment, dating from 1987. Therefore it was accepted as a candidate for HIPC relief in 1996, with a "completion point" set for 1998. In the interim, it underwent monitoring by the World Bank and the IMF, to ensure that it continued to implement structural reforms. The former included further reform of the financial sector, rapid advance in privatizing state enterprises, continuing civil service reform and strengthening the tax regime. The capital account was entirely liberalized in July 1997, and remaining non-tariff barriers to trade were lifted in April 1998. In the social field, the government adopted a Poverty Eradication Action Plan in June 1997.

Having satisfactorily completed these reforms, Uganda became the first country to be granted debt relief under the HIPC initiative, in April 1998. Through a series of negotiations, the total stock of debt (outstanding by end June 1997) was reduced by approximately 19 per cent.

Although this relief is welcome—amounting in the early years to $42 million annually—it is far from meeting Uganda's social development needs. President Museveni's Universal Primary Education initiative, for example, cost 120 million in 1997 alone. Such initiatives will remain dependent on external funding. Some of this will come in the form of grants, but the rest will be loans. As a result, the breathing space created by HIPC stands to be wiped out in a few years, as Uganda acquires more debts.

IMF, which was to demand not just proof of continued structural adjustment but also evidence of progress in poverty reduction. The annual cost to the G-7 countries of the Cologne reforms will be $2 billion to $3 billion—less than one third of the amount cut from aid budgets since 1992. Although international progress toward writing off all HIPC debt has been slow, individual countries have taken positive steps. Following earlier leads by the Nordic countries and the Netherlands, the governments of the United Kingdom, France and the United States announced plans in 1999 and 2000 to cancel all debts owed them by the poorest countries. But there is still a long bureaucratic and political road to travel before the infamous chapter of debt renegotiation can be closed. In the meantime, debt payments flow relentlessly out of poor countries toward creditors who have long since developed the financial means to write them off (box 2.2).

Debt relief for middle-income countries

Though the HIPCs are urgently in need of debt relief, they account for only around 10 per cent of total Third World debt. The remainder is owed by less-poor or middle-income developing countries whose development has also been shaped—and distorted—by decades of continuous restructuring under the discipline of debt.

The problems for these countries, typically in Latin America, originated in the 1970s. At that point, commercial banks were flush with capital from the oil exporting countries and lent fairly indiscriminately to many developing countries. This transformed financial flows to Latin America. In the period 1966–70, commercial banks had supplied only 8 per cent of the flow of resources from the United States to Latin America, but by 1978 they were responsible for 57 per cent.

The banks made minimal efforts to evaluate the risks associated with these loans. Many of the loans were used to finance investment in public and private enterprises, infrastructure and development programmes. But others were used to import consumer goods, to speculate on foreign exchange markets, or simply for private ends. The banks were sanguine about this. After all, much of their lending was going to governments, and "governments never default".

The debt crisis

Most of these loans were short-term, usually to be renewed annually, and the banks charged variable rates of interest. While interest rates remained low, repayment was less of a problem. But in 1979 the US Federal Reserve launched a historic assault on inflation. As a result, interest rates suddenly jumped to 20 per cent and, virtually overnight, projects whose business plans might have looked eminently reasonable—given their original assumptions—became unviable. A collapse in the prices of major Latin American commodity exports at this time further worsened the economic climate.

This was not just a crisis for the borrowers. It also threatened the stability of Northern commercial banks. In 1982, the Argentine debt alone represented 18 per cent of the capital of the nine biggest banks in the United States. Debtors and lenders thus found themselves locked into a classic debt trap: the banks had to continue lending to keep their debtors sufficiently above water to service earlier loans; and the debtor countries had to continue to accept additional loans at the new, high rates of interest.

The Third World debt crisis became headline news—a drama directed by the IMF that was to be played out in numerous acts. The plot was based on a series of threatened defaults that were followed by last-minute moratoria, most of which were conditional on debtors following the classic IMF prescriptions, devaluing their currencies to encourage exports and cutting public expenditure.

Over the course of the 1980s, the crisis eventually subsided—at least for the banks. They steadily set aside funds that would enable them to survive debt write-offs, while also exchanging some of the debt for stakes in state-owned enterprises. And by the early 1990s, the worst seemed to be over—particularly following agreement on the Brady Plan, which included an ingenious device that converted a considerable part of the remaining debt into bonds, backed by US government securities.

The banks were relieved at having outstanding loans transformed into bonds, which could be listed as an asset and traded in financial markets. But the debtor countries had less to celebrate. Their debt had not disappeared; it had merely changed form. Instead of paying interest to the banks, governments now had to pay it to holders of bonds. That meant continued sacrifices. People would need to tighten their belts still further. And governments would have to continue cutting public expenditure while stepping up exports, with the added pressure of keeping on the right side of the international investors, on whom they would depend for future funds.

The new bondage

Spurred by the unexpected success of the Brady bonds, for which there appeared to be a ready market, Latin American governments saw a way of relieving some of their problems by issuing yet more bonds on their own account. This transformed the debt picture yet again. Between 1992 and 1996, for example, Argentina's total debt rose from $43 billion to $100 billion. Of this, 3 per cent was owed to banks and 15 per cent to financial institutions, but 60 per cent now took the form of bonds.

These bonds still must be serviced—both the guaranteed interest, or coupon, and ultimately the principal. The crisis for the indebted middle-income countries has therefore become more diffuse. Now they must not only satisfy the IMF, when they need its support, but also keep the international capital markets on their side.

Since the bond markets in most of these countries do not accept large issues, governments can only borrow a few billion dollars at a time. This ensures permanent vulnerability. If international bond rating agencies, such as Moody's or Standard & Poor's, take a pessimistic view of a country's prospects, investors will require that the latter's next bond issue offer higher interest. Debt service will become still more costly. And the proportion of the national budget that can be allocated to non-debt-related projects will shrink. Borrowers thus find themselves continually dependent on the rating agencies.

This not only ties the hands of governments, but also dampens democratic debate. Citizens or politicians who protest against the effects of mounting debt now find they risk retaliation from market forces. Even to mention publicly that the debt overhang is a constraint on social spending—or that social and economic policy must change—will flash warning signals to investors around the world. This induces an unhealthy form of self-censorship throughout the political systems of many indebted middle-income countries. Both the general public and their representatives avoid touching on questions of elemental social justice that could promote yet another round of capital flight, or contribute to yet another period of economic instability.

The new bondage also makes it more difficult to present a united front when negotiating with creditors. When governments owed money to a small number of banks, they could exert some pressure by threatening a concerted default. But bondholders are highly dispersed and mobile. To negotiate with them is a far more daunting task.

Desperation can still lead to default. A portent of things to come appeared in September 1999 when Ecuador, with a foreign debt of more than $13 billion, defaulted on the interest payments due on one class of its Brady bonds. The government attempted to negotiate with bondholders but only persuaded 8 per cent to support a plan that would give Ecuador more breathing space. Instead, 25 per cent of them voted to demand accelerated payments.

Box 2.2 – Missing targets, the price of debt

The current levels of debt in the HIPCs make it virtually impossible for them to achieve the goals set at the Social Summit. The Summit target for child mortality by 2015, for example, was 52 deaths per 1,000 live births. UNICEF estimates, however, that in the HIPCs the child mortality rate at that time will be 134 deaths per 1,000—equivalent to 2 million additional child deaths annually. The prospects are no better in education. UNESCO estimates that up to 40 million primary school-aged children in HIPCs will remain out of school in 2010—a figure likely to rise further by 2015. On the basis of primary education trends since 1990, Oxfam estimates that only seven of the HIPCs are likely to achieve their 2015 goals.

Ecuador decided to default and suffered the consequences—which included a collapse in its currency and little prospect of attracting new funds. Other indebted countries were quick to distance themselves from Ecuador's action. Indeed, both Mexico and the Philippines at the same time bought back some of their own Brady bonds.

Confronting the problem of debt bondage in middle-income market economies is difficult and complex. Yet a way will have to be found both to head off impending crises and to protect the millions of people who are suffering long-term declines in their standards of living and in social welfare.

Fresh departures for debt

Continuing poverty and the likelihood of further crises in both HIPCs and middle-income countries demand not just urgent attention to their immediate debt problems but also a fresh approach to future borrowing.

New institutions for dealing with debt

Past debt activities have largely been driven by crisis and have resulted in ad hoc rescue packages. This is not only inefficient, but has caused untold, and unnecessary, suffering for millions of people. What is needed to lessen the seriousness of future debt crises is a new institutional structure. For this to emerge, however, the industrialized countries have to mobilize behind one clear idea.

A number of governments and international bodies, including UNCTAD and the Economic Commission for Latin America and the Caribbean (ECLAC), support the development of procedures for the orderly workout of debt, including a temporary suspension of payments by beleaguered governments—a move to be given legitimacy by an independent arbitration panel—combined with encouragement for further lending during the period of debt restructuring. Going further still, others have proposed the establishment of a treaty-based international bankruptcy court. A crucial element of such proposals is that the burden of restructuring should be shared between borrowers and lenders.

Sovereign debt and bankruptcy

When it comes to debts owed by enterprises, most industrialized countries have effective bankruptcy laws. These ensure that bad decisions or bad luck do not condemn debtors to paying for their mistakes for the rest of their lives. Indeed, the dynamism of the US economy is often ascribed to the opportunities it offers risk-takers to wipe the slate clean and start again. Should there not be something equivalent for sovereign debt?

Jubilee 2000 and others have proposed that states should have recourse to an international bankruptcy court. Rather than having debt problems discussed in the secretive corridors of the Paris Club or the international financial institutions, they should be aired formally and publicly in a new institution. This would have many advantages, but establishing such a mechanism will not be easy. It is not clear, for example, how such a court could establish the necessary jurisdiction over both creditors and debtors. And debtors might be tempted to capricious default.

But it can be argued that the present system, or non-system, has its own forms of moral hazard. In fact, unclear arrangements for dealing with crisis encourage all creditors to protect their own interests at the expense of someone else. The strongest creditors win such contests. And it is often ordinary taxpayers—including relatively poor ones—who foot the bill. Moreover, in both borrowing and lending countries, government bailouts of failing financial institutions frequently have to be paid for by cutting social expenditures—robbing the poor to pay the rich.

CONDITIONALITY

Attempts to deal with international debt have always been associated with conditionality—though lately the conditions have been changing. In the 1980s, debt renegotiation generally required the borrowers to carry out neoliberal reforms; in the late 1990s, these stipulations have been supplemented with requirements that any relief be targeted toward reducing poverty.

This is understandable. Some of the original debts were incurred by corrupt or authoritarian regimes that used the funds to benefit elites. Donor governments and NGOs want to ensure that future funds do not disappear down the same drain. Thus members of the Jubilee 2000 coalition link their proposals for debt cancellation to requirements that funds freed for use by debt renegotiation be used to improve health, education and other social benefits. Creditor countries also insist that debt forgiveness carry similar social conditionality.

But this raises a number of difficulties. The most familiar is fungibility—governments receiving relief may claim to be using the freed-up funds on social expenditure they would have made anyway.

A second, equally familiar concern is that of excessive interference in local decision making. Those involved in debt relief efforts need to use caution in the ways they monitor and influence the use of resources. Apart from stifling local autonomy, too much conditionality can also exhaust time and money that might be better employed elsewhere.

A further, less obvious issue is that social conditionality may be over-simplistic. All governments nowadays find their room for manoeuvre constrained by international markets. They are under constant pressure to keep wages, taxes and public expenditure low—and interest rates high. This can seriously limit their ability to invest, to stimulate employment, to fund essential infrastructure, and generally to promote longer-term development. Therefore, if they do get debt relief, governments may have good reason to use these resources to overcome key restraints on growth, and not simply to increase direct social expenditure. Rather than defining a specific use for the funds, it might be better to insist that governments make their decisions openly and democratically.

Indeed, one of the most important benefits of effective debt relief may be to open up larger democratic spaces. High indebtedness fosters a crisis mentality that inhibits open debate on public affairs. This allows lenders to collude with debtors in seeking solutions behind closed doors. The population at large feels disempowered and nervous about rocking a boat that always seems in imminent danger of capsizing. People may therefore swing between cycles of apathy and protest, rather than engaging in reasoned debate about how the country can best move forward (box 2.3).

Citizens should also have the opportunity to consider debt relief in a much broader context—seeing how it fits into the global economic system. Even if their country's debts are cancelled, this will not protect them from future drops in commodity prices, or wild increases in interest rates, or a sudden shift in investor sentiment—any one of which could again wreak havoc in their fragile economies and plunge them back into debt. It is vital to find a way out of the current crisis, but it is just as important to foresee, and prevent, the next one.

Development assistance

The poorest countries urgently need debt relief, but this is not enough. To strengthen their economies, there must be an inflow of new resources; and a large proportion of these can only be obtained in the form of development assistance. Aid is needed not just to fund critical development projects, but also to attract foreign private capital, which is unlikely to arrive in the poorest countries unless backed by guarantees from donor governments or multilateral agencies.

At the time of the Social Summit, prospects for development assistance were gloomy. Flows had already declined markedly, and only four donor countries—Denmark, the Netherlands, Norway and Sweden—were meeting or surpassing the agreed UN target of 0.7 per cent of their GNP. The Social Summit recognized the need to halt the slide, and delegates resolved to "strive for the fulfilment of the agreed target of 0.7 per cent of gross national product for official development assistance as soon as possible".

This resolve had little practical effect. Indeed, as indicated in table 2.1, official aid flows continued to dwindle. In 1995 the member countries of the Development Assistance Committee of the OECD gave $59 billion. But by 1997 the figure had dropped to $48.3 billion. In 1998 the figure improved—to $51.9 billion—but this is still considerably less than the 1995 level. The table sets this in the context of the military spending of DAC members.

Donor fatigue

The decline in ODA has commonly been attributed to "donor fatigue". One aid evaluation after another has pointed to wasted or misused funds, corruption in both public and private circles, and to the general institutional weakness in developing countries that makes it difficult for them to use aid effectively. As a result, donors have become increasingly dissatisfied. The World Bank, for example, in a widely read publication *Assessing Aid*, concluded: "Donors should be willing to cut back financing to countries with persistently low-quality public sectors".

But the problems with aid are not entirely due to the weakness of Third World institutions. In recent years, development assistance has had to operate in such a generally hostile global climate that its limited success is hardly surprising.

One of the most debilitating factors, as indicated in the previous section, has been debt. At the time of the Social Summit, around one quarter of bilateral aid was being used to repay multilateral lenders. And for World Bank aid the position was even worse. In 1993–94, out of every $3 that the World Bank offered as IDA loans and grants, it reclaimed $2 as debt repayment. Of the remaining dollar, the IMF pocketed part. Aid has also been diverted to cope with a string of humanitarian crises—some of

Table 2.1 – OECD aid compared with military spending

	1990	1991	1992	1993	1994	1995	1996	1997	1998
OECD official development assistance ($ billions)[a]	52.9	56.7	60.9	56.5	59.2	59.0	55.4	48.3	51.9
OECD military spending ($ billions)[b]	657	612	620	595	572	548	553	550	539
ODA as percentage of military spending	8.0	9.3	9.8	9.5	9.7	9.3	10.0	8.8	9.6
ODA as percentage of DAC members' GNP[c,d]	0.33	0.33	0.33	0.30	0.30	0.27	0.25	0.22	0.23
ODA average annual real percentage change, 1991-97[a]							- 4.6		

Sources and notes: [a] OECD/DAC, 1999b and 1999c; [b] SIPRI, 1999; [c] Randel et al., 1998 and 2000; [d] The target for overall official development assistance is 0.7 per cent of GNP (Commitment 9 (l) of the Copenhagen Declaration on Social Development).

them climatic, some of them man-made. The proportion of bilateral aid devoted to emergency relief rose from 1.5 to 8.4 per cent between 1991 and 1994.

Aid has also failed because of donor errors. An increasing proportion of aid has been used in co-ordination with the World Bank and the IMF to support policy reforms that ultimately have produced meagre results. Far too often, assistance has also been accompanied by such time-consuming demands for reporting that donor fatigue has probably been matched by "recipient fatigue". Each year, for example, Tanzania prepares as many as 2,400 progress reports per quarter for all its donor partners.

Reorienting development assistance

One way of reorienting development assistance is to require that a much larger proportion of aid be dedicated to social development. In the

Box 2.3 – Protests over social sector priorities

People in many poorer countries have become resigned to the cuts in public services they have had to endure. But as the press regularly reports, their anger frequently boils over into protests and strikes.

"Jamaica's capital, Kingston, was closed down as anti-government protesters blocked main roads across the island....The wave of protests was sparked by last week's budget, which increased the price of petrol by 30%. The government expects to spend 62% of tax revenue on debt service, and is struggling to protect spending on health, education and the police."—*The Economist,* 24 April 1999

"Since the fall of communism, academic freedom and government interest in higher education [in Russia] have mushroomed, although this has not been matched by increased resources. In response, student and industrial militancy have risen markedly. Besides strikes, demonstrations and pickets, students and lecturers have taken the state to court for unpaid salaries and begged outside Yeltsin's house. When in 1996 the government announced an indefinite delay in the payment of salaries and bursaries, 22 lecturers went on hunger strike. Within a week the government had given in. These are small victories against a background of defeat in a country where neoliberalism is running an education system into the ground."—*The Guardian,* 19 October 1999

"The strike [in Zimbabwe] began at the end of September when 400 junior doctors refused to go to work, demanding significant increases in their meagre monthly salaries and better hospital conditions. Nyasha Masuke, spokesman for the junior doctors, says: 'The hospitals are so badly equipped that we watch malaria patients die because there is no chloroquine. We see others die because there is no blood for transfusions.' Once the pride of Africa and a model for other developing countries, Zimbabwe's government health facilities have been starved of funds for nearly a decade.

A continuation of decline is likely as a result of Zimbabwe's new budget for 2000. The health ministry had requested Z$10bn ($250m) but was only allocated Z$6bn. In contrast, the defence ministry received a whopping Z$9bn. 'The government does not see any urgency in ending our strike,' says Dr Masuke. "The cabinet ministers and the rich can go to their private hospitals. It is the poor of Zimbabwe who suffer."—*The Guardian,* 1 November 1999

past, the bulk of non-military aid was used to stimulate economic development, through infrastructure projects, agricultural development, and various kinds of budgetary support. Social sector spending has lagged behind. Each country has had different priorities, but few have tried to ensure that large volumes of aid reach the poor. This was especially true while governments were preoccupied with adjustment. At that point, the best the poor could hope for were partial measures, such as social safety nets.

Moved by the desperate situation of large numbers of people deeply affected by crisis and adjustment, participants in the Social Summit focused a great deal of attention on the persistence of poverty. They committed themselves not only to reduce it, but also to eradicate it. And in consequence, all members of the international development community have now given poverty alleviation central importance in their programmes. But, given different traditions of social welfare and social policy in donor countries, it has not been easy for the aid establishment to develop an integrated approach to this goal. On one side are those who see poverty reduction in narrow terms—best achieved by targeting remedial action at the poor. On the other side are those of the welfare state tradition, who believe that poverty reduction should be a part of broader efforts by the state to improve social conditions and promote social justice. This division was clearly visible in the Social Summit's Declaration and Programme of Action and remains evident in the divergent policies of donors and their contrasting development assistance programmes.

The 20/20 initiative

The problems encountered in redirecting aid toward social development are well illustrated by experience with the 20/20 initiative. The final chapter of the Copenhagen Programme of Action includes a "mutual commitment between developed and developing country partners to allocate, on average, 20 per cent of ODA and 20 per cent of the national budget...to basic social programmes". Many people regard this mutual commitment as one of the most important achievements of the Social Summit. It has been taken up not just by bilateral donors and the major multilateral development agencies—including UNICEF, UNDP and the World Bank—but also by many NGOs in both North and South.

A great merit of the 20/20 approach is its apparent simplicity—which helps make it a sharp tool for advocacy. But the general unanimity starts to unravel when it comes to execution. There are problems right at the outset in agreeing on the definition of basic social services. While all donors agree that these include basic education, basic health, sanitation and clean water, not all of them see the need to deal with nutrition as a category separate from health. There are also different approaches to targeting. Some donors take 20 per cent as an overall target for their global development assistance programme, while others add the stipulation that it also has to be achieved in each recipient country. Then there is the question of conditionality. Some see 20/20 merely as a broad policy commitment—a long-term goal around which to organize collaboration. Other donors declare that if recipient governments to not achieve the 20/20 target they can expect to be penalized.

These disagreements make it difficult to coordinate donor activity or even to gauge progress. NGO monitoring projects, such as Social Watch and Reality of Aid, point to striking differences between reporting agencies. Not only do they employ different definitions, they also use incompatible accounting systems and statistical methods. This makes it almost impossible to determine the proportion of development assistance going to basic social services or to compare spending among donors.

The situation becomes even more complex when differences in reporting in Third World countries are taken into account.

Nevertheless, the 1998/99 Reality of Aid report attempted to measure the performance of bilateral donors. The project estimated what contribution bilateral aid should make to financing basic social services and what each donor's share should be, based on each country's GNP. The conclusion is summarized in figure 2.2. This shows that in 1995 the DAC countries as a whole were giving only 49 per cent of what was needed. Sharing out the overall bilateral target by country on the basis of GNP, the project found that only Sweden and Norway were contributing more than their fair share. While most countries fall short of what they should be contributing, however, it does appear that the proportions going to basic social services are slowly increasing.

But an increase in aid flows is only a part of the story. Much depends on the response of recipient governments. Here again there are problems of fungibility: governments that receive funds earmarked for basic social services may simply seize the opportunity to shift their own funds elsewhere. A World Bank study of 14 countries found strong evidence for this, though there was considerable variation between countries. Thus when Sri Lanka received aid for education and health, it took the opportunity to withdraw an even greater amount from these sectors—so the net effect was to reduce basic social sector spending. Indonesia, on the other hand, received a similar amount but supplemented this from its own funds, producing a substantial increase.

Regardless of the level of expenditure, one also has to take into account how effectively the funds are used. Again there can be enormous variations. In Bolivia, for example, donor contributions, along with national funds, appear to have been channelled very effectively to local groups for social services. But this case seems to be exceptional. More typical perhaps is Côte d'Ivoire, where reports indicate that most public services are failing to reach the poor.

Even when funds are used well, there can still be doubts about focusing so rigidly on basic social services. One danger is that other important social services will be sacrificed in order to meet imposed targets. A number of Third World governments, anxious to prove to donors and

Figure 2.2 – Providing basic social services for all: Bilateral donors' fair share, 1995

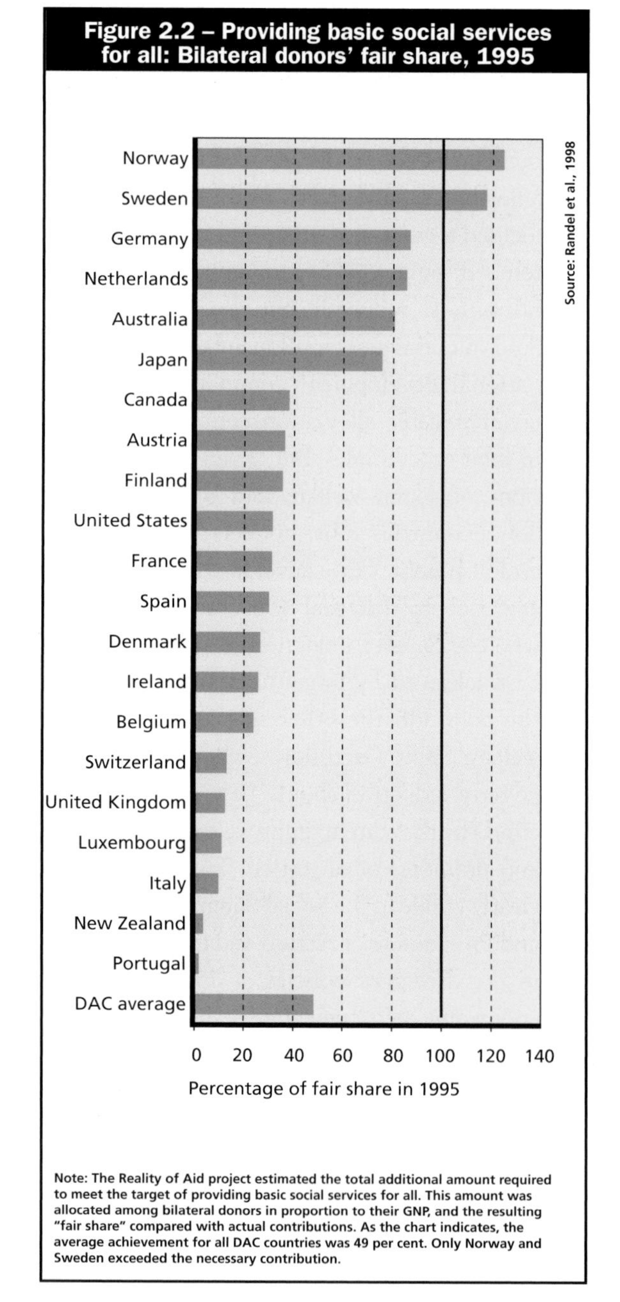

Note: The Reality of Aid project estimated the total additional amount required to meet the target of providing basic social services for all. This amount was allocated among bilateral donors in proportion to their GNP, and the resulting "fair share" compared with actual contributions. As the chart indicates, the average achievement for all DAC countries was 49 per cent. Only Norway and Sweden exceeded the necessary contribution.

international creditors that they are spending more on primary education—at a time when budgetary resources are not increasing—have achieved the goals required of them by reducing the coverage and quality of other social services, like secondary or vocational education. Some have met international goals by budgeting for many new primary school buildings without having the capacity to provide additional teachers (especially if the secondary and tertiary systems are starved of funds). Ensuring universal access to primary education is obviously extremely important. But single-minded insistence on this, within an environment of very limited resources, can distort social policy.

There is also a significant political price to pay when governments give special attention to improving basic education and health services at the cost of existing programmes that benefit a wider cross-section of the population. Working-class and middle-class citizens who depend on public services have often seen their levels of living decline sharply over the past decade or more; and they are justly upset by deterioration in public schools, clinics and social security systems. International advice that all but the poorest turn to the private sector for these services presents them with a new financial burden and an affront to their sense of citizenship. Pro-poor conditionality in the context of scarce resources can thus be an explosive political issue.

Alternatives to rigid targeting

Rigid targeting clearly has fundamental weaknesses. The data are unreliable, funds fungible, and long-term effects unpredictable. In the end, what seems to matter more is not how the international development community targets its funds, but how they are actually used. They are likely to achieve more if each society is allowed to pursue realistic and appropriate options.

Some donors who have recognized this, and concede their inability to influence the precise use of their funds, are now considering a change of tactics. Instead of being selective within countries, they are being more selective between them. In future they will be concentrating their aid in countries that have the greatest potential for progress—typically those with a commitment to economic reform, along with a good record on human rights. After choosing countries with which they share a common vision of progress, donors then enter into partnerships in which both states and citizens' groups exert greater control over the use of funds. Countries that do not meet the minimum requirements for good governance and economic reform will no longer receive aid.

This new approach—which is progressively reducing the number of countries to which bilateral donors provide assistance—has practical advantages, but like all aspects of the current development assistance framework it also poses difficult moral and practical dilemmas. A large number of poor people live under regimes that do not fulfil these requirements for effective use of aid. Eliminating development assistance to these countries is difficult to square with a broad-ranging commitment to poverty eradication.

Alternatives to aid

One way to avoid the dilemmas associated with foreign aid is simply to replace it. For example, instead of the current system of discretionary giving there could be a mechanism for automatic transfers from rich countries to poor. Much of the new thinking in this area is rooted in the principles of human rights. International conventions on human rights have long recognized the right of every human being to a minimum standard of living, for example—and asserted that the duty to fulfil human rights transcends national borders. Now a number of groups are trying to work out how this broader view of rights and responsibilities can be put into practice.

One proposal is to establish a new international development fund. Each high-income country could contribute a fixed percentage of its GNP to such a fund, which could be governed by representatives from both better-off and worse-off nations. This council would decide on the transfers required to bring each country's average per capita income up to an agreed minimum. Even if contributions to the fund never exceeded half the current UN target of 0.7 per cent of the GNP of rich countries, it would raise far more money than is currently available in conventional aid programmes.

A variant of this would have three "windows". Poor countries would achieve a basic social safety net through the first window. Through a second window, they could receive extra payments for services that benefit the whole of the global community, such as protecting biodiversity or fighting narcotic drugs. The third window would enable the richer countries to offer compensation for damage that they might continue to inflict on poor countries by maintaining trade barriers, for example, or by refusing to accept immigrants.

Figure 2.3 – Tax revenue and GDP

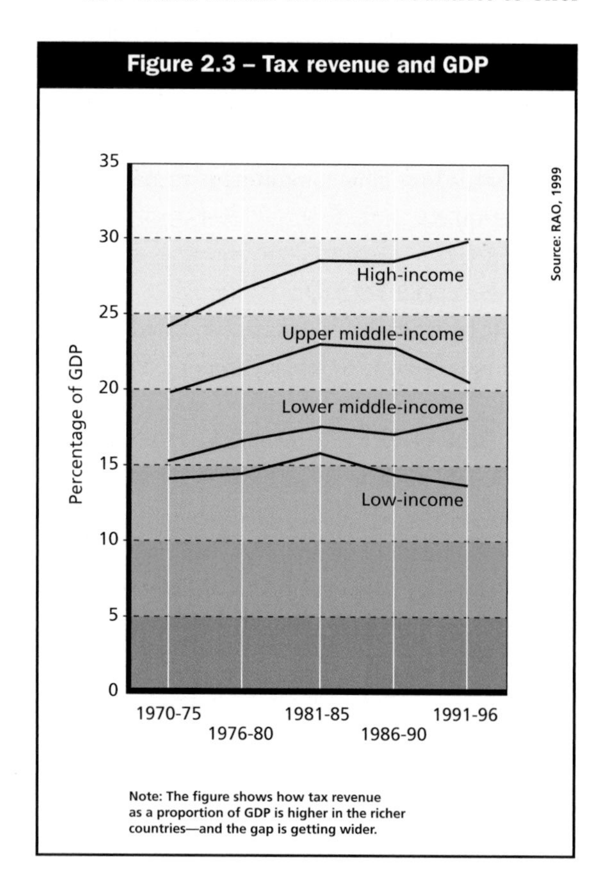

Note: The figure shows how tax revenue as a proportion of GDP is higher in the richer countries—and the gap is getting wider.

Another approach is to establish new forms of global taxation. One of the most familiar proposals is the Tobin Tax on foreign exchange transactions, which globally now run at $1.5 trillion per day. Similar suggestions have been made for taxing air travel, Internet use or other services that have strong international dimensions. Such charges could be levied by national tax authorities and some of the revenue used by national governments. But a certain proportion—perhaps half—could be allocated to the UN for a range of activities, including social programmes, environmental protection or humanitarian interventions. A part might also be distributed among developing countries, so that countries with the lowest per capita income received the largest amount.

New proposals on global citizenship and international taxation are likely to be aired at the Geneva 2000 meeting of the UN General Assembly, as well as at the 2001 Financing for Development conference. Most industrialized countries will doubtless oppose any such moves. But the idea of an international development fund is gaining greater support, particularly from NGOs. The growing intersection between human rights and poverty eradication could become a significant force for change.

Tax reform

Even if international taxation transferred some funds to developing countries, they would still need to rely primarily on generating their own resources. Unfortunately, governments in many of the poorer countries have seen their revenues eroded. Much of this is due to economic decline. When business enterprises are producing less, and more people are out of work, there is less income to tax.

The poorer countries are also generally less

successful at tax collection. Not only do they collect less in absolute terms, but they also gather less as a proportion of GDP. This is illustrated in figure 2.3, which shows that high-income countries collect more than twice as much as a proportion of GDP—and that the gap seems to be widening.

A second difference between richer and poorer countries is in the source of tax revenues. This is illustrated in figure 2.4. The limited extent of formal employment in developing countries reduces the potential for collecting social security contributions or personal income tax. In Bangladesh, for example, only 0.5 per cent of the population was liable for personal income tax in 1991. Many developing countries have had to make up for the shortage of personal taxpayers by focusing direct taxation on larger enterprises, particularly those involved in mineral extraction.

THE ERODING TAX BASE

But the main difference between rich and poor countries is that the poor rely more on taxes on imports and exports. This is partly because customs duties are easier to collect. The World Bank has estimated that levying trade taxes costs 1 to 3 per cent of the expected revenue—compared with 5 per cent for value added taxes and up to 10 per cent for income taxes. On average, developing countries derive around one third of tax revenues from taxes on trade, though in some cases the proportion is far higher: for Lesotho and Madagascar, the proportion is around one half.

The drive toward globalization and trade liberalization is therefore likely to hit developing country revenues hardest. As tariff rates have been falling, so have their incomes. Between 1993 and 1998, for example, India reduced average tariffs from 71 to 35 per cent. In 1998, however, a new government had to raise the tariffs again, claiming that this was not to protect Indian businesses but to protect government revenue. Even as staunch a free-trade advocate as Chile has worried about the revenue implications of trade liberalization. In 1997 the government postponed a reduction in import tariffs because the parliament could not decide how the anticipated $420 million cost was to be met.

A second revenue-weakening effect of liberalization is tax competition. Global competitive pressures make governments wary of raising taxes—for fear that foreign, or even national, businesses will flee elsewhere. This has resulted in falling tax rates around the world, both for individuals and corporations. Some experts suggest that in future this race to the bottom could see corporate tax rates sink to zero.

The tax base is also being weakened by the increasing informalization of economies. Even in the European Union, it has been estimated that between 7 and 16 per cent of the labour force now operates in the black economy. In developing and transition economies, the proportion is much higher and seems to be rising. In Latin America between 1990 and 1996, the proportion of the non-agricultural workforce to be found in the informal economy rose in almost

Figure 2.4 – Sources of tax revenue, 1991–96

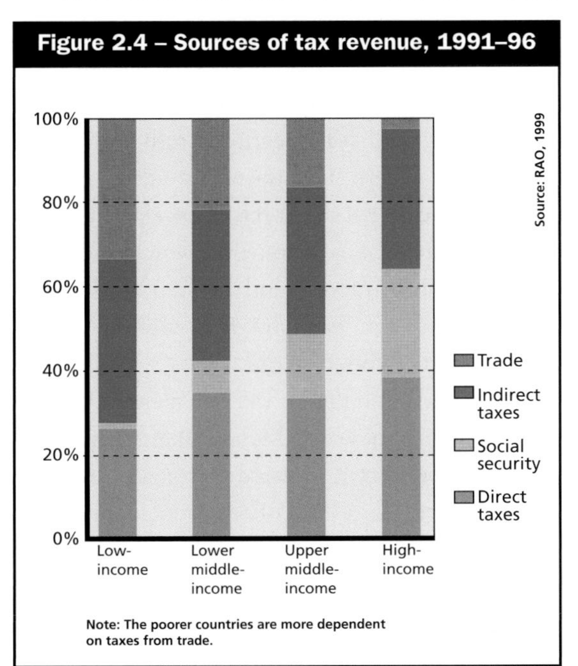

Note: The poorer countries are more dependent on taxes from trade.

every country: in Peru, for example, from 52 per cent to 58 per cent; and in Paraguay from 61 per cent to 68 per cent.

Taxing the consumer

Governments nervous about taxing businesses have set their sights elsewhere. Many have increased taxes on consumption, particularly through value added taxes—regressive taxes that hit hardest at the poor. One 1990 study of 39 countries undergoing structural adjustment found that almost all were shifting toward such indirect taxation. Pakistan is one of the latest countries to take this step. Here the ratio of tax to GDP is only 13 per cent—significantly below the 20 per cent ratio thought necessary to sustain public spending levels. Attempts in 1999 to introduce a sales tax faltered, however, after a general strike by small businesses. In Ghana, the imposition of a value added tax and subsequent price increases led to riots in May 1995 in which five people were killed.

A similar turn from taxing capital to taxing consumption is evident in transition countries. Hungary, for example, has been reducing taxation on corporations, particularly foreign ones: between 1988 and 1996, the contribution of taxes on business profits dropped from 30 to 10 per cent. Instead the government has increased personal taxation, which now accounts for 36 per cent of total revenue, and taxes on consumption, which now contribute one third of revenue. Payroll taxes are also high—the equivalent of more than half a worker's wage. Not surprisingly, Hungary also has a proliferating black economy—now estimated to account for around 30 per cent of GDP.

International avoidance

Another effect of liberalization is that individuals and businesses have increasingly sophisticated options for moving their funds internationally so as to elude, or at least minimize, taxation. The growth of electronic commerce will further expand opportunities for bypassing local and national tax systems.

Many of these funds are disappearing into tax-free offshore accounts. The IMF estimates that such accounts now contain around $8 trillion—equivalent to the GDP of the United States. If tax were to be paid on these funds, it could make an enormous contribution to social programmes. For example, if these deposits earned income of around 5 per cent per year and this were taxed at 40 per cent, around $160 billion annually would be raised—almost double what it would take for all countries to guarantee basic social services.

Recovering the resources lost through tax avoidance by the rich is thus essential to strengthening the resource base for social development. At the national level, one of the most important measures would be to improve the efficiency of tax collection. But the increasingly global nature of tax avoidance means that solutions must also be international.

One of the first steps in countering cross-border avoidance must be to ensure a better exchange of information among countries. In addition, states will have to consider harmonizing their tax systems to reduce the benefits of capital flight. They could, for example, agree on common ways to tax interest income, so that funds would not inevitably rush toward destinations where such taxes are either very low or non-existent. This has been a problem for Latin American governments, which find it difficult to tax interest and dividends while their citizens can earn tax-free interest on deposits in the United States.

States must also take concerted measures to eliminate tax havens. Major industrialized countries are working toward this goal. Since 1998, in fact, the OECD Forum on Harmful Tax Practices has been conducting a review of tax havens, defined as "tax poaching schemes... that impede the ability of home countries to enforce their own tax laws". Preliminary findings were presented to the senior tax policy body of the OECD in January 2000, and might be followed by public banking legislation prohibiting receipt of funds from tax havens. A number of international NGOs are lobbying for such an outcome.

Growing awareness of the international dimensions of tax avoidance also stands behind the proposal to create a World Tax Organization. Like the World Trade Organization, this would provide a framework within which governments could work out a set of rules they would be willing to observe. Such an institution is unlikely to emerge any time soon—and will encounter fierce opposition from transnational corporations and speculators. But in the longer term, the needs of governments could drive the international community in this direction.

Pension reform

Many of the same factors that have weakened governments' capacity to tax have also affected pension schemes—particularly in middle-income developing countries and countries in transition. These programmes are essential elements of social protection, shielding recipients from hardship in old age. They are often the largest social transfer schemes and, along with health and education, absorb the largest amounts of social expenditure. But like taxation, they are vulnerable to economic crisis, rising unemployment in the formal sector and the growth of the informal sector.

Pension schemes are also affected by demographic changes. If the proportion of older to younger people in the population covered by any programme rises, the government needs to make appropriate adjustments to contributions and benefits. The industrialized countries' populations have aged markedly over the past few decades. But, as figure 2.5 shows, populations are also set to age rapidly in less developed regions in the first half of the twenty-first century.

During the past two decades, public pension schemes have been hit by a combination of shrinking resources and growing needs. Rather than undertaking wholesale restructuring, the advanced industrial democracies have responded with a number of innovative reforms. For the developing and transition countries, however, the international financial institutions have demanded far more radical change. And, as in the case of many prescriptions for institutional reform meted out during the 1980s and early 1990s, this advice has often proved misguided.

The central element in international prescriptions for pension fund reform in indebted middle-income and transition societies has been privatization. Encouraged by the Chilean experience during the 1980s, neoliberal reformers at both national and international levels have attempted to replace public social security systems with private retirement accounts. Their approach was supported by an influential 1994 World Bank report, *Averting the Old Age Crisis*. And it was backed up by the exercise of conditionality: discussions of structural adjustment loans gave a high priority to privatizing pension funds.

Figure 2.5 – Population over 60, 1990–2050

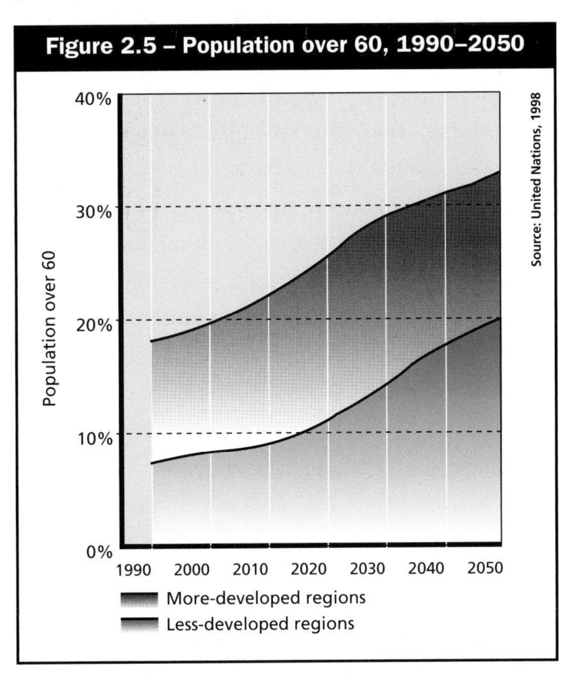

In Latin America, this pressure proved least effective in the more democratic countries. In Costa Rica, for example, citizens preferred to reform the public system—eliminating the last pockets of privilege for public sector workers and ensuring that new levels of contribution would be adequate to provide minimum benefits for the aged and infirm. In Uruguay, citizens forced a public referendum, through which they rejected a proposal for privatization. At a later stage, they did permit the introduction of private investment accounts, but not at the cost of eliminating the public programme. In Argentina and Peru, after the legislature refused to authorize partial privatization, it was eventually pushed through by presidential decree. Only in Chile and Mexico has there been a complete shift to private pension funds—but interestingly enough, in both cases influential sectors of the elite, including the military, have been allowed to keep their previous, publicly managed funds.

The struggle over pension reform reflects a broader debate about the meaning of solidarity and the nature of risk. First, should there be room in old-age protection schemes for some degree of redistribution between those who are better-off and those who are not? Almost all public pension systems have an element of redistribution, but privately managed individual accounts do not. Second, should pension programmes ensure some degree of security for all members, whatever the immediate circumstances surrounding their retirement? Public pension schemes establish a minimum benefit, based on the length and magnitude of contribution, and bear the risk for delivering that benefit. In fully private programmes, the amount of each pension depends entirely on the size of the individual's investment and the performance of the market.

There is, of course, no reason why the pension programmes developed in any country should be either entirely private or entirely public. Combinations of both abound. Indeed, some of the most creative attempts to deal with an aging population and falling tax revenue have involved innovative combinations of public and private spheres. Thus some industrial democracies have added individually funded accounts to basic public pension schemes; some private investment accounts are managed by business or trade union associations; and some public schemes invest in private markets. In addition, many countries have chosen not to dismantle their public system but have raised the pension age or introduced incentives for later retirement.

It is time to introduce a note of caution and realism into what has often been a highly ideological debate. This shift in thinking has already begun, as practical lessons are drawn from 20 years' experience with full privatization in Chile (box 2.4). In addition, a number of people are re-examining the technical arguments—economic and actuarial—for radical privatization. A recent paper from the Office of the Chief Economist of the World Bank insists that "the complexity of optimal pension policy should caution us against believing that a similar set of recommendations would be appropriate in countries ranging from Argentina to Azerbaijan, from China to Costa Rica, from Sierra Leone to Sweden". And it goes on to address "10 myths" that underlie past Bank support of mandatory private pension schemes.

OTHER ISSUES IN SOCIAL PROTECTION

Public pension programmes are generally part of broader social protection schemes, including sickness, accident and unemployment insurance. Of the 172 countries included in the 1997 edition of *Social Security Programs throughout the World*, only six (Bangladesh, Botswana, Malawi, Myanmar, Sierra Leone and Somalia) lack any kind of public social insurance programme. But in the poorer countries, coverage is often restricted to a relatively

Box 2.4 – Salutary pension lessons from Chile

In the 1990s, Chile was in the forefront of pension reform—phasing out the public system and shifting all formal sector workers above a minimum poverty line from public to private pension schemes. Countries tempted to follow the same path should consider the discrepancies between claims originally made for this experiment and the reality after almost 20 years of experience. Discrepancies have emerged in the following areas.

- ***Efficiency***—Though it was claimed that privatization would improve efficiency, this is highly questionable. Private individual accounts have proved more expensive to manage than collective claims. In fact, according to the Inter-American Development Bank, administration of the Chilean system was, by the mid-1990s, the most expensive in Latin America.

- ***Yield***—Private pension funds were supposed to offer pensioners a good rate of return. But between 1982 and 1998—and after deducting administrative costs—privately held and administered pension funds in Chile showed an average annual real return of only 5.1 per cent. Since part of the fees and commissions are charged at a flat rate on all accounts, these charges have also proved highly regressive. When levied against a relatively modest retirement account, standard fees reduced the latter by approximately 18 per cent. When applied to the deposit of an individual investing 10 times more, the reduction was slightly less than 1 per cent.

- ***Competition***—Since the public pension system was a monopoly, it was assumed that privatization would promote efficiency by opening the way for sharp competition between pension providers. In the event, Chile's "pension industry" has become highly concentrated. The three largest pension fund administrators handle 70 per cent of the insured. And account holders have limited opportunities for transferring between them: to reduce spending on advertising, public regulators are limiting the number of transfers that any individual can make from one company to another.

- ***Coverage***—It was assumed that a private scheme would draw more people into the pension system by offering the prospect of profitable investments. This has not happened. Coverage and compliance rates have remained virtually constant.

- ***Stronger capital markets***—Another claim was that the conversion of the public pension system into privately held and administered accounts would strengthen capital markets, savings and investment. But a number of studies have recently concluded that, at best, this effect has been marginal.

- ***Gender equity***—Pension benefits in private, funded systems are determined strictly by the amount of money contributed. Since women typically earn less money and work fewer years than men, they receive considerably lower benefits. Public pension systems—as in Sweden, for example—can counter this disadvantage by providing credits for child care. Private pension systems cannot.

small group of formal sector workers and civil servants. And hundreds of millions of people—particularly in developing countries—have been affected by more generalized reductions in the coverage and quality of services.

As an alternative form of support for those in greatest need, some countries provide social assistance pensions. Governments, which finance these small payments not through contributions but through taxes, thus aim to support those whose income is too low to qualify for social security. But like other areas of social protection in the 1990s, the real value of such pensions in developing and transition countries has often plummeted; and the number of people receiving benefits has declined. The ILO estimates that about one third of all the world's people lack any type of formal social protection—whether contribution-based social insurance or tax-financed social assistance. In Africa, this applies to 90 per cent of the population of working age.

The social protection agenda in the years ahead must include efforts to deal with this problem. This could be achieved by extending existing social security programmes to cover informal sector workers. Or it could be done by supporting innovative voluntary initiatives. Many self-employed people in developing countries have devised schemes that provide some hedge against risk: co-operative insurance schemes, communal grain storage programmes, savings clubs and rotating credit societies. Many NGOs and donors are supporting these efforts.

In the last analysis, however, voluntary, community-based schemes will always be vulnerable to external shocks—sharp shifts in the economic environment, for example, or in the weather. And they can be fundamentally affected by changes in social relations among members as well. If they are to be more resilient they need to affiliate with large, professionally run institutions. Public social security systems are the obvious choice in this regard, though many now lack the financial or administrative capacity to incorporate a broad range of low-income, self-employed groups.

Mobilizing resources at the grassroots

Hit by rising debt repayments, declining development assistance and falling tax revenues, many Third World governments find it increasingly difficult to provide social services and social protection. They have therefore been trying to decentralize—to shift the burden of obtaining and managing resources from national to local authorities, often as part of structural adjustment programmes.

But there is a limit to what this can achieve. When governments decentralize, they may, of course, be strengthening democratic governance. But they may also be using this as a pretext for cutting financial support. And they may be demanding too much of local administrations whose institutions are ill prepared to take over. Decentralization is thus as likely to encourage inefficiency as efficiency, and can compound, rather than offset, the difficulties associated with declining social spending.

Another way of rationalizing the use of scarce resources for social development is through targeting. But this, too, has proved problematic. Most countries use targeting to some extent, and it does seem logical to direct scarce resources toward the neediest. In many situations, however, it is difficult to locate the individuals or households that have the best claim. Moreover, a growing number of studies have shown that in many areas of the developing world, targeting is not only haphazard but also expensive: often it would be cheaper to provide benefits to the population at large. And in towns or villages where the majority of the population obviously requires assistance, this form of rationing makes little sense.

A further option is to charge for social services. Donors and creditors have encouraged cash-strapped governments to recuperate a part of the cost of social services by charging, or increasing, fees for public education and health services. Of all the measures proposed for raising revenue from local people, this is probably the most ill advised. One study of 39 developing countries found that the introduction of user fees had increased revenues only slightly, while significantly reducing the access of low-income people to basic social services. Other studies have shown that fees reinforce gender inequality, particularly in education. When forced to choose which child can go to school most families are likely to favour boys.

Many citizens' groups and NGOs made these points forcefully at Copenhagen, and their views are now broadly accepted the international development community. Yet, in fact, more governments are resorting to such charges than ever before.

Micro-finance

Governments can attempt to mobilize resources at the grassroots. But so can local people. And they are increasingly likely to do so, with the help of NGOs, donors and international financial institutions that are either investing in micro-credit or attempting more generally to strengthen grassroots financial systems.

Influenced by pioneering experiments like the Grameen Bank in Bangladesh, micro-credit organizations provide small loans at relatively low interest rates to poor people—most frequently women who use the loans for money-making projects. They organize borrowers into small groups and their loan officers monitor the clientele. Although no collateral is required, repayment is virtually guaranteed by peer pressure. Clients with good records are also eligible for better terms on future loans.

Thousands of small enterprises have been started with micro-credit; and by the time of the Social Summit, proponents of this approach were claiming that in the next few decades micro-credit could entirely eliminate poverty. At the Micro-Credit Summit of 1997, presidents and prime ministers, business and financial leaders, and representatives from 1,500 NGOs pledged to provide 100 million of the world's poorest families with small loans by the year 2005. Their programme was noted and approved by international bodies ranging from the Non-Aligned Movement and the Commonwealth Heads of Government to the G-7. In December 1997 the UN General Assembly adopted a resolution recognizing the importance of micro-credit in fighting Third World poverty.

Nevertheless, activists involved in the movement are becoming increasingly sceptical. Small loans may help many people live better in poverty, but they are generally not sufficient to provide an escape from poverty. Nor do they offer clear answers to poor women's deeper problems of disempowerment, since other members of the family frequently use loans made to women. One study of Grameen Bank villages in Bangladesh found that men used 60 per cent of loans granted to women, and that three quarters of the loans were not used in the ways that the Grameen Bank had sanctioned.

There are also doubts about long-term viability, since many micro-credit ventures are financially unsustainable and would collapse without continuing outside support. If these programmes did charge rates of interest sufficiently high to enable them be self-supporting, their loans would be too expensive for most poor borrowers.

Micro-credit is an important tool but, on its own, it is no solution to poverty. Communities do need access to affordable credit, but they also need a broader range of services, including facilities for saving small amounts, as well as institutions that can turn those savings into investments. Thus efforts to improve grassroots financial services in areas that are vastly underserved may provide more solid foundations for social development than targeted micro-credit schemes can ever build.

Such institutions would be particularly useful for investing remittances—income sent back home by migrant workers in foreign countries. The amount of money pumped into the economies of developing countries by nationals working abroad has been growing rapidly. Between 1970 and 1995, global flows of remittances increased from $2 billion to around $70 billion—considerably greater than flows of development assistance. Remittances serve as vital lifelines for hundreds of millions of families. Yet they could have a much greater impact if they could be captured by local financial institutions operating along modern lines, rather than flowing into traditional money-lending circuits or leaking out into large corporations in distant cities.

To meet this need, local institutions would have to count on greater expertise and sufficient start-up capital. They would also need to see changes in national regulatory structures and banking laws. The growing micro-finance movement is attempting to deal with these issues, and it is receiving support from many international organizations. For example, the Asian Development Bank has recently announced that it intends to shift the emphasis in its lending from large infrastructure projects to micro-finance, rural electrification and farm-to-market roads. It will not give money directly to small banking organizations, but instead will promote regulatory reform so that local financial institutions can flourish.

Grassroots co-operative banks and mutual societies were motors of local progress in today's advanced industrial democracies. Can this experience be repeated at the turn of the twenty-first century, when electronic banking is erasing financial borders? Development organizations need to look more closely at the connection between micro-finance and the rapid evolution of the global financial industry.

A balance sheet

Individuals, households and communities have always taken the primary responsibility for financing social development. Their success depends, however, on broader economic and political trends. They will be in a much stronger position if their national economies are growing and if their social rights are being met. And they will advance more consistently and rapidly in a society that encourages solidarity and redistribution.

In many ways, the current environment is not encouraging. National debts are rising, aid is falling as a proportion of donors' GNP, and social protection and social services have weakened. Difficulties in taxing immense wealth have grown more severe, and—relatively speaking—those with less income are paying more.

But the picture is not entirely bleak. At least people in many parts of the world are more aware of the dangers of globalization and are mobilizing to confront them. Creditors and donors are offering debt relief in fits and starts. Governments are considering ways to make better use of the world's wealth by working together to curb tax abuses by individuals and transnational corporations. And even the international financial institutions are starting to doubt many of the hitherto unquestioned truths of neoliberal social policy—including privatization, user fees and targeting.

More generally, there seems to be a greater openness and a willingness to reassess some of the older and increasingly discredited preconceptions of development finance. This is certainly related to increasing pressure from those who have borne the burden of economic crisis and restructuring over the past few decades. They are often struggling to create or strengthen democratic governance under very difficult conditions—a subject to which we now turn.

Fragile democracies

Masai women casting their votes. Kajiado, Kenya

Associated Press AP

Today the vast majority of countries have formally democratic systems of government. But gains remain fragile—vulnerable to voter disillusionment, ethnic conflicts and takeover by technocrats.

As the Social Summit emphasized, social development requires more than additional funds or better economic and social policies. It also requires a supportive environment—in particular, vigorous democratic institutions that allow citizens to participate freely in decision making.

On this point at least there has been some advance. One of the most cheering developments of recent decades has been the spread of democracy. Progress has been uneven, and democratic principles may not always have percolated very deeply into the national consciousness. But the direction of change has been positive.

The number of sovereign states has been increasing rapidly. Between 1900 and 1950, an average of 1.2 new states were created per year. Between 1950 and 1990 the rate was 2.2, but between 1990 and 1998 the rate increased to 3.1. By 1998 there were 185 sovereign members of the United Nations, and in 1999 they were joined by Kiribati, Nauru and Tonga.

Many of these states are now formally democratic, as reflected in increased electoral activity around the world. Over the period 1990–99, there were about 300 competitive elections in 160 of 185 states—an average of 1.9 elections per country. Some regions have had more intensive activity than others, as indicated in figure 3.1, which shows the number of elections per country to be greatest in the industrialized countries and least in North Africa and the Middle East.

Nevertheless, there have also been some reversals of democracy, in the form of military coups: between 1990 and 1999, sub-Saharan Africa had 15 coups, Latin America had one (in Haiti), and Asia also had one (in Pakistan).

The United Nations has played a key role in the extension of democracy. In addition to sponsoring conferences on democracy, the UN has provided technical assistance to electoral commissions, helped supervise elections and supported national and international election observers (box 3.1).

The governing dilemma

Representative democracy is a solution to a fundamental dilemma. In a democracy everyone is presumed to have equal rights. Ideally, each citizen should be able to express his or her

Figure 3.1 – Elections per state, 1990–98

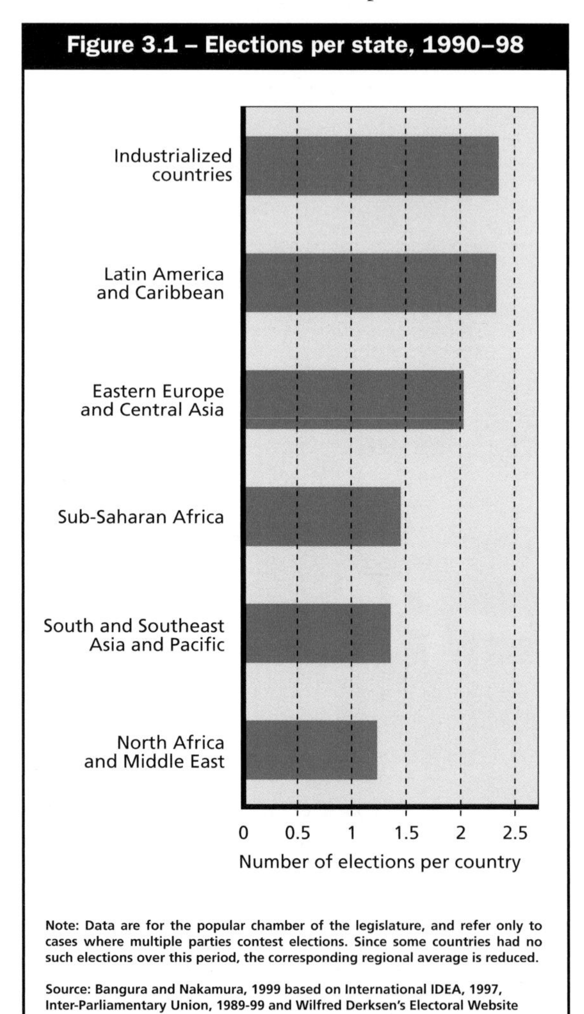

Note: Data are for the popular chamber of the legislature, and refer only to cases where multiple parties contest elections. Since some countries had no such elections over this period, the corresponding regional average is reduced.

Source: Bangura and Nakamura, 1999 based on International IDEA, 1997, Inter-Parliamentary Union, 1989-99 and Wilfred Derksen's Electoral Website

preferences directly. Even for the 78,000 people of the UN's smallest member, Kiribati, this is impractical. Instead people have to aggregate their interests through political parties and pressure groups. And they delegate power to politicians to formulate public policy and deliver services.

At a basic minimum this demands that elections are free and fair, and that citizens enjoy full civil and political rights, particularly the rights of organization, assembly and expression. Were all the elections of the 1990s free and fair? Not all of them—but a reasonable proportion, at least if a change of government counts as success. One common danger is that the ruling party may use its current power to retain future power—directly, by controlling the electoral authority so as to falsify the outcome, or

Box 3.1 – The United Nations promotes democracy

The UN Charter and the Universal Declaration of Human Rights have guided the UN's work on democratization. More recently, in 1988, the General Assembly adopted a resolution supporting the principle of free, fair and periodic elections. Other activities promoting these ideals have included three UN-sponsored conferences on "new and restored democracies"—1988 in Manila, 1994 in Managua and 1997 in Bucharest. A fourth is planned in Cotonou for 2000.

In 1995, the World Summit for Social Development also focused on the importance of democracy, declaring that the promotion of social development "requires democratic institutions, respect for all human rights and fundamental freedoms, increased and equal economic opportunities, the rule of law, the promotion of respect for cultural diversity and the rights of persons belonging to minorities, and an active involvement of civil society". Between 1994 and 1998, the Secretary-General prepared four special reports on the various ways in which the UN system could help governments to promote and consolidate new democracies.

In terms of direct assistance, the UN has helped organize, supervise and verify elections and has also provided technical assistance and support for national and international election observers. In Cambodia in 1993, for example, the UN trained about 5,000 Cambodians as election officers. In Namibia in 1994, a special representative of the Secretary-General supervised the electoral process during the period leading to Namibian independence. In Mozambique in 1994, the UN assisted with the establishment of a national electoral commission and an electoral tribunal for the elections that ended 16 years of civil war.

In the field of technical assistance, the UN has provided training and education, as well as logistics, to about 50 countries. Between 1989 and 1996, the UN also sent election observer missions to 24 states. During the same period, it received 187 requests from 69 states for various forms of electoral assistance. Around half of these took the form of technical assistance, and most activities were concentrated in Africa, Latin America and the Caribbean, and Eastern Europe—the three regions where the wave of democratization has been strongest.

indirectly, by intimidating the electorate and opposition groups or controlling the media. A good indication of fairness, therefore, is that the ruling party loses. Having the same party in power for a long time does not necessarily imply fraud—in Japan and Sweden, for example, the same parties have remained in government for 20 or even 30 years. But for new democracies, a change of government does indicate a degree of flexibility and maturity in political processes.

As figure 3.2 indicates, the region whose elections were least likely to result in a change in the ruling party was sub-Saharan Africa. Significantly, this was the region where the opposition was most likely to have contested election results. This was also the region where opposition groups were most likely to refuse to participate—they boycotted around one-quarter of elections.

In Asia and Latin America, the picture appears healthier. Here elections are more likely to have produced changes of government and election results are less likely to have been contested. In the industrialized countries during this period, no elections were boycotted by major parties and no results were contested.

Incomplete transitions

Though most countries have been moving in a democratic direction, many are still some way from mature democracies. Autocratic regimes often find ways of retaining much of their power even in a formally democratic environment.

Latin America—military impunity

In Latin America, most transitions from military rule to democracy took place in the 1980s. But former military rulers often found ways to retain some vestiges of power or to protect themselves from prosecution for crimes committed during their regimes. They extracted these concessions as the price of a peaceful handover of power and of avoiding future military insurrections. But such guarantees have not necessarily proved sufficient. The attempt to prosecute former Chilean President Augusto Pinochet is the sharpest reminder of the limits of impunity. Argentina now seems less forgiving of its ex-dictators as well: since 1998 a number of former military leaders have been prosecuted for kidnappings and "disappearances".

The concessions in Latin America's transitions were not made solely to the military. Probably more enduring were those offered to the traditional elites who managed to hold on to much of their power. In Brazil during the mid-1980s, elites supported the change to democracy in exchange for political posts, state jobs and money for specific projects.

Figure 3.2 – Alternations in power and disputed elections, 1990–99

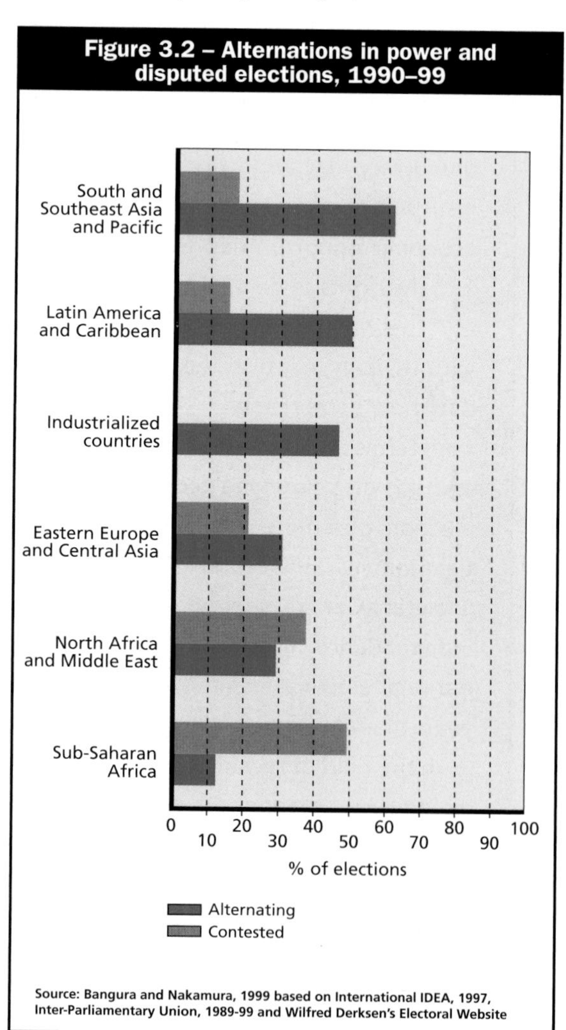

Source: Bangura and Nakamura, 1999 based on International IDEA, 1997, Inter-Parliamentary Union, 1989-99 and Wilfred Derksen's Electoral Website

Another development in Latin American democracy is the attempt to change rules that forbid the re-election of incumbent presidents. Leaders cite the unfinished business of economic reforms as justification for passing *continuismo* legislation that will enable them to run for second terms. More than half of the countries in Latin America were governed by *continuista* regimes in 1998.

Overcoming opposition in Africa

Africa's autocratic regimes were often able to retain power because opposition parties were not sufficiently well organized to replace them. In Côte d'Ivoire, for example, President Houphouet-Boigny had ruled for decades and caught opposition leaders by surprise in 1990 when he announced an instant election that gave them little time to prepare. He won the ensuing election comfortably; and though he died in office in 1993, his appointed successor also maintained a strong grip, banning opposition rallies and jailing members of the opposition until ousted in a coup in 1999. As one of Côte d'Ivoire's opposition leaders has pointed out, this kind of repression of opposition in Africa is a way not just to retain power, but also to avoid the humiliation of defeat.

The nomenklatura of Eastern Europe and Central Asia

In Eastern Europe, transitions have often been managed by the old party bosses, the nomenklatura, who have managed to hold on to power, or at least wield enormous influence. In Belarus, the Central Asian republics and Ukraine, they influenced the way in which public assets were privatized; and they remain active in the region's rapidly growing criminal gangs. In Turkmenistan, for example, the

B.K. Bangash, Associated Press AP

Troops seize control. Islamabad, Pakistan

Turkmen Communist Party has been renamed the Democratic Party and remains the only legal political party. Most of the opposition is exiled. The former communist leader is still the country's president. He has ruthlessly suppressed all dissent and enforced a personality cult—calling himself the "Turkenbashi" (leader of the Turkmen).

The progress of political parties

The basis of all democratic systems is the political party, which organizes people who share a common interest or purpose. Often this has been based on an economic or social philosophy—typically set somewhere along a left-right, socialist-capitalist spectrum. Most Western European parties organize on this basis—reflecting divisions that emerged many decades ago, following the enfranchisement of the working classes. In the United States as well, the differences between Republican and Democratic parties have reflected the interests respectively of capital and labour. Political culture in Latin America has developed in a similar way: parties often align themselves with business interests and landlords on one side and trade unions on the other.

Another party rallying point is religion. European Christian Democratic parties are a residue of religious affiliations. But religion is still a live political force as well. India, for example, has since 1998 been governed by a Hindu-dominated party.

Many countries, such as Bangladesh, Indonesia, Pakistan and Turkey, have Islamic parties that compete with other parties in democratic states. But there is always a concern that Islamic parties ultimately seek absolute rule. Non-religious parties are understandably alarmed by the prospect of an Islamic party victory, which can be interpreted as a challenge to secular democracy itself—a prospect that led in 1991 to a military coup in Algeria, and civil war and bloodshed in the years since.

Another familiar basis for party organization is ethnic identity. In some cases this may be linked with religion, as in former Yugoslavia. And it may have a strong regional character. But the most ethnically diverse countries are typically found in Asia and Africa.

Other parties may be based not on divisions of class or religion but on personalities, as people align themselves behind one powerful or charismatic figure. Such parties often emerge after a period of dictatorship, when a military leader seeks to legitimate authority by creating a new party. In Ghana, for example, the military takeover by then flight-lieutenant Jerry Rawlings in 1981 resulted in a Provisional National Defence Council. But after a new constitution in 1992, Rawlings won the presidency at the head of a newly created party, the National Democratic Congress.

Another personality-based system emerges when an individual with a strong following, or at least a strong will, enters politics on his or her own account and creates a party to provide support. One example is President Alberto Fujimori of Peru.

In principle, all these systems of party organization are valid. All respond to the representational dilemma—resolving the tension between individual and group rights. But they also have to settle differences and conflict in an equitable and peaceful fashion. On the whole the systems that have achieved this with least disruption have been those based on class interests. Most industrialized countries have maintained a reasonable balance between left- and right-wing parties. Both left and right have acquired mass followings and over the long run have alternated in power. Indeed, a greater worry in industrialized countries is that this process is now too smooth—that modern parties anxious to claim the centre ground have been discarding their class characteristics and becoming virtually indistinguishable, leading to disillusionment with the democratic process itself.

Democracies are less stable when parties are based on ethnic groups or regional identities. Ethnic or religious parties seem to have greater potential for intolerance and violence, and strong regional identities can lead to conflict or secession. Mindful of this, some constitutions, such as those of Kazakhstan and some African countries, forbid the formation of parties that have an ethnic or religious basis.

Least stable of all are the democracies based on individual personalities or narrowly constituted interest groups. Many of these tend not to be programmatic. Rather than attempting to carry out any popularly agreed mandate, they pursue the self-interests of individuals or elites.

President or parliament?

States differ not only in their party systems, but also in their systems of government. Democratic countries have to choose whether to vest executive power in a president or in a parliament led by a prime minister. They can also operate somewhere in the middle—distributing power between an executive president and a prime minister. A strongly presidential system tends to be more centralized: the president is generally elected for a fixed term and is difficult to remove. He or she can thus exercise power in a more single-minded way. A prime minister, on the other hand, is more beholden to a political party and can be removed at any time after losing a vote of confidence. This means that more time will have to be spent cultivating political support.

Industrialized countries

Of the major industrialized countries, the United States and France are the only ones with executive presidents. Both operate on the balance of power principle, and in both cases the president has recently had to cohabit with an elected assembly controlled by an opposition party. In France,where there is both a president and a prime minister, the latter enjoys enormous powers in the making of economic and social policies. In the United States, cohabitation has sometimes led to gridlock and a failure to take important decisions. But the US system functions thanks to a long democratic tradition bolstered by strong institutions, including the judiciary and the press.

Most other industrialized countries have opted instead for parliamentary systems. They, too, have their weaknesses and can centralize power. If the prime minister is a powerful personality with a large parliamentary majority—as was the case with Margaret Thatcher and the Conservative government in the UK in the 1980s—he or she has considerable freedom of action. On the other hand, a parliamentary system that generates a multiplicity of small parties can lead to weak government. Italy is the most notable example among the industrialized countries—the constantly shifting allegiances among dozens of small parties have given Italy 59 governments since the Second World War.

Developing and transition countries

Developing countries have generally opted for a presidential system. Most have done so as a way of solidifying national unity—particularly when the integrity of their societies is weakened by multiple ethnic cleavages. Unfortunately, this also means that they risk electing autocrats who subsequently pay scant heed to the rules and procedures that brought them to power.

As in the United States, the president may come into conflict with the legislature. But in the absence of strong institutions, particularly the judiciary and the press, the president may be tempted to undermine parliamentary powers or to rule by decree. Latin America borrowed the institution of the presidency from the United States, but a number of elected presidents have eventually chosen to ignore even their own parties and rule directly through personalist movements and media appeals—as was the case with Carlos Menem in Argentina, and Fernando Collor in Brazil.

Developing countries with parliamentary systems should in principle be more protected from autocrats. But autocrats can also surface as prime ministers, especially when they enjoy large majorities. Nawaz Sharif operated in a fairly dictatorial fashion within a parliamentary system in Pakistan until ousted by a coup in 1999.

At the other extreme, parliamentary systems with a plethora of parties can also be difficult to manage in developing countries. Benin, for example, is seen as one of Africa's leading democracies. Nevertheless, in 1999 more than 17 parties were represented in its parliament, the largest of which had only 25 per cent of the seats. Suriname, a country with less than half a million people, had eight parties represented in its 51-member parliament in 1999 and was run by a five-party coalition.

Some Eastern European countries emerging from communism sought to build more democratic societies by opting for parliamentary systems. Since then, however, several have retreated. Albania, the Czech Republic and Poland have subsequently weakened their parliaments. In Poland, for example, Lech Walesa, the Solidarity leader, changed the constitution to a mixed system that gave substantial power to the presidency.

A presidential system may seem particularly attractive when the government feels it has to push through unpopular reforms—which can be easier if there is a strong president who can employ trusted technocrats insulated from popular pressure. Whether this produces long-term stability is doubtful. Parliamentary systems certainly demand greater efforts to build working coalitions. But once achieved, these broadly based governments can prove more durable. Even junior partners in coalitions have an incentive to prevent the collapse of the government—especially if they are nervous about the prospect of a snap election they might not win. One study of 53 non-OECD countries over the period 1973–79 found that governments based on parliamentary systems had a 61 per cent survival rate, compared with a 20 per cent rate for presidential systems. Presidential systems were also twice as likely to suffer a coup d'état.

Democracy as means or end?

Democracy is usually seen as an end in itself. It allows people to express their opinions freely and make their own choices. Democracy thus offers a way of fulfilling basic human rights. But many people see systems of government in more limited, instrumental terms. For them, a system of government is merely a means to an end—a way of achieving social stability and economic development. If democracy serves this purpose, all well and good. If it does not, then it might be better to have a more autocratic system.

There is always, therefore, a risk that underperforming democracies will harden into autocracies. An analysis of Freedom House data for Latin America in 1996 concluded that while six out of 22 countries had registered some increases in freedom, 10 others had experienced significant declines. The most recent dramatic example is in Venezuela, where President Hugo Chávez has weakened Congress and greatly expanded his presidential powers.

A preference for more authoritarian government has also been attributed to cultural predisposition (box 3.2). Some people argue that Asian societies place a high value on consensus and are thus less keen on the adversarial style of Western democracies. The "Asian values" of East and Southeast Asia have been used to justify autocratic governments and to account for their economic success. Former President Lee Kuan Yew of Singapore has been one of the

Box 3.2 – Human rights controversies

The Copenhagen Declaration places human rights at the centre of development. This is understandable. The principles of human rights offer rallying points that even the most regressive governments find difficult to deny completely. And though these rights may previously have been seen as abstract formulations, they are now being elaborated in much greater detail and have been supported by numerous decisions of courts and tribunals. Claims based on human rights have been putting greater pressure on governments and the international community.

But this apparent consensus hides a number of sharp disagreements. The first is over whether rights are genuinely universal. Government leaders in Asia and Africa, for example, say that Western societies have been preoccupied with rights, while their own societies place special importance on duties. And many people point to a similar theme in the world's major religious and spiritual beliefs. Leaders in Southeast Asia say that they owe their political stability and economic development to Asian values oriented toward harmony and the community.

This kind of cultural relativism conveniently insulates societies from external criticism, and serves to consolidate privilege and hierarchy. It ignores the many commonalities between cultures and the ways in which they interact and change. And while government leaders often espouse the distinctive values of their societies, many of the neediest are more attracted by the egalitarian and redistributive dimensions of universal human rights.

The other main argument is over what should be regarded as rights. Some governments in the West, particularly in the United States, have objected to considering economic and social benefits as rights, a principle they have associated with communist ideology. On the other hand, many governments in Asia and Africa have resisted the implementation of civil and political rights on the grounds that they are less important and urgent than economic and social rights.

Some of this gap has been bridged in recent times. The conventions on the rights of women, children and migrants, for example, recognize that improvement in their situation requires progress on both sets of rights. But many disagreements remain, and the tensions and contradictions between different sets of rights have become more evident—for example, the tension between the right to freedom of expression and the need to protect communities from hate propaganda or incitement to war.

One strategy has been to pair the traditional bundle of rights with the right to development. The 1993 Vienna Conference on Human Rights endorsed this approach. The West withdrew its objections to the right to development in return for the acceptance by Asian states of the hallowed formula that human rights were universal, indivisible, and interdependent.

Such tensions are reflected in the Copenhagen Declaration itself, where the commitment to human rights is qualified with "full respect for the various religious and ethical values and cultural backgrounds of people".

most vociferous advocates of such a position.

This case is weakened by the sheer diversity and heterogeneity of Asian countries. As Amartya Sen has noted, "the so-called Asian values that are invoked to justify authoritarianism are not especially Asian in any significant sense". Most Asian countries have also had opposition to autocratic government. In the Republic of Korea, this has frequently been organized by trade unions. Even China had a widespread movement for greater democracy prior to the massacre in Tiananmen Square in 1989. The few social science surveys done since then in China show a strong desire for more democracy, although hardly anyone questions the legitimacy of the state.

The developmental state

One of the supposed advantages of autocratic government is that it makes it easier for a country to be a developmental state—one that is strong and coherent, and focuses all its efforts on economic and social development. Developmental states are assumed to have a number of core elements. The first is autonomy—the government can operate free from the pressures of particular interest groups. The second element is high capacity—the country's political elite is supported by an efficient bureaucracy, and these two work together in pursuit of their agreed goals. A third element is nationalism: the political elite develops a nationalist project of industrialization that is different from current notions of free trade and capital movements.

The tiger economies of Southeast Asia could be considered developmental states—as could the People's Republic of China in the 1960s, and also post-war Japan. All were authoritarian to some degree, but they did not rely simply on the exercise of authority. These governments were deeply embedded in their societies, and they maintained strong links with social forces conducive to development.

Authoritarianism that is not similarly embedded tends to lead not to development but to predation. In many African countries authoritarianism has been profoundly anti-developmental. Mobutu Sese Seko in Zaire, for example, had sufficient autonomy to create a developmental state. Instead, he exploited his power to amass a huge fortune for himself and his cronies while leaving his country in ruins.

The "soft authoritarian" states of East and Southeast Asia were historically unique. Many of the fundamental changes, such as land reform in Japan, that laid the foundation for equitable development arose during US occupation and were shaped by the disciplines of the Cold War. Authoritarianism on its own rarely creates these egalitarian circumstances or generates progressive political leadership.

The democratic alternative

Authoritarian regimes cannot be relied upon to be developmental, but neither can democratic ones. In theory a liberal democratic government should be responsive to the electorate—and thus meet basic needs and fulfil rights. This does happen in some cases. The industrialized countries are generally democratic, and their people have the lowest levels of poverty. A number of developing countries, such as Botswana and Mauritius, also manage to combine democratic rights with growth that may lead to poverty reduction. Figure 3.3 illustrates this and other possible combinations in developing countries.

Unfortunately, there are many counter-examples. Indeed, most countries that have recently moved toward democracy also seem to have suffered reverses in economic growth and human development. Eastern Europe and Central Asia, in particular, have seen devastating rises in poverty: between 1987 and 1998, the number of people living on less than $1 per day rose from one million to 24 million. Why is this? A number of reasons have been put forward.

• ***Illiberal democracies***—Achieving democracy is a complex business that requires several stages of democratic deepening. Unfortunately, many countries appear to be stuck in the early stages. Elections may take place, but the press is often muzzled and the courts corrupt, and many sections of state power lie beyond democratic control. Incomplete transitions produce illiberal democracies. And because democracy has not got very far, neither has social development.

• ***Weak institutions***—The essential institutions of democracy do not materialize overnight. In many sub-Saharan African countries, for example, state institutions remain inadequate. Badly paid civil servants are often obliged to concentrate not only on public duties, but also on extra income-earning activities. In Latin America as well, many of the old problems survive; traditional clientelism remains strong. Eastern Europe has confronted the additional challenge of having to dismantle one set of institutions and create another. Where institutions are weak, one of the most serious outcomes is rampant corruption—as reflected in Transparency International's corruption perception index. The bottom 10 countries (out of 99) in the 1999 index were, in order of increasing corruption: Kenya, Paraguay, Yugoslavia, Tanzania, Honduras, Uzbekistan, Azerbaijan, Indonesia, Nigeria and Cameroon. Developing countries and transition countries do not, of course, have a monopoly on corruption, which in recent years has become an issue in Italy, the United Kingdom, Japan and, more recently, Germany.

• ***Elite domination***—Even when countries move toward democracy, the old elites may remain in control through strategies of compromise or force. African countries that are formally democratic maintain entrenched systems of personal rule that frequently channel resources to individuals in favoured ethnic groups. They also mutate according to shifting power allegiances. In Kenya, for example, the ruling Kenya African National Union party was originally dominated by the Kikuyu; but President Moi has steadily transformed the party into one that primarily serves the needs of members of his own group, the Kalenjin. In Latin America, the military managed to retain much of its authority, even if some of this is now unravelling. In Guatemala the same landed and business oligarchies have had considerable influence over the economy for 80 years or more, and in the democratic era remain firmly in charge.

The rise of the technocrats

Local political circumstances push some countries toward autocracy. But external influences also play a part in dampening democracy. They can encourage more technocratic forms of governance that weaken the position of elected politicians and concentrate day-to-day decision making in the hands of a few national experts or institutions operating beyond democratic oversight and control.

One of the main pressures in this direction is the increasing predominance of the financial markets. All countries now find themselves at

Figure 3.3 – Democracy and economic performance in developing countries

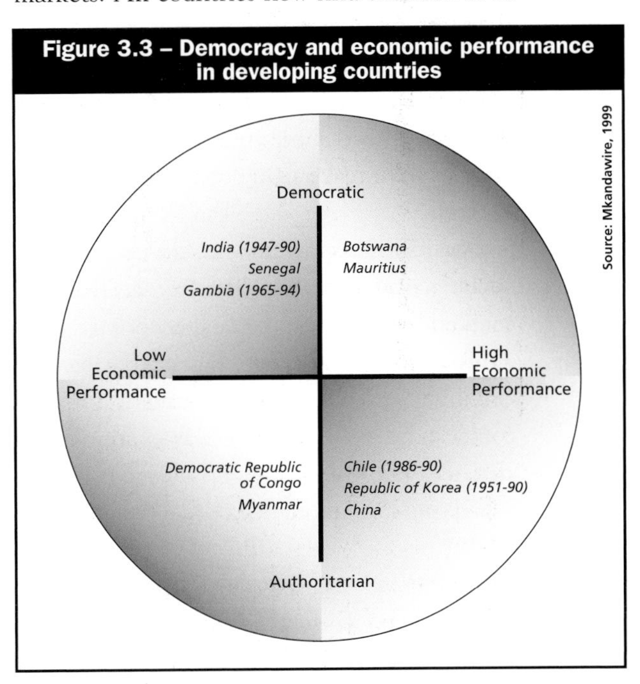

the mercy of international financiers. This applies particularly to those that have attracted large amounts of private funds—the OECD countries, Latin America, East Asia and parts of Eastern Europe. In the past, most such flows were the result of companies making foreign direct investments—whether in factories or mines or other enterprises. These companies were making fairly long-term commitments; and in order to protect their investments, they tried to establish good relations with governments, trade unions and other local institutions. They were not particularly sensitive to immediate changes in the macroeconomic environment. Indeed they might welcome a bout of inflation if it helped stimulate local demand for their products. Even when there were deeper economic problems in the country, each company's physical investment retained much of its value.

Now, however, as described in chapter two, more capital is coming from financial investors—those buying equities or bonds. Portfolio investors and traders in bonds or currencies will always be more nervous about inflation, or about any development that depreciates the currency in which their bonds or equities are denominated. They have no way of recovering their position other than to sell. And they have short time horizons: indeed, they have to make many of their decisions in seconds.

Aware of this, governments are permanently looking over their shoulders to see how the markets react to their macroeconomic decisions—particularly those that have a bearing on inflation. A government might prefer a looser monetary policy as a way of stimulating demand. But even a rumour of such a change could cause capital to flee.

The rise of the central bank

In these circumstances, governments may believe that the best approach is to remove monetary policy from the political arena altogether and to pass all decisions on monetary and even fiscal policy to technocrats in the central bank.

Independent central bankers are presumed to have several advantages over politicians as far as consistent monetary policy is concerned. First, they are less susceptible to immediate popular pressure and so can steer a steadier course. Second, since they are likely to be in office longer than politicians, they can have a long-term strategy that does not need to be in tune with electoral cycles. Third, they are not distracted by other considerations, such as popular pressures to boost growth and employment.

The delegation of authority to central banks is well advanced in industrialized countries. The United States and many Western European countries have now given varying degrees of autonomy to their central banks, and a similar process is under way in developing countries. In Chile, for example, the Pinochet dictatorship in 1989 gave independence to the central bank as a way of tying the hands of the incoming government and preventing a reversal of its own neoliberal economic policies. And during the 1990s, Colombia, Mexico and Venezuela also granted substantial autonomy to their central banks. The trend is less advanced in Africa, though in most of Francophone Africa price stability is delivered by membership in the Franc Zone.

For the transition countries of Eastern Europe, one of the strongest forces encouraging technocratic decision making is the drive toward the creation of a common currency for the European Union. This requires countries in Euroland to converge toward similar rates of interest, budget deficits and inflation. While the transition countries wanting to join the EU are not expected to meet the same convergence criteria, they still have to pass some rigorous tests on economic management before they can be admitted to the club. They must demonstrate clear progress in a number of areas, including liberalizing capital flows and establishing independent central banks.

THE RISE OF THE TECHNOCRATIC FINANCE MINISTER

Finance ministries have always been important, but in most governments they have now been catapulted to positions of dominance. Pressures for economic stabilization and balanced budgets have drained power away from the spending ministers and pushed it toward finance ministers. And in an increasingly complex world economy, finance ministers themselves are now required to be specialists. Gone are the days when the job could be filled by any politician. Today, the candidate is expected to have academic training in economics, or at least to be fully conversant with complex economic issues. Ministers such as Leszeck Balcerowicz of Poland, Yegor Gaidar of Russia, and Kwesi Botchway of Ghana were all highly trained economists or academics. This trend is particularly evident in Latin America. Alejandro Foxley in Chile, Domingo Cavallo in Argentina and Pedro Aspe in Mexico received doctorates from US universities. On returning home, these technocrat-politicians—"technopols"—then assembled cadres of like-minded people and built a power base in their respective political parties.

THE NEW MANAGERIALISM

The drift to technocracy is also evident in the reorganization of government bureaucracies. Here, the trend is shifting responsibilities from government departments to executive agencies. Although staffed by civil servants, agencies are headed by chief executives, on fixed-term contracts, who have independent boards of directors. This trend is furthest advanced in OECD countries, notably in the United Kingdom, where by 1995 two thirds of civil servants were employed in agencies—dealing with everything from teacher training to the issuing of passports. Developing countries have been following the same path—notably Ghana, Jamaica, Sri Lanka, Uganda and Venezuela.

The same impulse has also led to the establishment of independent systems for tax administration. These are run separately from the Ministry of Finance, and sometimes even from the regular civil service. Uganda, for example, followed this path and as a result managed to raise tax revenue over the period 1992–94 from 0.9 to 1.7 per cent of GDP—an example that has encouraged neighbouring Kenya and Tanzania to follow suit.

Executive agencies can operate with greater managerial discipline and more direct incentives than government departments. But even when agencies succeed, they do so at the expense of day-to-day democratic control.

Shizuo Kambyashi, Associated Press AP

G-7 finance ministers and central bank governors. Tokyo, Japan.

Encouragement from Washington

Moves toward more technocratic control in developing countries have been encouraged by the IMF and the World Bank. From their point of view, insulating governments from democratic pressures is an advantage when carrying out structural adjustment programmes (SAPs). Such programmes are often highly unpopular—which is understandable, since they generally increase unemployment, reduce wages and cut government services. In a number of cases, they have provoked riots in the streets.

Unpopularity was not a handicap when SAPs were being imposed by military dictatorships or single-party regimes; but in a more democratic era, public participation can make such programmes more troublesome. The Bretton Woods institutions tended, therefore, to confine policy discussions to a small group of people. In Latin America, for example, they worked through business groups and the technopols with whom they had close relationships. In Africa, the situation was slightly different. Since governments had fewer trained people who were enthusiastic about market reforms, the Bretton Woods institutions had to supply most of the technocrats themselves—placing experts in key financial and economic ministries. When, as democratization proceeded, there was greater pressure for local autonomy, this international staff was gradually replaced with local technocrats who could be relied upon to support adjustment.

Technocracy and democracy

Citizens in emerging democracies may not object to more technocratic government if it delivers economic stability and development. But this assumes that the technocrats get things right. When they get things wrong, they may undermine not just their own position but the legitimacy of democracy itself. In Eastern Europe, for example, where much public policy has been put into the hands of finance ministries and technocrats, the public response to economic failure and collapsing welfare systems is to aspire not to greater democracy but to the old certainties of communism. Surveys in Bulgaria, Slovakia, Belarus and Ukraine all show good ratings for the defunct regimes.

But the main danger of technocratic control, and of isolating policy makers from popular sentiment, is that it can alienate quite a large proportion of the population and thus block the way to future progress. Experience has shown that the best way to achieve durable support is through democratic processes of participation, dialogue and compromise. They should not merely promise long-term prosperity but also take care to compensate the short-term losers. In 1999 the European Bank for Reconstruction and Development, reviewing 10 years of transition, concluded: "It is commonly believed that successful reform requires a stable, strong government of technocrats committed to reform, but the experience of the last 10 years of transition has contradicted this view. A high degree of political competition, rather than a government insulated from electoral pressures, has promoted reform in many countries".

Without these processes of adjustment and adaptation, countries also risk lurching into political volatility, low voter turnout and a regression to primordial and sectarian forms of politics. Even industrialized countries such as Sweden, Italy, Austria and the US have seen the rise of new parties and charismatic figures with few or no links to established parties. In Eastern Europe it is noticeable that countries pushing ahead most rapidly with reform have had more frequent changes of government than those that moved more slowly. Poland, for example, had seven prime ministers and three presidents between 1990 and 1997.

Technocratic government poses serious problems for old and new democracies. It empowers narrow elites and undermines both democratic accountability and popular sovereignty. Clearly, policy making does now require greater technical expertise. But such expertise should still be open to democratic oversight.

Interest groups and social pacts

The most direct form of oversight is via elected representatives and the ballot box. But citizens have many other ways of influencing governments, through membership in other organizations and institutions of civil society. Many of these contacts are sporadic and involve trying to influence governments on particular issues. But there can also be more formal arrangements that culminate in social pacts—as individual interest groups pledge support or restraint in the national interest.

These efforts fit into a corporatist model of government in which different interest groups are incorporated into the political process. In exchange for having an influence over the formulation of public policies, these groups then have to assume responsibility to help implement them.

The most important of these interest groups have been the trade unions and employers' associations—the social partners who have entered into tripartite relations with government. Such negotiations flourished in the Keynesian era, when governments felt more confident about manipulating their economies to achieve high growth with low unemployment and low inflation. Trade unions could, for example, be offered better working conditions in exchange for wage restraint. In many cases this process involved an annual round of wage negotiations—as in Germany or the United Kingdom in the 1970s. But there have also been more formal social pacts, particularly in smaller countries like Sweden and Switzerland. In Latin America, such pacts have a long history.

The era of liberalization and globalization might have been thought to have done away with corporatism. Governments are less confident about controlling their economies. Trade union membership rates have gone into freefall. And employers' associations are being overtaken by the spread of multinationals.

In Mexico, for example, corporatism has been assailed from many different directions. The long-dominant Institutional Revolutionary Party is slowly loosening its grip on political life. And the central labour organization, the authoritarian Confederation of Mexican Workers, is seeing its influence eroded. Faced with lower wages and rising unemployment, workers are now forming smaller independent unions.

Yet the idea of social pacts seems far from dead in countries that are attempting to build more stable and more democratic political systems. In 1997, for example, the government of the Republic of Korea established a tripartite commission consisting of the state, labour and other forces of civil society. This reached an impasse when the government refused to accept union proposals for wide-ranging social safety nets. Probably the best example of a social pact in the developing world is South Africa's National Economic Development and Labour Council, which is attempting to bring together the state, organized labour, business interests and community groups in an elaborate set of corporatist institutions (box 3.3).

Ethnicity and democratization

States may become more technocratic and centralized. But along with the centripetal forces drawing power to the centre, there are also centrifugal forces tending to wrench democratic states apart. One of the most evident in recent years has been ethnicity. The Balkan wars, the secessionist claims in Indonesia, and the continuing struggles across Africa, from Western Sahara to Somalia, are all evidence of continuing ethnic tension.

All states are multi-ethnic, though some have many more groups than others. On the basis of language, European political systems include among their citizens only around 9.5 ethnic groups per state, compared with 21 in Latin America and the Caribbean. But the most ethnically segmented states tend to be found in Africa, Asia and the Pacific, where

Box 3.3 – Social pacts in South Africa

The ANC was elected in 1994, pledging to build a more egalitarian society. It had long maintained an alliance with the main trade union organization, the Congress of South African Trade Unions. But the ANC government also recognized the importance of protecting the country's industrial base and its international competitiveness. How could it transform South African society while maintaining industrial peace? One response in 1995 was to establish the National Economic Development and Labour Council (NEDLAC)—a multipartite body designed to reach consensus on economic and social policy between organized labour, organized employers, community groups and the government.

One of its most important achievements has been the Job Summit in 1998. This created possibilities for a negotiated social pact that would include wage and price increases, the distribution of the benefits of productivity improvements, and agreement on macroeconomic policy, social welfare and the investment regime.

But on some issues consensus has proved elusive, and at times NEDLAC has been bypassed in favour of bilateral negotiations. The Social Plan and Basic Conditions of Employment Act, for example, caused a major dispute. Employers were worried that it would affect their global competitiveness; and some of their views were reflected in the final Social Plan, which provides for the active management of workforce reduction when large-scale job losses are unavoidable. The trade unions wanted full protection against job losses, and in 1997 they staged a series of strikes to achieve a 40-hour week—though in the end they compromised in return for government commitment to resist employers' demands for greater flexibility in working hours between sectors.

NEDLAC faces a number of problems. Its members do not represent all the affected parties—notably those who are not trade union members. Some of its members have stronger negotiating skills than others. Also, although NEDLAC requires the government to bring its major policies to the negotiating table, it does not require the same of the other social partners.

The wide-ranging public sector strikes of the last few months of 1999 suggested that unions were becoming disenchanted with their limited scope to influence policy. But NEDLAC does provide the institutional basis for South Africans to engage with the new global order. This process, which may be called liberalized bargaining, assumes that participants accept the need to open up the economy; but it also offers them the opportunity to influence the terms on which this is done.

the number of groups per state averages 50 or more. In some countries there are many hundreds—Nigeria has 470, India 407, Indonesia 712, and Papua New Guinea 817.

In the majority of countries, one ethnic group tends to dominate. Even in ethnically diverse Asia, one group makes up more than half the population in 34 of 46 states, and the same is true in 19 out of 26 states in the Pacific. The only region to break this pattern is sub-Saharan Africa where, if the small island states are excluded, a single group dominates in only 12 out of 34 states.

A useful way of considering the ethnic structures of different countries is in terms of polarity. This is illustrated in table 3.1, which classifies countries in five types. The simpler cases are unipolar, bipolar or tripolar. A unipolar structure refers to cases where one group enjoys an overwhelming majority. A bipolar ethnic structure may either be composed of only two main ethnic groups or, as in Sierra Leone, it may contain a multiplicity of groups in which two roughly equal groups account for more than 60 per cent of the population. In a tripolar ethnic setting, there are either only three ethnic groups or three large groups in a multi-ethnic setting. Then there are multipolar countries—either concentrated or fragmented. In the concentrated multipolarity case, one ethnic group may constitute half or 40 per cent of the population, but still not be large enough to outnumber clusters of smaller groups. In the case of fragmented multipolarity, no group is large enough to dominate the political system. The conflicts that are often difficult to manage are those that occur in bipolar or tripolar settings. Government reforms should aim toward moderation, weakening polarity, and revealing multiple cleavages.

Ethnic diversity is not in itself a problem. Individuals and states can be enriched by cultural and ethnic diversity. Nor is ethnicity fixed and thus likely to store up trouble for the

Table 3.1 – A typology of ethnic structures

	Number of groups	Percentage of population made up of		
		largest group	two largest groups	three largest groups
Unipolarity				
Botswana	30	70	80	82
Equatorial Guinea	12	75	77	79
Cambodia	17	90	94	96
China	205	70	78	82
Viet Nam	85	87	88	89
Bulgaria	9	85	94	96
Bipolarity				
Rwanda	2	90	99	100
Burundi	2	85	99	100
Belgium	4	57	90	91
Fiji	10	49	95	99
Guyana	6	51	82	93
Sierra Leone	20	31	61	69
Tripolarity				
Switzerland	4	74	92	99
Nigeria	470	19	38	54
Malawi	15	32	47	58
Fragmented multipolarity				
Cameroon	279	5	9	11
Namibia	27	7	13	17
Tanzania	131	15	30	34
Papua New Guinea	817	4	7	8
Solomon Islands	66	5	10	13
Vanuatu	109	4	7	9
Concentrated multipolarity				
India	407	50	57	64
Congo[a]	60	51	64	73
Niger	20	43	61	70
Kenya	61	20	34	47
Togo	43	21	33	42
Ethiopia	82	29	36	44

Note: [a] Republic of the Congo

Source: Bangura and Nakamura, 1999, based on Grimes, 1996 and Premdas, 1995

future. Ethnicity is constantly adapting: it is a variable and shifting attribute that can never pin a person down to a precise identity. Many ethnic markers—physical characteristics, language, religion and culture—are very fluid. And while some societies consider religion, say, or language to be defining characteristics, others may ignore such considerations altogether.

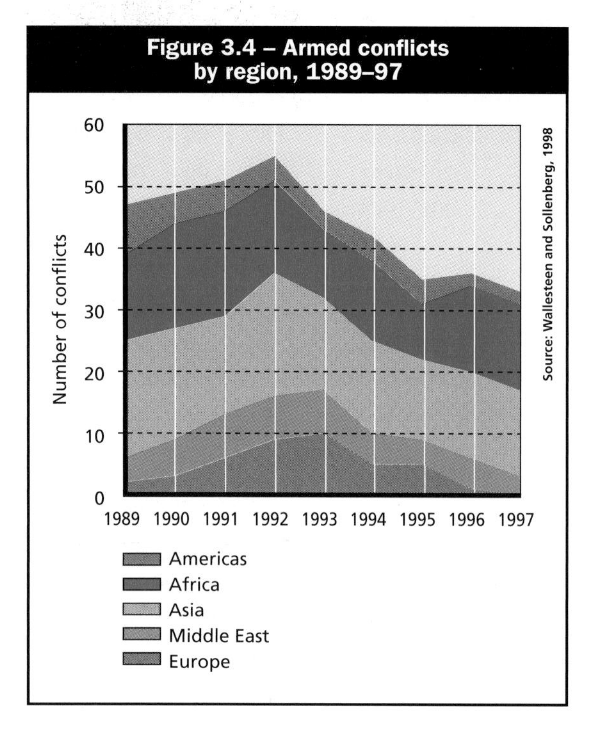

Figure 3.4 – Armed conflicts by region, 1989–97

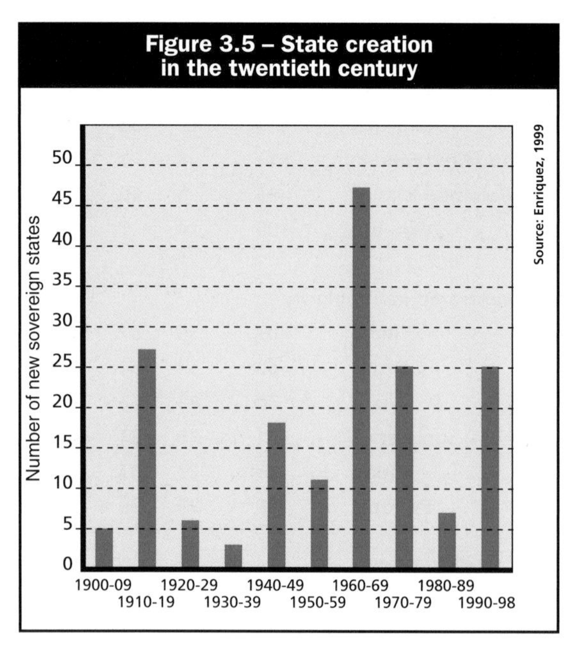

Figure 3.5 – State creation in the twentieth century

The problems arise only when ethnic identity is politicized—at which point it can be used to provoke behaviour that is insular, xenophobic and destructive. It has this power because, *in extremis*, ethnic identity overrides all other loyalties and obligations.

One of the clearest indicators of the increase in ethnic strife was the alarmingly high number of civil wars in the 1990s, even though these decreased between 1992–94, and 1996–97. In the 1990s most wars were not inter-state but intra-state. These may not have started as ethnic conflicts, but ethnic identity certainly came to the fore once they were under way. Such conflicts typically originate in the maldistribution of resources or jobs, or in abuses of cultural or human rights. Those who struggle to preserve or overturn these inequalities often use ethnicity as their focal point.

As figure 3.4 illustrates, most of these conflicts have been in the more ethnically diverse regions—Africa and Asia. These are also the regions that have produced the majority of refugees: of the 11.4 million refugees in 1998, 41 per cent came from Asia and 28 per cent from Africa.

The risk of secession

Inter-ethnic strife may end in the crushing of an insurrection or a change in the national power structure. But it can also lead to secession and the creation of a new state. Figure 3.5 indicates the rate of sovereign state formation in the last century. The peak in the 1960s and 1970s represents the period of decolonization and independence, while that in the 1990s largely corresponds to existing states breaking up. The most dramatic sequence was in East and Central Europe in the 1990s, when 22 new states appeared, most of which had been parts of the former Soviet Union or Yugoslavia. Few new states have been created elsewhere: none in the Americas, and only one in Asia—East Timor.

Paradoxically, despite the turmoil in Africa, only one fully recognized state has been created (Eritrea), though two others—Anjouan (which seceded from the Comoros in 1997) and Somaliland (which has effectively become a separate state within Somalia)—may be recognized in the near future.

The main reason for Africa's slow rate of state formation is the degree of ethnic fragmentation. Africa has more than 2,000 ethnic groups, whose average size is less than one million. It is hardly practical for each of these to have a state of its own. Instead, political leaders have tried to forge new states within their inherited colonial boundaries. The reluctance of political leaders to seek new nation states has been reinforced by the Charter of the Organization of African Unity, which forbids redrawing of colonially inherited borders and makes it difficult for secessionist movements to gain recognition. In fact, sub-Saharan Africa has only three states where ethnicity has been linked to statehood—Lesotho, Swaziland and Somalia, though the third is in the process of breaking up.

The African situation is mirrored to some extent in Asia. All the larger states—China, India, Indonesia and Pakistan—are multi-ethnic. Of these, probably only Indonesia, where ethnic fragmentation is compounded by geographical dispersion into islands, is at serious risk from secession.

Electoral systems and ethnic diversity

Governments have adopted a number of strategies for accommodating ethnic diversity within single states. In some cases they have done so by altering the structure of the state in ways that allow distinct groups to have greater autonomy. Some of the larger and most diverse countries, such as India, have federal structures that devolve considerable authority to state or provincial assemblies. Many states have also made efforts to decentralize—deconcentrating their activities, or delegating administrative tasks, or in some cases devolving considerable authority to local governments. The primary purpose of decentralization is usually to make the government more responsive to regional and local sensitivities. But since most ethnic groups also tend to be concentrated in specific regions, this effectively permits greater ethnic autonomy.

Uganda, for example, has since 1994 been decentralizing authority to 46 districts, whose activities now account for 30 per cent of government expenditure. In many respects this is thought to have been a success and to have consolidated national unity. But there have also been complaints that the districts were actually created along ethnic lines, so that decentralization has intensified ethnic politics—making it difficult for civil servants to work outside their home areas.

In addition to changing the structure of their states, governments have also tried to accommodate ethnic divisions by devising more appropriate voting and governance systems. Here there are two main options. One, the "alternative vote", encourages political parties to be multi-ethnic. The other, the "list system", accepts that parties will be rooted in ethnic identities but tries to make these parties share power.

Pluralistic parties and the alternative vote

One electoral system that encourages parties to appeal across ethnic lines is the alternative vote. This system requires voters to rank candidates in an order of preference. If no candidate receives more than 50 per cent of the vote in the first count, the last candidate is eliminated and his or her second-preference votes are transferred to the remaining candidates. The process is repeated until a winner emerges. This system can still allow candidates who adopt an ethnically extreme position to be elected, but it reduces their chances of success—and improves the prospects of those who adopt more centrist positions and are prepared to appeal to people outside their own core group.

The alternative vote was initially devised for fairly homogenous industrialized countries—to address some of the weaknesses of the first-past-the-post system, where a candidate may be elected even if heartily disliked by the majority of voters who split their vote between two or more other parties. The main Western democracy to use this system is Australia.

But the alternative vote could also be of value in ethnically diverse developing countries. So far, it has not been used extensively. Papua New Guinea used it in early elections but subsequently replaced it with a first-past-the-post system. Sri Lanka has a variant of the alternative vote for presidential elections, and Fiji adopted it in 1996.

Consociation and the party list

A diametrically opposed approach accepts that citizens will vote along ethnic lines but obliges the ethnically based parties to share power in a government of national unity. This "consociation" model thus tries to promote diversity not within parties, but within governments.

Consociation typically requires a system of voting based on party lists. A country is divided into very large constituencies—or may even be treated as a single constituency, which is usually the case in a presidential election. In the case of a parliamentary election, voters do not choose an individual candidate, but instead vote for a party. Parties are then allocated parliamentary seats according to their proportion of the total vote—nominating their representatives from a previously prepared ranked list of candidates.

The consociational governments that this system permits ideally have four key elements. First, they are coalitions that reflect all segments of society. Second, they distribute public sector jobs proportionally to each ethnic group. Third, they offer a high degree of territorial autonomy—through federalism or decentralization. Fourth, they allow minority groups a veto on important issues. This system effectively encourages each key group to form its own party in order to gain representation in both the government and the civil service.

Consociational systems are to be found in Austria, Belgium and Switzerland, and also in developing countries such as Malaysia and South Africa. They are also a popular choice for negotiators trying to devise solutions for war-torn societies, as in Bosnia-Herzegovina and Northern Ireland. But this does not always work. There have been failures in Cyprus and Lebanon, for example, and the consociational agreement for Angola was never fully implemented because of the recalcitrance of the rebel leader, Jonas Savimbi.

The merits of different systems

There has been considerable debate about the relative merits of these two approaches. This has centred on four main issues.

- ***Promoting moderation***—The alternative vote will only be biased toward moderate candidates if each constituency has an ethnically mixed electorate across which candidates are obliged to appeal. If constituencies have one dominant group, then ethnically extreme candidates can still be elected. In this case, the party list and consociation may be a better option.
- ***Voter empowerment***—The alternative vote has the advantage of allowing voters to identify with a particular candidate and monitor his or her performance. The party list system discourages accountability to voters. After the election, successful candidates are more likely to respond to the wishes of their party, particularly those of the party leader.
- ***Ease of use***—Illiterate voters may find the alternative vote system too complex, though

this can be alleviated by the use of separate and differently coloured ballot papers to indicate second and third choices. Ballot boxes can also be arranged in a rank-ordered way for voters to express their preferences.

- ***Strong government***—The alternative vote system is majoritarian—electing people who appeal to a broad spectrum. Opposition parties and more extreme groups are thus excluded, but this may provoke them into extra-parliamentary activity that could destabilize the government. Also, when groups are sharply polarized voters may refuse to exercise their second-preference votes. The consociational approach, conversely, will draw in even the most extreme groups. This may build stability, but it will not necessarily produce strong government.

The two basic models have their strengths and weaknesses. And of course they do not exhaust the possibilities. Countries contemplating a new electoral system can spend many years mulling over a plethora of options. Another popular choice is the "single transferable vote", where voters list their preferred candidates in order; when the leading candidate has received sufficient votes to be elected, his or her surplus votes are transferred to other candidates. Under the single transferable vote system more than one candidate may be eligible for election in a constituency: this offers opportunities for smaller parties to be elected into parliament. Elections may also be conducted in a series of separate rounds, progressively eliminating weaker candidates.

There are other ways of modifying party behaviour. There can be a ban on ethnic or religious symbols, for example, or parties may be obliged to establish offices throughout the country rather than exclusively in their home territory. There are also many variations on the rules of consociation. Thus party lists may be required to have a minimum number of individuals from more than one region, or the presidential and vice presidential candidates of political parties may be chosen from different regions—as in Sierra Leone. And there can be various forms of affirmative action, including reserved seats for minorities, as in New Zealand.

In practice, states have a broad palette of options and tend to mix and match systems of voting with different structures of government. Very few adopt all elements of the ideal consociational model. They are unlikely to allow a minority veto, for example, or to distribute civil service posts on a strictly proportional basis. And there are many forms of power sharing. The Swiss model is based on strong, multi-ethnic parties. Nigeria rotates the presidency among individuals from different regions. And Malaysian political parties create their "grand coalition" prior to the election.

The choice of solutions depends very much on ethnic make-up. Consociational or power-sharing instruments may be unavoidable in bipolar and tripolar ethnic structures, but may not have the same urgency in unipolar or multipolar settings. And there are many forms of power sharing. Thus bipolar states such as Rwanda, Burundi and Cyprus are likely to opt for some form of power sharing, although there may have to be specific provisions to allow the minority group to provide the prime minister or president at some stage. In Rwanda and Burundi, where there are mixed settlements, this may best be combined with an alternative vote system to encourage the formation of plural political parties. In Northern Ireland, the Good Friday Agreement was based on power sharing using the single transferable vote system. Under this scheme, the more moderate Ulster Unionist Party increased its share of parliamentary seats by 4.6 per cent through second-order preference votes; and the strongly anti-war Northern Ireland Women's Coalition won two seats despite its poor showing in the first-order preferences. The major pitfall of Bosnia's power sharing government, which is based on the party list system, is that it offers no incentives for parties to attract votes outside of their ethnic enclaves. In tripolar structures such as Nigeria, which has a very large number of ethnic groups, there is more room for manoeuvre. Nigeria has a non-ethnic-based party system that has power sharing within a federal structure.

When considering the possibilities, the designers of institutional systems should be careful not to freeze existing ethnic cleavages, but always to allow citizens room to change their affiliation or express multiple identities. They should also promote institutions that are likely to reflect cross-cutting cleavages—such as trade unions, professional associations, and other civic organizations. Whatever system is chosen should aim to build a pluralistic state that will promote economic development and deliver social services to all, without prejudice or discrimination.

The democratic process

People who live in democratic societies tend after a while to become complacent—to forget that democracy involves a constant process of negotiation, and that its institutions need to be regularly reassessed and reinvigorated. The older democracies in Europe, from Austria to Sweden, frequently hear disturbing echoes of the fascism and racism that they thought had long been banished. And the United States, which is in the forefront of media technology, has yet to address the serious democratic implications of the fact that it takes a great deal of money to be elected to the highest office.

Many other societies have more fragile democracies that could yet slide backward. Latin America appeared to have banished the era of military coups, but Ecuador started the twenty-first century with something that came very close, and Venezuela seems to have settled for an old-fashioned centralized presidency.

Elsewhere, many developing and transition countries have yet to be convinced of the value of democracy. They seem prepared to experiment with participation and accountability, but also to set these aside if they do not deliver economic progress or social peace. Probably the most difficult circumstances arise when people feel they do not have enough in common to be willing to share a common government—and threaten to fracture their states along religious or ethnic fault lines. And all over the world there is a risk that even the most mature democracies can ossify into technocracies that place many functions of the state beyond the control of ordinary citizens.

All these possibilities underline the need for governments to maintain their vigilance, to develop new constitutional devices and instruments that not merely proclaim grand ideals but also help to meet people's immediate needs, and to fulfil their basic human rights. Democracy is not a static condition; it is a constantly evolving process—and one that can always mutate in unpredictable and unsettling directions.

A new mission for the public sector

Seeking a job in the public sector.
Athens, Greece

Eurokinissi, Associated Press AP

Many efforts were made in the 1990s to reform the public sector. In developing countries, inappropriate schemes often served to weaken the capacity for effective governance. But the tide may now be turning—with a more realistic appreciation of what states can and should achieve.

Between 1945 and 1980, the public sector expanded at an unprecedented pace. Most people wanted the state to play a central part in national development. The OECD countries wanted government to redistribute wealth, protect the vulnerable and stimulate economic demand. The developing countries wanted states that crystallized national identity and built modern economies. Meanwhile, the Soviet Union and the countries of Eastern and Central Europe had already built states that controlled virtually every aspect of their citizens' lives.

During the 1980s and 1990s, however, some states disintegrated and many were affected by free-market reforms. In a globalizing world, public sector reform became a central preoccupation of citizens and governments. The previous chapter looked at governance from the vantage point of democracy. This chapter looks more closely at public sector management—at the state's ability to deliver the public services needed in the twenty-first century.

Pressures for reform

Over the past two decades, states have come under pressure from many different directions. But four main issues seem to have predominated.

- ***Rising deficits***—Governments all over the world had been sinking deeper into the red. In the 1960s the OECD countries managed to keep their budgets more or less in balance, but by the 1970s their annual budget deficits were rising to 4 per cent, and by the 1980s to 6 per cent or more. The situation was even worse in developing countries. In Asia, countries managed to keep their deficits down to 3 per cent, but by the 1980s many countries in Latin America and Africa were facing deficits above 10 per cent. This caused increasing alarm. Many people accused the deficits of stifling economic development, and they demanded cuts in government expenditure.
- ***Financial globalization***—More governments now finance their activities not by borrowing directly from a specific bank or institution, but by issuing bonds. This can trigger an international chain of events. Thus the city authority in Jakarta might finance public works by issuing a bond, which is then funded in Amsterdam, serviced in London and ultimately held by a pension fund in New York. This extended intermediation may smooth the process of fund raising, but it also weakens the links between borrowers and lenders. Lenders who have less direct contact with borrowers will require more general forms of reassurance, which they can only get if they feel that the borrowing institutions are operating in a sound and transparent fashion. The growth of international finance thus tends to foster a standardized, and fairly small, public sector that is well integrated into the global economy.
- ***Economic ideology***—In the 1980s, many economists became increasingly critical of the public sector, which they accused of sustaining inefficient and unaccountable monopolies—whether in industry or in service delivery. This was the stance of the Bretton Woods institutions; and since they held the purse strings, they were in a powerful position to impose these ideas on debtor countries. The international financial institutions advocated privatization, decentralization and market delivery of public services. They also argued that governments should reorganize their civil services and demanded that they control their expenditure

and reform their tax systems in order to achieve balanced budgets.

- *Democratization*—In today's more democratic atmosphere, citizens have been demanding more and better public services. Yet at the same time, the revenue base of many states is shrinking. This leads to a search for more efficient ways of using public funds. It also generates struggles between potential winners and losers. The disruptive demands of more open societies have created a more fluid and uncertain environment for public policy.

Fiscal stability

The most pervasive and far-reaching reforms in both industrialized and developing countries are those that aim for fiscal stability. Governments have made some changes on the revenue side. But most have concentrated their budget-balancing energies on cutting public expenditure, which is typically expressed as a proportion of GDP. During the 1960s, in most countries this proportion was maintained at around 20 per cent. But by the 1980s the figures had risen rapidly. Most developing regions were averaging around 25 per cent, while the industrialized countries were averaging considerably more.

Public expenditure targets

There were also differences in the pattern of expenditure. By and large, the developing countries were devoting their funds to capital expenditure (30 per cent), public sector wages (25 per cent) and government administration (20 per cent), and spending relatively little on education (11 per cent) or health (5 per cent). The industrialized countries, on the other hand, were devoting more of their expenditure to social security transfers and social services (45 per cent)—with a particular emphasis on health.

So when it came to cutting expenditure, industrialized countries attempted to reduce expenditure on welfare. They tried various approaches, sometimes reducing benefits, and sometimes making an effort to limit the number of potential claimants—through reforming their labour markets, for example, so as to maximize employment, if at lower wages. Even so, the industrialized countries did not succeed in cutting expenditure by much. Indeed, in the 1980s they seemed to be spending more—public expenditure rose from 45 to 47 per cent of GDP. Governments faced stiff resistance to cuts in the public services on which their citizens had come to rely. While they did not manage to cut the totals, however, they did change the distribution—devoting more to welfare payments, while trying to restrain expenditure on health.

Developing countries were more successful at cutting expenditure, as indicated in table 4.1. They also reduced fiscal deficits. Latin America did so first—achieving stability by the early 1990s. Other regions brought deficits under control during the mid-1990s, chiefly by reducing expenditures. One reason why they had more "success" is that they did not face such powerful popular resistance—those who

Table 4.1 – Public expenditure as a percentage of GDP

	1980	1990	1997
Sub-Saharan Africa[a]	25.5	26.3	22.3
North Africa	39.0	29.4	30.4
Latin America	n.a.	24.5	23.6
South and East Asia	29.4	37.3	26.2[b]

Notes: [a] Excludes South Africa; [b] Data are for 1996
Sources: World Bank, 1998f; ECLAC, 1997; ADB, 1998

suffered most had few options for expressing their dissatisfaction. Governments also had their resolve stiffened by the IMF and the World Bank. When giving structural adjustment loans, the Bretton Woods institutions applied a fairly consistent set of conditions. Table 4.2 summarizes these and indicates the priority given by the World Bank to expenditure reforms.

One of the main instruments of these reforms in developing countries has been the public expenditure review. This is generally prepared for loan recipients by World Bank staff or foreign consultants. More than 200 reviews were carried out between 1987 and 1998. Another important technique has been "cash budgeting"—which means that finance and line ministries are permitted to spend only what they have in the bank: they are not allowed overdrafts. In Zambia, for example, a monitoring committee meets daily to ensure that this discipline is being followed.

Such techniques have certainly cut deficits: in Zambia during the first year of cash budgeting, a deficit of 69 billion kwacha was turned into a surplus of 24 billion kwacha. But here, as elsewhere, such techniques may be unsustainable. At times they have caused wild fluctuations in expenditure, provoking political crises. In 1993–94, for example, the Zambian government had to violate these principles—intervening to lend money to traders in order to stave off a food crisis.

Budgetary discipline can also distort patterns of expenditure and make it difficult to achieve consistent planning. In Zambia, the expenditure overruns of the office of the presidency in 1994 were roughly the same as the 12 per cent shortfalls experienced by the Ministry of Health. Similarly, in Uganda, expenditure overruns by the president's office were almost equal to the combined shortfalls of the Ministries of Agriculture (51 per cent) and Education (29 per cent).

Table 4.2 – World Bank loan conditions, 1980–94

Condition	Number of countries where imposed
Expenditure reforms	126
Social-sector restructuring	60
Privatization and marketization	43
Streamlined budgetary processes and accounts	42
Civil service reform	42
Poverty alleviation	10
Participation	1
Others	26

Source: World Bank, 1997b

Expenditure cuts in the social sector

One of the main targets for cuts has been the social sector. For a group of 21 countries in Africa, social expenditure between 1980 and 1990 fell from 4.6 to 2.7 per cent of GDP. The World Bank also cut some of its social spending. A comparison of 1972–82 and 1982–88 shows that its education expenditure (in 1990 dollars) fell from $0.5 per person to $0.3. Following widespread criticism, the Bank subsequently rethought its policies. Now it requires borrowing countries not only to reduce expenditures, but also to restructure them, with more emphasis on basic education and primary health care. This appears to have had some effect. The IMF has concluded that 32 low-income countries receiving structural adjustment loans have been devoting more resources to health and education: between 1985 and 1996, they increased their real per capita expenditure on these services by an average of 2.8 per cent per year—though even this is a small increase when set against overall needs. Given the new policy focus by the World Bank and the IMF on basic education and health provisioning, these gains may also have been achieved by shifting funds from tertiary education.

THE SOCIAL EFFECTS OF PRIVATIZATION

One of the priorities for governments carrying out structural adjustment has been to privatize public enterprises—partly as a way of raising funds and partly to reduce subsidies paid to loss-making enterprises. Between 1990 and 1996, developing and transition countries divested $155 billon of their assets to the private sector (figure 4.1). Governments in Latin America led the way—accounting for more than half of these sales, which they used largely to finance their deficits. Sales in Africa were much slower. The transition countries were more active but did not raise much revenue, since governments effectively gave away many enterprises via voucher schemes or sold them at low prices to a privileged elite.

There is a sound case for privatizing many manufacturing enterprises, which will generally perform better in the private sector. But the case is less strong for public sector utilities. These are frequently monopolies that, after privatization, may be tempted to raise prices, with disastrous consequences for the poor. In principle, this danger can be minimized through a strong regulatory system. But even industrialized countries have had problems regulating private utilities, and developing countries find it even more difficult. In Argentina, for example, the regulators have proved less powerful than the utility companies and have effectively been colonized by the interests they were designed to control.

Another damaging social outcome of privatization is unemployment. Public enterprises in developing countries usually account for a high proportion of formal sector employment—22 per cent in Africa. Prior to sale, governments frequently lay off workers as a way of making the company more attractive to buyers, and afterward the privatized companies continue the process as a way of cutting costs. To stave off potential backlashes, many Latin American governments have required guarantees of continued employment—most of which seem to have been honoured. The more militant workers have also been able to protect employment to some extent. But this has not been easy. Despite the fact that trade unions in Ghana strongly opposed workforce reduction, employment in the country's 42 largest state enterprises was cut by almost two thirds between 1984 and 1991.

Welfare implications of a shrinking public sector are even greater in the transition economies, since enterprises there provided not just employment, but also extensive welfare services—from health care to pensions. The disappearance of public enterprises has not only cost jobs, but also removed much of the social infrastructure in these countries.

Figure 4.1 – Privatization revenues

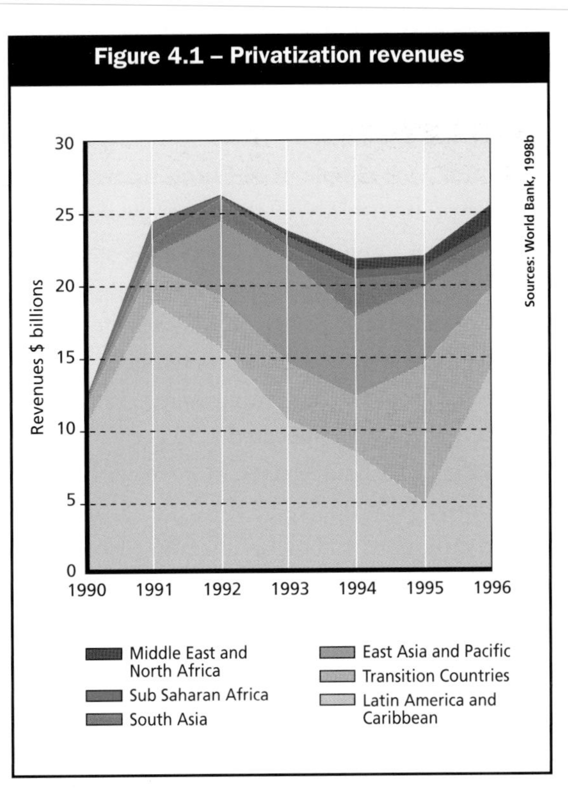

Carlos Eduardo, Associated Press AP

Street theatre at a demonstration against privatization of Brazil's telecommunications system. Brasilia, Brazil

Privatization has also altered the social landscape because the process has frequently been distorted in favour of powerful groups. In transition countries, privatization has often benefited managers and workers in the most viable enterprises. After privatization in Russia, one sample of 314 firms suggested that almost two thirds of the shares were in the hands of "insiders". In developing countries, privatization can benefit individuals from more powerful ethnic groups. In Malaysia, for example, there were concerns that Chinese business groups would take most advantage of sales, so the government allocated a 30 per cent quota to the indigenous Malays. More recently, white South Africans have been taking advantage of privatizations to buy up assets in Mozambique and Zambia—acquisitions that may eventually cause a racial backlash.

Managerial efficiency

In addition to privatizing many public sector activities, governments have also attempted to improve managerial performance. In doing so, they have frequently been guided by the "public choice" theories in vogue in the international community. These approaches analyse political and bureaucratic processes by applying principles of economics. Public choice theorists argue, for example, that civil servants have few incentives to improve performance or reduce costs, and that the only way to get them to perform better is through reforms that introduce techniques and disciplines from the private sector.

Most reforms aim to break up bureaucratic activities into more manageable parts, which may be insulated from political control in the hope of achieving optimal services. They are part of the technocratic revolution discussed in chapter 3, and have a number of common elements.

- ***Agencies***—Central ministries continue to set policy, but divest responsibility for carrying out these decisions to autonomous agencies. Agencies generally operate in a corporate fashion, with a chief executive and a board of directors.

- ***Contracts***—Agencies deal with ministries and each other on a contractual rather than an administrative basis. The new management systems also include performance contracts between governments and service providers, requiring that the latter achieve specific targets.
- ***Quasi-markets***—This involves creating a buying-and-selling relationship in what had previously been one department. Thus, within a health service, doctors and local health bodies can be allocated a budget to buy services for their patients from hospitals.
- ***Contracting out***—This is regarded as the most advanced stage of reform. Governments may, for example, hire companies or NGOs to manage hospitals or water systems, or even prisons.

These ideas took hold in the industrialized countries in the 1980s with the advent of neoliberal governments in the United States and the United Kingdom, and they seem to have been pursued with greatest vigour in New Zealand. They have been slower to arrive in developing countries, but are likely to become much more prevalent now that they are being advocated by the World Bank and have become the standard prescription of international management consultants.

In the early years, these ideas of decentralized management were confined to one or two sectors. One of the first targets has typically been the tax-collection office. Many countries have now separated this office from the national civil service. The staff have different rules of employment and are paid according to performance (box 4.1).

But donors are requiring far broader reforms. Tanzania began following this path in the 1990s: it has reduced the number of ministerial departments by around one quarter and now has 47 agencies. Uganda has been going through a similar process: it has removed around half the functions of many ministries and created more than 100 new agencies. By the end of the exercise, 54,000 Ugandan civil servants will have lost their jobs.

Box 4.1 – Tax reforms in Peru

By 1990, a bout of hyperinflation and serious macroeconomic mismanagement had reduced Peru's tax revenues to 4.9 per cent of GNP. The tax office, with 3,000 staff, was riddled with corruption.

Under strong external pressure, the new government introduced a radical reform and created a new tax authority, SUNAT, independent of the Ministry of Economy and Finance and accountable only to the presidency. Two thirds of the previous staff were dismissed and replaced by recent graduates on short-term contracts, who were evaluated every six months. SUNAT also introduced a new, simplified tax system and a strictly level playing field for the treatment of taxpayers. This produced swift results; and by 1993, the tax ratio had risen to 13 per cent of GDP. SUNAT became an elite corps of the civil service.

Since then, however, some of the old problems have returned. As the macroeconomic situation improved, some of the pressure was reduced; and SUNAT started to acquire traditional features of public administration—with evidence of favouritism to certain taxpayers. The government repeatedly changed the head of SUNAT, which weakened managerial cohesion. In 1997, plans for a wider reform of public administration were abandoned.

In Latin America, the reforms have been more piecemeal. Brazil has tried to create a range of agencies, but the results have been meagre. By 1999, there was still only one executive agency—the National Institute of Measurements and Technical Norms. Reforms have met stiff opposition from well-organized public sector unions, not only in Brazil but in many other Latin American countries as well.

THE RESULTS OF REFORM

Do these reforms work? Most evaluations have taken place in industrialized countries. In New Zealand, for example, the reforms are considered a success—having reduced costs and improved public sector performance and efficiency. In the United Kingdom, the conclusions are more mixed. Though some agencies have performed well, others have been severely criticized: thus the child support agency, which gathers payments from separated fathers, has been roundly criticized, and more recently the passport agency has been through a major crisis. The "internal market" in the National Health Service has now largely been abandoned.

These experiences may be contrasted with those of the Netherlands. Here, too, the government embarked on a process of "agencification" but changed tack when it became concerned about the lack of democratic control over agencies. Public sector reforms subsequently went ahead, but they were based less on market principles and more on proper supervision of agencies, democratic accountability and social pacts with trade unions. Reforms in labour markets combine flexibility with generous welfare protection for workers if things go wrong. As a result, the Netherlands has gained many of the benefits of a more efficient public sector, including good rates of economic growth and low inflation, without heightening social divisions. It currently has the second lowest unemployment rate in the industrialized world.

Experience in developing countries has been more limited. Efficient agencies and decentralized management can only succeed if there is close monitoring based on sound budgeting and regular flows of accurate information. In most developing countries these capacities are weak, and governments frequently fail to establish clear objectives. Managers may then be able to manipulate information on performance indicators. In these circumstances, decentralizing the systems may foster arbitrariness or corruption. Gross abuses have been detected in Ghana; and in Zimbabwe, the performance management system had to be discontinued because ministers feared that civil servants would use it to create personal empires and ethnic enclaves. Nigeria's reforms in the late 1980s gave far greater powers to heads of ministries but did not create adequate systems to monitor their performance.

PUBLIC ACCOUNTABILITY

Accountability is a central problem with the use of agencies. In theory, this is provided by market discipline: bad providers will be punished by users, who will spend their funds elsewhere. In practice, these new "markets" frequently fail—allowing powerful interest groups and managers to take advantage of their positions and offer low-quality services.

In the industrialized countries, this has led to calls for additional forms of accountability. The UK government, for example, created a Citizens' Charter, which seeks to ensure that service users have full information on the performance of service providers and have adequate means of redress. This is now being adopted in other countries. The system of ombudsmen that started in Scandinavia also offers ways of receiving public complaints and forwarding them to governments. Another approach is the service delivery survey, which is being carried out in a number of developing countries by the NGO CIET-International.

The most advanced application of this technique is in Indian cities, where citizens' views are sought on a wide range of services, from the telephones to the police.

Capacity building

Reforms in most developing countries soon run into capacity problems. Even when governments and bureaucracies are committed to reforms, they often lack the skills or experience to carry them through.

If anything, these skills are disappearing. The next generation of senior officials should now be passing through the universities and institutes of public administration. But in the poorest countries, most systems of tertiary education are in crisis. Buildings are decaying, equipment is non-existent and teachers are joining the private sector, taking on extra jobs or migrating abroad.

It is ironic that the World Bank, which is a champion of decentralized public sector management, has done much to undermine the very institutions needed to make it work. Structural adjustment has eroded education systems generally, but it has been particularly hard on tertiary education. This has been evident in Africa, where World Bank lending for universities fell steeply. In the period 1969–79, it was $0.38 per capita; by 1980–87, it was down to $0.10.

Not surprisingly, many governments have had to rely heavily on expatriate staff. This is partly because of the unpopularity of structural adjustment programmes, but it is also because there have not been sufficient numbers of skilled local people. In the 1980s, Africa had around 100,000 resident foreign advisers—who cost roughly 35 per cent of foreign assistance to the region.

Since the 1990s, the World Bank, UNDP and other donors have been trying to address the problem—putting greater emphasis on capacity building and local "ownership" of projects. There has also been much talk of rebuilding African universities and research institutes.

Kent Gilbert, Associated Press AP

Protest by public employees for a fair wage increase. San José, Costa Rica

But not much has happened. Many of the resources are being channelled through the new African Capacity Building Foundation, based in Harare. By 1998 this foundation, which has close institutional ties to the World Bank, had supported 36 projects in 29 institutions in 20 countries. But the funds are meagre in relation to the need, and even these do not seem to have been used very effectively.

One of the most important issues that capacity building programmes will have to tackle is the level of salaries. It is significant that the developmental states in Southeast Asia were able to call on a skilled cadre of public servants. They also paid them well. In Singapore, for example, many civil servants earn more than their counterparts in the private sector. Public servants in low-income, crisis-ridden states, on the other hand, have seen their real wages fall steeply. As a result, they are not only more open to corruption, but also have to spend more time on second or third jobs just to earn a living wage. Yet the problem is not just low pay. Systems of remuneration can be quite opaque—and there is often no clear relationship between pay and responsibility or performance.

Some governments have started to address these issues. Uganda, for example, has been trying to clarify its payment system by including the real market value of additional benefits, such as housing, transport or health benefits. One of the most radical options would be performance-related pay. Malaysia is one of the few governments to have tried this.

In the past, systems of remuneration also suffered from compression—a narrowing of differentials between top and bottom. Immediately after independence, many African countries moved toward more egalitarian pay structures. Recently, however, this trend has been reversed: in Ghana, for example, between 1984 and 1991 the ratio between the salary scales of the top civil servants and those in the lowest grade increased from 2:1 to 10:1.

Steps toward wage decompression have often been linked with retrenchments. Governments that wish to escape from the low-wage, low-morale, corruption trap would prefer to employ fewer people but pay them better. Uganda, Bolivia and to some extent Ghana have attempted this, but with some difficulty. In addition to resistance from civil servants, there can be high severance costs. And frequently, those who retire subsequently reappear as consultants.

Low pay is also associated with the more general problem of financing recurrent costs. On the whole, donors prefer to invest in new physical or social infrastructure, such as schools or hospitals, leaving recipients with the burden of maintaining them and paying salaries. For projects in the poorest countries, it has been estimated that annual recurrent costs can be up to 70 per cent of the initial investment. Seeing the possibility that their projects will collapse, some donors have had to create and finance parallel structures within bureaucracies, just to keep their projects alive. Zambia's Educational Materials Project, for example, was largely run by an enclave of foreign experts.

In its Public Investment Programme, the World Bank has tried to address these issues by urging ministries to develop budgets that reflect operating and maintenance costs. But this is not an easy task.

The future of public sector reform

Developing countries do need to reform aspects of their public sectors. Many have done so, reducing the size of their workforces and cutting budget deficits. The range of reforms is outlined in box 4.2.

But if reformers want to make greater progress in future, they will need to look more closely at local circumstances and apply more appropriate remedies. Many of the principles of reform assume that there is some standardized

Box 4.2 – Public sector goals and reforms

Public sector reforms around the world have four main goals. International agencies attach primary importance to fiscal reform and managerial efficiency, but have paid less attention to capacity building or accountability.

1. **Fiscal stability**
   - Expenditure reduction
   - Privatization
   - Tax reform
2. **Public accountability**
   - Citizens' charters
   - Ombudsmen
   - Service delivery surveys
   - Plural parliaments
   - Press freedom
   - Independent judiciary
   - Mass-based political parties
   - Civic action
3. **Capacity building**
   - Human resource development
   - Policy analysis and monitoring
   - Management of recurrent costs
   - Management of public investment
   - Pay reform
4. **Managerial efficiency**
   - Decentralized management
   - Executive agencies
   - Quasi-markets
   - Corporate boards of directors
   - Performance contracts
   - Contracting out

or ideal form of government—and that even if this has not yet been achieved, there is some global process of convergence as all countries move from Old Public Administration (OPA) to New Public Management (NPM).

Many of the poorest countries have yet to achieve the OPA stage. They lack a professional civil service and rely more on patronage and informal systems. In these circumstances, trying to transform the existing arrangement into an NPM system may create little more than an empty managerial shell.

These reforms also assume that there is a right size for the state: small. It is argued, for example, that state expenditure will always crowd out private investment. Certainly, over-expenditure and excessive borrowing can undermine price stability. But where there has been little industrial development, state expenditure can also build the infrastructure that will attract private investors.

Another argument is that state growth will require higher taxes, which will undermine incentives and discourage people from keeping their funds in the country. However, most of the poorer countries have very low rates of both corporate and income tax. All governments should try to keep their budgets balanced; but when the poorer countries are in trouble, it is more likely to be because of their weak position in global markets—as they are blown off course by collapsing commodity prices.

Reforms of the public sector cannot simply be managerial or technocratic exercises. They need to be firmly grounded in what citizens see as the mission of their state. The state's mission will inevitably vary according to local circumstances and the stage of development. At its heart, the mission is not managerial; it is social. People want to move toward societies that are more prosperous, equitable and harmonious. Having ambitious managerial targets may be a part of this—but only a small part. Indeed, focusing too rigidly on market reforms is likely to perpetuate the incidence of failed states, civil wars and developmental stagnation.

The basis for any reform must be broad political consensus. While public sector reforms may appear technical, they are always highly political and conflictual. Few governments in crisis-ridden developing countries had a popular mandate for the policies that the IMF and the World Bank required them to carry out. Most of these countries are also grappling with complex problems of democratization—trying to lay the ground rules for the way their societies are governed.

Even industrialized countries that have entrenched democracies and single-party governments have struggled with these changes. Many of the developing and transition economies have not only fragile democracies, but also fragile governments. In most cases, the leading parties in government do not have parliamentary majorities. Given the fractured nature of political systems, and the ambiguous or contentious mandates of governments, it is hardly surprising that there is only a weak commitment to reform.

The reform of public services can only succeed when it is an integral part of overall democratic reforms—each reinforcing the other. This means having parliamentary parties that pursue broad social interests, supplemented with a free press and an independent judiciary. The aim should be to deepen and defend the civil rights of citizens, who will then be in a much better position to demand the highest standards from their politicians and from all public servants.

Calling corporations to account

John McConnico, Associated Press AP

Protest on the 15th anniversary of the Union Carbide Bhopal disaster. New Delhi, India

The huge and growing social impact of transnational corporations requires that they take corresponding responsibility. While they would prefer to comply through voluntary initiatives, the public interest can only be fully served through stronger regulation and monitoring.

Until recently, transnational corporations (TNCs) seemed to be little concerned with social development. Governments, NGOs and international development agencies took the prime responsibility for social issues, while TNCs operated mainly in the economic arena. Corporations always had a social impact of course, at best generating employment, income and community services, at worst disregarding labour standards and the communities in which they operated. But they were rarely called on to have explicit social policies.

Much of that has changed. Today, TNCs find themselves embroiled in many of the most vexed social issues, from global warming to child labour to genetically modified foods. Indeed, almost every international development issue is assumed now to have a corporate dimension.

To some extent, this is a consequence of corporate success. TNCs straddle the globe as never before. Some 60,000 corporations now account for one third of world exports. Their annual turnovers dwarf the gross domestic products of many countries. In 1998 the top five corporations had annual revenues that were more than double the total GDP of the 100 poorest countries (table 5.1). In recent years the number of TNC affiliates has more than doubled, from around 200,000 in 1994 to over half a million in 1998. Over the same period, the sales of foreign affiliates increased from $6.6 trillion to $11.4 trillion. But the global reach of TNCs is extending not only through direct control of affiliates, but increasingly through joint ventures, strategic alliances, sub-contracting and outsourcing. By the time of the Social Summit, it was clear that globalization and economic liberalization had granted corporations far greater freedom—without any commensurate increase in responsibility.

Another reason why companies have found themselves in the spotlight is the rise of environmental awareness and related NGOs. In the 1960s, environmentalism was a fringe pressure-group phenomenon, but by the end of the 1990s these ideas had pervaded the economic and political mainstream—making consumers more sensitive to problems such as deforestation, pesticides and pollution. They were also making people more aware of the ways in which their patterns of consumption were degrading and exhausting the planet.

Consumers are scattered and largely anonymous, but producers are easier to identify; and the largest corporations offer an obvious outlet for frustration. Their profile has been further raised by incessant flows of information. Floods of data, analysis and comment wash around most international companies and organizations. These information flows have peaked around a series of shocking incidents—including Union Carbide's gas leak at Bhopal; the Exxon Valdez oil spill in Alaska; and Shell's links with human rights abuses in Nigeria.

Today, corporations find it much more difficult to argue that their sole purpose is the pursuit of profit on behalf of shareholders, restrained only by the law of the land. They have to respond more broadly to many other stakeholders—employees, customers, suppliers, host communities, the general public—and to future generations. As "corporate citizens", they are being asked to assume responsibility for their actions.

Some corporations argue that this is nothing new. In the United States, during the early decades of the 1900s, companies such as Ford and Carnegie took measures to improve their workers' living conditions and contribute to the communities in which they operated. In the United Kingdom, companies such as Lever Brothers and Cadbury built model housing estates for their workers. The largest corporations also established huge and respected philanthropic organizations—the Ford Foundation, for example, or the Wellcome Trust.

But most companies, most of the time, concentrated on their primary purpose of making profits. They regarded the social context as incidental—the arena of governments, which were expected to provide the regulations to constrain corporate excess. In the industrialized countries, governments were well placed to do this. They had the resources, skills and sufficient autonomy to develop and enforce standards. But governments in developing countries were in a much weaker position: many were barely able to provide minimum services, let alone control powerful corporations.

Table 5.1 – Corporate power

Corporate revenues and gross domestic product, selected companies and countries[a]

Rank	Company	Revenue $ billions 1998	Country[b] (Approximate GDP equivalent)
1	General Motors (US)	161.3	Denmark/Thailand
10	Toyota (Japan)	99.7	Portugal/Malaysia
20	Nissho Iwai (Japan)	67.7	New Zealand
30	AT&T (US)	53.5	Czech Republic
40	Mobil (US)	47.6	Algeria
50	Sears Roebuck (US)	41.3	Bangladesh
60	NEC (Japan)	37.2	United Arab Emirates
70	Suez Lyonnaise des Eaux (France)	34.8	Romania
80	HypoVereinsbank (Germany)	31.8	Morocco
90	Tomen (Japan)	30.9	Kuwait
100	Motorola (US)	29.4	Kuwait
150	Walt Disney (US)	22.9	Belarus
200	Japan Postal Service (Japan)	18.8	Tunisia
250	Albertson's (US)	16.0	Sri Lanka
300	Taisei (Japan)	13.8	Lebanon
350	Goodyear Tire & Rubber (US)	12.6	Oman
400	Fuji Photo Film (Japan)	11.2	El Salvador
450	CSX (US)	9.9	Bulgaria
500	Northrop Grumman (US)	8.9	Zimbabwe
Top Five Corporations (revenue)		708.9[c]	
100 Poorest Countries (GDP)		337.8	

Notes: [a] A more accurate comparison of countries and companies would be based on value added as opposed to corporate revenue data, but not many companies include value added information in their annual reports. [b] Based on 1997 data. [c] General Motors, DaimlerChrysler, Ford Motors, Wal-Mart Stores and Mitsui.

Source: Utting, 2000 based on *Fortune*, 1999 and World Bank, 1999b

During the 1970s, pressure built up from governments, trade unions, academics and some NGOs. Techniques were developed to take on the multinationals. In 1974, for example, a powerful campaign against the harmful marketing of baby formula in developing countries was launched. But it was the environmental groups, such as Greenpeace, appealing to everyone's self-interest, who were to become the heavy hitters—confronting corporations with charges of deforestation, pollution and global warming, and mounting campaigns of "direct action".

From confrontation to partnership

These pressures came to a head in 1992 in Rio de Janeiro at the Earth Summit—an event that focused public and corporate minds as never before. The Summit's programme of action, *Agenda 21*, called on the world's governments, business leaders, international organizations and NGOs to work together to minimize the trade-off between economic growth and environmental protection. The Earth Summit also signified a change of philosophy and tactics—a shift from confrontation to co-operation. The UN in particular took a more conciliatory tone, closing its Centre on Transnational Corporations, which had been trying to design an international code of conduct. The UN turned instead to encouraging partnerships with business, and agencies like UNCTAD promoted developing countries' access to foreign direct investment.

TNCs also experimented with a different line: rather than waiting to be reined in by government regulations, they vowed to become more proactive—engaging in corporate self-regulation and working with their critics. In 1991 the International Chamber of Commerce presented a Business Charter for Sustainable Development, and in 1992 the founder of the Business Council for Sustainable Development published *Changing Course*, which called on corporations to rethink their strategies. In the years that followed, a number of companies also came together in "green" business networks, some of which subsequently merged: one of the largest is the World Business Council for Sustainable Development, formed in 1995.

At the same time, TNCs have been forming various kinds of partnerships with NGOs. In 1996 Unilever, which is the world's largest buyer of frozen fish, entered into a partnership with WWF-International to promote sustainable fishing. Similarly, in 1998 British Petroleum allied itself with the Environmental Defense Fund, and General Motors started to work with the World Resources Institute. By the end of 1998, 17 Fortune 500 companies were working through the Pew Center on Global Climate Change, set up that same year to promote awareness of climate change and reductions in emissions of greenhouse gases.

Many corporations have also expanded their links with UN agencies. In 1999, some 15 TNCs participated in the preliminary phase of a UNDP project to establish a Global Sustainable Development Facility. In the same year, the International Chamber of Commerce endorsed a call by the UN Secretary-General for a compact through which corporations would voluntarily comply with UN standards on environmental protection, labour conditions and human rights.

Codes and verification

These exercises in greater corporate responsibility take different forms, but they have a number of common features. Many are based on codes of conduct—sets of ethical principles and standards that guide a firm's social performance. Thus in 1997 the World Federation of the Sporting Goods Industry and the International Council of Toy Industries adopted codes relating to working conditions, and in particular the use of child labour.

At the same time, corporations are being

asked to adhere to more universal standards. The best-established are the ILO conventions, which cover a wide range of labour issues. But a number of other organizations have been working to create universal standards in new areas. Prominent among these is the International Organization for Standardization, whose members are national standards bodies. This organization produces a series of standards prefixed by ISO. The ISO 14000 series deals with environmental issues (box 5.1). The Forest Stewardship Council issues more specific standards on forestry.

National and regional bodies have also produced standards. In the United States, the Council on Economic Priorities Accreditation Agency, an interest group based in New York, has produced Social Accountability 8000, which is based on UN and ILO standards on human rights and labour conditions. The European Union also has an Eco-Management and Audit Scheme, whose standards are more rigorous than those of the ISO. Various industrialized and developing countries have eco-labelling schemes, such as the Blue Angel scheme in Germany and the Thai Green Labelling Scheme.

All these codes and standards need to be backed up with systems of verification. While a company's own inspectors should, in theory, be capable of doing this, they may not have much credibility outside their own offices. Some companies have therefore been hiring firms of independent auditors. This has offered a profitable new line of business for many international accounting and consulting firms, like Ernst & Young, KPMG and PricewaterhouseCoopers.

Such audits may achieve even greater credibility if they are backed up by independent NGOs. The toy company Mattel, in addition to setting up an independent monitoring committee for its factories, also invites local activists to interview workers.

This kind of auditing can result in official documentation that can be extremely beneficial for a company's reputation and competitiveness. Those adhering to ISO standards, for example, can apply for certification, which is becoming increasingly important for trading internationally. And a number of auditing systems offer labels that can be attached to qualifying goods. One of the earliest of these, which originated in Germany, is the Rugmark, which certifies that carpets have not been produced by children. Garment makers have also become regular users of labels. And following the discovery of Pakistani children stitching soccer balls, many of the balls sold in the United States now carry a label: "No child or slave labor used on this ball".

These forms of voluntary regulation can bring many benefits, but they can also have damaging side effects, particularly in the developing world. Companies in richer countries may exploit certification as a disguised form of protection. Western companies get little sympathy if they claim that foreign competition is draining away their profits. But they are more likely to be heard if they argue that the competing goods are inherently flawed—of doubtful quality or produced under dubious conditions. Certification will also tend to favour the larger enterprises, which can afford it, over the smaller ones for which the processes and requirements may appear too complex. And eliminating one problem can sometimes result in something worse. Thus banning child labour sounds inherently virtuous; but unless child workers have a genuine alternative to that work, they may simply be displaced into even more dangerous circumstances.

Corporate motivation

Why have companies started to take ethical considerations on board? The most optimistic view is simply that they have seen the light and chosen to behave more responsibly. Some individuals in corporate hierarchies certainly take these issues seriously. And in some cases the corporation as a whole may adopt a more moral stance. Well-known examples are The Body Shop and Ben & Jerry's Ice Cream, which openly profess their ethical standards.

A more utilitarian explanation is that corporations have learned that ethical forms of operation also enhance efficiency, profitability and a company's competitive edge—a "win-win" strategy. Treating workers well is indeed likely to make them better and more efficient. And striving to produce goods in a more eco-efficient fashion could lead to savings and new opportunities, and thus add to productivity. Those professing ethical standards may also make this a selling point that allows them to capitalize on growing ethical or green markets. Some corporations thus claim to be pursuing a "triple bottom line"—profitability combined with environmental and social goals, the three legs of a tripod, each of which adds stability.

Unfortunately, the win-win arguments are often inflated. Many companies are unconvinced. Globalization is creating such a harsh competitive environment that they feel under more pressure to lower costs. Some go out of their way to seek locations where labour and environmental regulations are weak; others simply find reforming management systems too costly.

There is, indeed, an ethical goods market. In Europe the retail sale of fair-trade goods was worth a quarter of a billion dollars by 1995. But

Box 5.1 – Questioning corporate lingo

Corporate responsibility is generating as many new terms as it is questions about its effectiveness.

- ***Certification***—An evaluation system designed to provide proof of a company's environmental or social performance. But who sets the standards and who does the certifying?
- ***Code of conduct***—A set of ethical principles and standards designed to guide a company's performance. But does the code progress far beyond a piece of paper? Is it even shown to the company's workers, let alone enacted?
- ***Corporate social responsibility***—The requirement that a company behave ethically toward the whole society—not just to shareholders, but to all stakeholders who have a legitimate interest in the company's activities. But does the assertion of responsibility have any impact in the real world? Does it merely involve statements of intent, or does it imply real changes in behaviour?
- ***Eco-efficiency***—A process of adding even more value while steadily decreasing resource use, waste and efficiency. But does this involve technical fixes to clean up after the fact, while encouraging even greater production and consumption?
- ***ISO***—The International Organization for Standardization is made up of national standards-setting bodies that may be governmental, private or hybrid organizations. ISO standards can be used by third parties as a basis for issuing certificates. But who is setting these standards, and are they being over-influenced by business and Northern interests?
- ***ISO 14000***—A series of standards that establish rules for environmental management. But do companies complying with these standards do more than put in place an environmental management system? Do they actually reduce the impact of their activities on the

this remains a niche market. Research in Canada indicates that while 30 per cent of shoppers say they are willing to pay extra to ensure justice for producers, only 5 per cent actually do so.

A more realistic analysis would suggest that at the heart of most corporate ethical moves is "reputation management"—defending profits and market share by massaging a company's image. Consumers may not be willing to pay more for ethically traded goods, but they are at least starting to demand an ethical component to the goods they normally purchase; and unless corporations satisfy this demand, or at least appear to, they will risk losses of sales or even consumer boycotts. In 1997, Nike was accused of paying low wages and maintaining dangerous working conditions in its Asian factories, and was faced with a consumer boycott. While denying the charges, the company moved swiftly to protect its public image, joining with other companies to draw up a code of conduct and severing relations with a number of contractors.

But all companies with a high public profile are vulnerable. Although a Japanese lumber company cutting down forests in Myanmar, in league with the dictatorial regime, may not be too worried about its public image, companies with consumer brands to protect are more exposed. Companies such as Levi Strauss, Macy's, Eddie Bauer and PepsiCo withdrew from Myanmar after being criticized for doing business there. And Texaco and Amoco did so as well.

environment? And should companies that produce environmentally dangerous products be able to obtain ISO certification?

- ***Stakeholder***—Any group or individual who can affect, or is affected by, the achievement of an organization's objectives. The stakeholders of corporations include not only employees and stockholders, but also neighbours, public interest groups, customers, suppliers and the general public. While corporations may claim to be accountable to everyone, do some stakeholders hold a much more powerful stake than others?
- ***Triple bottom line***—The notion that companies should have not just one bottom line, which registers a profit or loss, but two others: one related to environmental protection; the other to meeting social needs. But are these three goals in any way equal, or are companies really just conducting business as usual by concentrating on financial aspects while paying lip-service to the others?
- ***Voluntary initiatives***—A wide range of measures that are seen as an alternative to the command and control regulations set by governments. They go beyond following the letter of the law to include concerns for environmental and social protection. These initiatives can originate in industry, governments or NGOs, or a combination of two or more. But do these initiatives really imply serious changes to company behaviour? Are they a substitute for tighter legislation?
- ***Win-win strategy***—A corporate strategy that enables a company simultaneously to improve its environmental and social record while reducing costs, and increasing competitiveness and profitability. But is such a strategy really available? Does greater social responsibility not inevitably cost money?

Those who do worry about timber extraction methods are more likely to be retailers. Thus campaigns against logging for years had little impact on companies or governments. But when European activists targeted retailers of furniture and timber products, they had much more success. Now chains like B&Q in the United Kingdom make a point of displaying their environmental credentials.

Piecemeal progress

Perhaps it does not matter why corporations are behaving more ethically, providing that they are actually doing so. At present, however, it is very difficult to judge how far their behaviour has changed. The evidence tends to be anecdotal, piecemeal and often contradictory.

The vast amount of writing and publicity surrounding corporate social responsibility and best practices would suggest that big business has turned over a new leaf. But many companies continue to behave perversely. Through mergers and acquisitions, downsizing, outsourcing, and the "feminization" or "flexibilization" of employment, many corporations are laying off workers, weakening unions and shifting to sites and systems with lower social and environmental standards.

Only a small proportion of companies have introduced codes of conduct. And these tend to be narrow in scope. Typically they highlight issues to which consumers are particularly sensitive, such as environmental protection and child labour, but avoid other issues, such as freedom of association or the right to strike. One study of the codes of Canadian corporations operating abroad, for example, found that the majority made no reference to the most basic human rights.

Even when they produce promising codes, industry associations or corporations may not take the matter much further. In 1996, UNCTAD reviewed the guidelines set by 26 industry associations for their member firms and found that most did not ask the signatories to commit themselves to any of the recommended principles or activities, and only a handful required any kind of compliance. Many companies that are aware of such codes seemed reluctant to share the detailed information with their employees or consumers.

This reluctance also extends to adherence to other internationally agreed standards, such as the ISO 14000 system on environmental management. By the end of 1998, only 7,887 certificates had been issued worldwide. By way of comparison, the ISO 9000 series, which is concerned with quality management systems, generates around 50,000 certificates in one year alone. The limited commitment to environmental standards is also evident in those concerned with forestry. By early 1999, only 15 million hectares of forests had been certified by bodies accredited by the Forest Stewardship Council—less than 1 per cent of the world's forests outside protected areas.

Inflated claims

For many corporations, one of the main purposes of a more ethical stance is to create a friendlier public profile. But inevitably, in an era dominated by advertising and public relations, rhetoric tends to spin well beyond reality. Many companies publish reports that declare their ethical credentials. But few offer much hard information. A 1994 study by UNEP of 100 "pioneering" companies found that only 5 per cent of their reports contained meaningful performance data.

Even when companies are being monitored and certificates are being issued, it may not be clear what is being measured. Some forms of environmental certification relate more to policies and management procedures than to their effects. They may certify that the company has an environmental policy but say nothing about its actual impact—the extent to which a company has reduced its emissions, say, or its use of energy.

In some cases, companies have gone out of their way to make more specific claims that look weaker on closer inspection. After the Bhopal disaster in 1984, the international pesticide industry, for example, made efforts to establish ethical credentials through its Responsible Care programme and Safe Use projects in several developing countries. The International Union of Food and Agricultural Workers investigated the impact of one such project in Guatemala. It found that although one third of a million people had indeed been trained in pesticide use, the training itself was limited and did not extend to agricultural workers, who are the main users. The companies targeted primarily the farm owners who bought their products, and paid little or no attention to alternatives to pesticides, such as integrated pest management—which could suggest that the project was also a marketing exercise.

Company claims that they are taking great strides to improve working conditions and wages also need to be examined closely. Nike and Reebok claimed that in 1998–99 they had raised the wages of their sports-shoe workers in Indonesia by 40 per cent. According to the NGO Clean Clothes Campaign, however, the companies had failed to note that an inflation rate of 70 per cent offset any gain.

The problem of inflated claims also affects other aspects of corporate responsibility. A seemingly positive development of recent years involves the rapid growth of ethical investing. Social investment funds now manage over $1 trillion, roughly one half of which is in socially screened portfolios. But a recent analysis by Credit Suisse and the journal *Tomorrow* shows that the most popular stocks targeted by ethical or green mutual funds are not the pioneers of sustainable business but the big technology companies like Cisco Systems, Intel and Microsoft, stocks favoured by the traditional investing world.

Perhaps the most inflated claim of all is that companies are contributing to sustainable development. Initiatives that are couched in the language of sustainable development usually only involve measures for environmental protection. Even the World Business Council for Sustainable Development has, until very recently, tended to concentrate its energies on promoting eco-efficiency. Of particular concern are the all-too-common cases of companies that have double standards—cultivating their public image through, say, an environmental initiative while disregarding human rights (box 5.2).

A strategy to promote sustainable development presumably implies a multi-faceted agenda that embraces progress in a number of different directions, including the following.

- ***Environmental protection***—in the interests of all the earth's inhabitants and of future generations.
- ***Employee empowerment***—with full labour rights and participation.
- ***Economic performance***—sustained profitability, employment and fair wages.
- ***Ethics***—with codes of conduct, transparency and stakeholder accountability.
- ***Equity***—fair trade, and fair treatment of stakeholders.
- ***Education***—dissemination of information and participation in campaigns.

Companies that espouse sustainable development seldom address these issues comprehensively. Indeed, the most basic criticism of these corporate measures is that the changes are taking place at the margins, leaving the fundamental problems undisturbed.

Few corporate environmental initiatives involve a major change of policy. Energy companies could, for example, be paying much more attention to solar power. BP Amoco did

Box 5.2 – Jekyll, Inc. and Hyde Ltd.

Corporate behaviour is often confusing. Companies may behave responsibly in some parts of their business, while lapsing in others.

- ***Aracruz Celulose***—This Brazilian producer of bleached eucalyptus wood pulp supplies 20 per cent of the world market. The company is frequently praised for its efforts to promote sustainable development through its tree-planting, harvesting and pulp-production methods. But it has also been accused of displacing people and food production, and destroying local fauna.

- ***Asea Brown Boveri***—The Swiss-Swedish engineering company sponsors the Global Sustainable Development Facility and is a world leader in developing eco-efficient technologies. It has been criticized by environmentalists and human rights campaigners for its involvement in controversial hydro-electric projects, including the Three Gorges project in China and the Bakun Dam in Malaysia.

- ***Chiquita Brands***—The US banana corporation has attempted to improve its environmental reputation by complying with standards that allow it to use the Eco-OK label. Trade unions claim that the company not only continues to pursue environmentally damaging practices, but also restricts such basic human rights as freedom of association of workers.

- ***Dow Chemical***—According to UNDP, Dow abides by "the highest standards of human rights, environmental and labour standards and norms". According to the Transnational Resources and Action Centre, an NGO, Dow is probably the world's largest source of the toxic chemical dioxin and has regularly exported pesticides unregistered in the US for use in developing countries.

- ***General Motors***—The US company is the world's largest TNC. General Motors is involved in a number of environmental initiatives, and in 1998 entered into a partnership with the World Resources Institute to define a long-term vision for protecting the earth's climate. At the same time, it supports the Global Climate Coalition and the Business Roundtable, organizations that oppose the Kyoto Protocol designed to reduce greenhouse gases.

- ***Mitsubishi Group***—The Japanese conglomerate has a number of environmental projects and cultivates an image of responsibility. However, it has also been identified as a leading destroyer of tropical forests and was, until recently, under fire for plans to build a huge salt plant in an environmentally sensitive area of Mexico. The Mexican government cancelled this project in early 2000.

- ***Novartis***—The Swiss life-science corporation is frequently praised for its social awareness and philanthropy. But its active promotion of genetically modified crops seems to contradict the precautionary principle established at the Earth Summit.

indeed expand its interests in solar energy in 1999, with the purchase of Solartex for $45 million. But this fades into insignificance when compared with the rest of the company's activities and acquisitions. Greenpeace has estimated that for every $10,000 BP Amoco spent on oil exploration and development in 1998, it spent only $16 on solar energy. And when companies like Shell initiate multi-stakeholder dialogues to discuss their latest proposals for oil extraction, the issue is generally how the project should be implemented rather than whether it should go ahead at all.

Many critics argue, therefore, that there is little of significance happening—that the TNCs are using publicity to paint over an unsavoury reality—not with whitewash but with greenwash.

Alternatives to confrontation

The most powerful influences on corporate behaviour are external—government regulations, consumer pressure and civil society activism. But the corporations argue that the best way ahead is less confrontational. Rather than having stronger regulations to contend with, they prefer to engage in corporate self-regulation or voluntary initiatives. And instead of waiting for NGOs and others to criticize them, they want to enter into partnerships.

Voluntary initiatives

Corporations are not the only ones who would prefer light regulation. The general ideological and political drift in the 1980s and 1990s has been to reduce state intervention and leave corporations free to create as much wealth as they can. Developing country governments are generally competing to attract foreign direct investment—and regulations on TNCs might impede those efforts.

The United Nations has also been moving in this direction. Not only did it close its Centre on Transnational Corporations, it also abandoned efforts to draft various codes of conduct. In fact, of some 30 codes proposed in previous decades, only a few were ever adopted.

David Guttenfelder, Associated Press AP

Cleaning up the Niger Delta? Oil pipes running through a neighbourhood near Port Harcourt, Nigeria

These included codes relating to the marketing of breastmilk substitutes, pesticide use and medical drug promotion.

The UN also seems to be moving toward the view that the World Trade Organization should not be overly concerned with social and environmental issues. When the Secretary-General met representatives of big business gathered at the World Economic Forum in Davos in 1999, he implied that the UN would support the idea of a trade and investment regime largely free of social and environmental clauses. In return, he called on the business community to take voluntary initiatives to uphold human rights, and labour and environmental standards (box 5.3).

Such initiatives would be welcome. But their effectiveness should not be overestimated. Codes of conduct tend to be stronger on rhetoric than delivery. Even when they are put into practice, they can degenerate into closed systems, opaque to external inspection or participation. And there will always be the temptation to greenwash.

Codes also tend to have less impact in developing countries. In industrialized countries, they can be reinforced by sophisticated and well-organized consumer surveillance, as well as by independent verification, but the chances of effective consumer and civil society pressure in the poorest countries are slim. More plausible at present is that consumer activists

Box 5.3 – The UN-business Global Compact

"There is enormous pressure from various interest groups to load the trade regime and investment agreements with restrictions aimed at reaching adequate standards in human rights, labour and environment. These are legitimate concerns. But restrictions on trade and impediments to investment flows are not the best means to use when tackling them. Instead, we should find a way to achieve our proclaimed standards by other means. And this is precisely what the compact I am proposing to you is meant to do. Essentially there are two ways we can do this. One is through the international policy arena. You can encourage States to give us, the multilateral institutions of which they are all members, the resources and the authority we need to do our job....The second way you can promote these values is by tackling them directly, by taking action in your own corporate sphere....You can uphold human rights and decent labour and environmental standards directly, by your own conduct of your business....But what, you may be asking yourselves, am I offering in exchange? The United Nations agencies...all stand ready to assist you, if you need help, in incorporating these agreed values and principles into your mission statements and corporate practices. And we are ready to facilitate a dialogue between you and other social groups, to help find viable solutions to the genuine concerns that they have raised....More important, perhaps, is what we can do in the political arena, to help make the case for and maintain an environment which favours trade and open markets."

Kofi Annan
World Economic Forum, Davos
31 January 1999

in the rich countries will have an effect on corporate behaviour in poorer ones by pressuring TNC headquarters to impose stricter standards on their affiliates and suppliers in developing countries. To minimize the risk of consumer boycotts or tarnished reputations, some TNC headquarters are now adopting a more hands-on approach throughout the supply chain. What this can mean, however, is that the poor countries are following an agenda set by Northern consumer groups or NGOs, who are well intentioned but often fail to work in tandem with Southern NGOs. It may also mean that smaller companies in developing countries, which lack the managerial and financial resources needed to comply with stricter standards, are being replaced by larger companies in the networks controlled by TNCs and the big Northern retailers.

Partnerships

In an age of liberalization, governments have ceded many of their functions to the private sector and civil society. Similarly, in the field of corporate responsibility there have been efforts to move away from regulation and confrontation and instead to build new partnerships between governments, the private sector and civil society.

This has a pragmatic appeal, and not just to the corporations. Even the most determined activist can eventually grow weary of issuing condemnations from outside corporate fortresses. Better, perhaps, to engage directly and have some influence over day-to-day activities.

Partnerships create new opportunities, but also new risks. One of the most familiar is that of co-optation, as activists find they have been absorbed into the corporate machine. Many NGOs have now become consultants, selling technical advice and other services. As one activist put it: "Having had to work so closely with chief executive officers of corporations, I am beginning to sound like one. At some point a new generation of NGOs is going to have to come along to check on people like me".

International organizations face similar problems when they try to work with corporations. They may, for example, find themselves involved with an unsuitable partner. Some UN agencies seem to have lax criteria and guidelines for selecting partners, and can quickly find themselves the target of NGO criticism for having teamed up with companies associated with environmental and human rights abuses. UNDP has been criticized for its choice of partners for the Global Sustainable Development Facility. UNHCR has also come under fire for some of its relationships within the recently established Business Humanitarian Forum (box 5.4).

In addition to the risks that may arise from new alliances, there is also the danger that corporations will gain excessive influence over existing regulatory bodies—achieving "institutional capture". This is a familiar problem for many governments, which often find that most of the experts in a particular field, even the academics, have corporate links of one kind or another. At the international level, there is concern that some standard-setting bodies are unduly influenced by big business—for example, the International Organization for Standardization, the WTO and the Codex Alimentarius Commission (a joint FAO/WHO body on food safety and quality standards).

Some of these new partnerships will also be at the expense of old ones. There have always been splits in NGOs and pressure groups between the radicals and the reformers. Now they have another opportunity to diverge. Some will choose to work with corporations; others will reject any kind of link.

Another danger of NGO-business partnerships is that of marginalizing trade unions. Not so long ago, trade unions were the main force motivating improvements in working conditions. But trade unions in the industrialized countries have suffered a steep drop in membership and influence, and in the developing countries TNCs often manage to shut them out completely. Developing closer relations between NGOs and business may appear constructive and conciliatory; but if this also serves to marginalize trade unions, it will be removing one of the main engines of social progress.

From hard to soft

With the arrival of newer and "softer" approaches, the corporate responsibility scene nowadays is more complex and ambiguous. But it would be a mistake to replace the hard with the soft. The world needs both. Most corporations will ultimately only respond to tight regulation and enforcement, and close monitoring by NGOs, trade unions and consumer groups. Yet there is a danger that corporate self-regulation, as well as various partnership arrangements, are weakening the role of national governments, trade unions and stronger forms of civil society activism.

There is also a danger that the debate about how and by whom corporations should be regulated is diverting attention from another key mechanism through which corporations have historically contributed to social development: taxation. Corporate social responsibility should not just be about standard-setting and compliance. It should also be about companies paying—rather than avoiding—taxes to welfare-minded states. As indicated in chapter 2, much of the rapidly escalating wealth of corporations is not being tapped by the state for social purposes.

In some cases effective controls on corporate activities can be achieved through various

Box 5.4 – The watchdog on the Web

The online magazine *Corporate Watch* has aired NGO concerns about some UN-business partnerships.

"...We write today to express our disappointment at seeing the name of UNHCR associated with that of Unocal Corporation...and with Nestlé as members of the Business Humanitarian Forum....The arrangement with the BHF allows Unocal, a company that is currently involved with one of the worst human rights situations in the world, to enjoy the benefits of associating itself with the UN without actually taking steps to protect human rights. The arrangement affords Nestlé, a company still targeted by consumer boycotts in 18 countries because of its violations of WHO's International Code of Marketing of Breastmilk Substitutes, the benefits of associating with WHO's sister agencies....Unocal is a partner, with French-based Total and the Myanmar Oil and Gas Enterprise, in the construction of the Yadana gas pipeline in Burma. EarthRights and other organizations have documented horrendous human rights abuses associated with the construction and maintenance of the pipeline."

Excerpt of a letter signed by Instituto del Tercer Mundo, Institute for Policy Studies, Third World Network, Earth Rights International, Transnational Resource and Action Center, Brazilian Institute of Economic and Social Analysis, and International Baby Food Action Network.

forms of co-regulation. Governments and businesses, for example, can work together through negotiated agreements to design and implement programmes that both sides consider useful—but that retain an element of state sanction. Another possibility is civil regulation, through which businesses comply not only with legislation but also with standards set and monitored by civil society.

Effective and relevant standards not only need to be devised, they also require updating and improvement. Thus environmental regulations will need to move beyond "end-of-pipe" monitoring, which tries to cope with pollution, to measures that avoid generating pollutants in the first place. And future regulations will also need a stronger information component—requiring companies to publish data in a standard form so that performance can be accurately monitored.

Independent verification will be an increasingly important issue (box 5.5). The existence of new groups to check on corporate activity widens the scope of verification, but may also cause some confusion. The fact that the NGO or accounting firm involved may be formally independent may not be a guarantee of capacity for rigorous critical appraisal. In addition, the lack of hard data and clearly defined indicators to measure corporate performance may compromise the monitoring process.

The proliferation of codes of conduct and reporting systems has created a rather chaotic environment that calls for much greater harmonization. Corporate environmental and social standards need to be measured against internationally defined benchmarks—such as those in *Agenda 21*, and in ILO and human rights conventions.

When codes are well defined, whether binding or not, they can also be an important tool for global citizens' action. The 1981 Breastmilk Substitutes Code, for example, targeting companies like Nestlé, helped to raise and maintain public awareness, and build public pressure on companies to change the marketing practices that threatened people's health and lives in developing countries.

Box 5.5 – What makes a good voluntary initiative

The NGO Taskforce on Business and Industry (ToBI) highlights the essential components of a productive voluntary initiative. It should:

- ***Be substantive***—It must solve problems not avoid them. And its ideas and language should be unambiguous and undiluted.
- ***Offer incentives***—It must have ways of encouraging companies to adopt and accept the measures.
- ***Be fully incorporated***—Social and environmental values need to be completely integrated into all policies and operations.
- ***Be independently verified***—To gain credibility among all stakeholders, performance needs to be monitored independently.
- ***Invite participation***—All stakeholders should be drawn in, especially those directly affected by a company's operations.
- ***Be transparent***—Companies need to provide adequate and timely information.
- ***Offer full accountability***—If necessary, it should be backed up by effective regulations.

This is an area in which the United Nations could play a more constructive role. International governance in this field has been relatively weak since the 1980s, but is showing some signs of revival. The Commission on Sustainable Development, for example, is currently supporting a review of voluntary initiatives aimed at defining a coherent set of guidelines. In August 1999, the Sub-Commission on the Promotion and Protection of Human Rights—an independent panel of experts linked to the UN Commission on Human Rights—agreed to a three-year inquiry into the activities of transnational corporations, and to consider the establishment of a code of conduct based on human rights standards. UNDP's 1999 *Human Development Report* calls for a multilateral code of conduct, arguing that TNCs are "too important for their conduct to be left to voluntary and self-generated standards".

Outside the UN system, in January 2000 the OECD published a revised set of draft guidelines on TNCs that proposes some new standards on corporate governance, workplace conditions and environmental safeguards. Although not legally binding, these guidelines, once approved, would be expected to apply to the activities of TNCs based in the OECD and in Brazil, Argentina and Chile. Some NGOs and private foundations are also taking a lead with initiatives such as SA 8000, mentioned earlier, and with international standards for ethical trading (the Ethical Trading Initiative) and sustainability reporting (the Global Reporting Initiative).

If international organizations, whether UN agencies, the ISO or the World Bank, are to play a greater part, they can only do so legitimately if they operate in a transparent fashion, opening their doors or decision-making processes to participation from civil society, and particularly to representatives from developing countries.

This also requires that the organizations of civil society be prepared to behave in a more cohesive and co-operative fashion. For example, tensions have arisen between environmentalists and trade unions. Many trade unions need to pay more attention to the environmental agenda. And some environmental NGOs pay little attention to labour standards. If these NGOs focused more on social issues, they might get more support from trade unions for, say, forest certification schemes. Furthermore, where democratic trade union structures exist, NGOs should attempt to co-operate with, rather than substitute for, unions on issues relating to workers rights.

Left to their own devices, TNCs are likely to fulfil their responsibilities in a minimalist and fragmented fashion. Their strategies may be conducive to economic growth and the stability of their operating environment, but not necessarily to sustainable human development. They still need strong and effective regulation and a coherent response from civil society.

Civil societies

M. Cassetta, Associated Press AP

Human rights activists. Rome, Italy

People are banding together to influence state policy and have a stronger voice in the international arena. They are building new partnerships and employing new tactics for dealing with globalization and its risks. The results of their actions have been mixed.

The Social Summit, like many other international gatherings before and since, placed a lot of trust in civil society. This is a rather amorphous category covering myriad groups that belong neither to government nor to the profit-making private sector. A civil society organization (CSO) could therefore be anything from a community-based organization (CBO), like a village savings group, to an international trade union federation (box 6.1). Confusingly, civil society also includes non-governmental organizations (NGOs)—which sound as though they could be identical, but are actually a subset of CSOs. NGOs are understood to be the larger and more professionalized CSOs that aim to deliver benefits not to their own members but to the wider community.

As social and political conditions mutate over time, so do the components of civil society and the ways in which they link up and interact. Many would argue that today there is even an international civil society, reflecting the special concerns, habits and cultural norms of the people who come together at international gatherings or who take international collective action.

The industrialized countries have a long tradition of CSOs. The United States, for example, has an estimated two million. In Eastern Europe and the former Soviet Union, the situation has been very different. Their all-encompassing states left little room for such organizations. But with the transition to democracy, CSOs have proliferated: by 1995 there were thought to be around 100,000. Developing countries also have huge numbers of CSOs. Brazil, for example, has some 100,000 church-based CSOs; and India is thought to have over one million grassroots groups. But reliable numbers are hard to obtain: by various estimates, the Philippines has either 21,000 CSOs or 60,000. Then there is the category of international CSOs—defined in statistical terms as those that operate in three or more countries. Between 1990 and 1995 these are thought to have increased from 10,000 to 20,000.

Not all the organizations of civil society are truly civil. Some groups have decidedly antisocial aims. This chapter discusses those CSOs that are seeking to influence the path of social development positively through service delivery; through various forms of partnership; and through advocacy at the international level. These are three areas where CSOs have achieved a high profile in the 1990s.

Civil society and service delivery

Some CSOs, like trade unions, have a long history in the field of social policy. What is different today—particularly in developing countries—is the extent to which governments and aid agencies expect NGOs to provide social services, either independently or in collaboration with the state. The organizations most likely to be involved are non-governmental development organizations—NGDOs. While NGDOs tend to operate differently from governments, they form a very heterogeneous group—and have evolved in different ways depending on the local context.

- ***Latin America***—Many NGDOs emerged as a reaction to military regimes and were often linked to trade unions, peasant organizations, popular movements and the Catholic Church, which afforded them protection in an era of commitment to liberation theology. They were among the first to receive bilateral aid from

Box 6.1 – A glossary of civil society terms

- ***Civil society organizations (CSOs)***—These are groupings of individuals and associations, formal and informal, that belong neither to government nor to the profit-making private sector.
- ***Non-governmental organizations***—NGOs are often and mistakenly equated with civil society. In fact, they are only the most visible tip of the civil-society iceberg. They work in a broad spectrum of fields, from humanitarian aid, to human rights promotion, to environmental protection. NGOs may or may not be membership organizations.
- ***Non-governmental development organizations***—NGOs that specialize in channelling development funds are often called non-governmental development organizations (NGDOs). Some work at the international level channelling aid from North to South—such as Oxfam, Save the Children, World Vision, CARE, Caritas and Novib. Most Southern countries have their own NGDOs. These too can be extremely large and influential: some of the better-known include the Bangladesh Rural Advancement Committee (BRAC) and the Orangi Pilot Project in Pakistan. Unlike many Northern organizations, Southern NGDOs engage directly with other local-level civil society entities in carrying out development projects or in mobilizing the local population.
- ***Community-based organizations***—CBOs are the invisible mass of the CSO iceberg under the NGO tip. CBOs are typically membership organizations whose constituency—both activists and beneficiaries—resides within a recognizable geographic entity, such as a neighbourhood, a village or a district. CBOs may or may not be formally constituted or legally recognized. They include neighbourhood associations, tenants' associations, women's clubs, parent-teacher associations, burial societies, micro-credit circles and community kitchens. CBOs rely mainly on the voluntary contributions of labour and material resources of their members—though they may also receive funds from NGOs.
- ***Advocacy NGOs***—These do not usually have individual members. More often they are professionally staffed, or they second staff from like-minded entities wishing to expand their voice through a collective effort, as in a federation of labour unions or neighbourhood associations. Their constituents may be spread over neighbourhoods, urban or rural districts, regions or even across international boundaries. They provide services to their members, such as research and training, information gathering and dissemination, and advocacy. The most common forms of advocacy NGOs are chambers of commerce and federations of CBOs. At the international level, they include the International Council for Social Welfare, Amnesty International, and the World Business Council for Sustainable Development.
- ***Interest group associations***—These include associations of professionals, such as lawyers or doctors or architects. They also include producer and consumer co-operatives, and associations for business executives or retired persons. The CSOs in this category that have the most comprehensive mandate are the trade unions, whose primary function is to protect the interests of their members at the workplace. The most important distinction between trade unions and NGOs is that trade unions consist of dues-paying members who can hold the organization to account, while NGOs are usually answerable, formally, only to themselves.

those donors who opposed military governments. NGDOs thrived even more during the democratic era, as donors looked for ways of consolidating democracy and channelling aid through non-state agencies. Some also benefited from structural adjustment, since donors were keen to include them in the operation of social funds—intended to mitigate the social costs of structural adjustment programmes.

- ***Sub-Saharan Africa***—Here NGDOs arose in a very different context. They emerged in the 1960s and 1970s when governments, engaged in nation building, promoted self-help schemes such as the Kenyan Harambee. These were essentially community-based organizations that were heavily influenced by both government and the ruling party. NGDOs grew more rapidly in a few multi-party states like Senegal than in one-party states like Tanzania. Even so, not all were indigenous; many were connected with Northern NGOs, and particularly with the churches. The number of NGDOs increased markedly in the 1980s in response to economic crisis and the weakening of the state. They have continued to proliferate in recent years as a result of aid flows to Africa, political liberalization and retrenchments of civil servants who must look for alternative employment.
- ***Middle East***—The Middle East has a history of peasant organizations, co-operative movements and trade unions, often with links to the state or ruling party; but NGDOs were traditionally few in number. During the past two decades this situation has changed dramatically, with the rise of Islamist movements and urban-based NGDOs. Some Islamist movements have contributed directly to social welfare by providing services such as health care, education and financial aid. They have also contributed indirectly: other religious or secular organizations, including state institutions, feel obliged to compete for support by implementing social programmes in favour of the poor. In addition to many religious welfare associations, other types of NGOs have proliferated since the 1980s—in response to public sector restructuring, foreign funding and a broad political consensus on the important role they can play. They include NGDOs managed by middle-class professionals and those with strong links to the state, such as the Egyptian Community Development Associations or the Iranian Foundation of Dispossessed.
- ***Asia***—Here the situation is more diverse. On one hand, countries like India have a strong tradition of philanthropy and voluntary action. On the other, communist states like China and Viet Nam have little perception of civil society, let alone NGDOs. Different again are countries like Thailand and the Philippines, which are closer to the Latin American model—many NGDOs emerged in response to civilian or military dictatorships, so their leaders tend to be very politically aware. With democratization, many have shifted their focus from human rights to social and environmental concerns. The end of international isolation saw a sharp increase in NGDO activity in Cambodia in the 1990s. Bangladesh proved to be a special case. The circumstances of the country's birth in 1971 nurtured NGDO leaders determined to operate on a large scale to meet the needs of their new nation. Bangladesh now has the largest indigenous NGDOs in the South.
- ***Transition countries***—Here NGDOs remain something of an unknown quantity. Organizations that sound similar in function to NGDOs —such as national women's organizations—were in the past actually agencies of the state. Some countries, such as Hungary, have seen new organizations emerge, in certain cases recalling previous expressions of civic organization. But in most countries they are very underdeveloped. NGDOs are highly restricted in Kazakhstan, Kyrgyzstan and Turkmenistan; and in Russia some are even suspected of being mafia fronts.

While NGDOs have proliferated in many

countries, their influence on government policy has been limited. This is partly the result of their limited capacity. Organizations like Oxfam and World Vision in the Northern countries often have extensive research departments whose experience and skills equal—and sometimes surpass—those of government departments. But few NGDOs in developing countries can afford such investment. Many Southern NGDOs have gathered valuable expertise in specific areas—such as environment, gender, debt, micro-credit and landmines—but most are not involved in setting the broad framework and standards for social policy.

Where they do have a more consistent impact is through service delivery at the local level. A few decades ago, NGDOs in developing countries got most of their funds from NGDOs in Northern countries. Today, however, they are also likely to receive funds from their own governments, as well as from bilateral and multilateral aid agencies. Current estimates suggest that NGDOs disburse annually about $13 billion, of which official development assistance accounts for 50 per cent—up from less than 30 per cent a decade ago.

As discussed in chapter 4, this reflects the new public management philosophy—shrinking the state and passing more responsibility to the supposedly more efficient private sector, including NGDOs. This is now taking place on a significant scale. Half of the World Bank's projects now involve NGDOs at the implementation stage, and by the mid-1990s, NGDOs disbursed approximately 15 per cent of total public development aid.

Nevertheless, the balance between public and private provision varies greatly according to local circumstances. In Latin America and in India, the state is still the major service provider; NGDOs are junior partners. In many African countries, NGDOs have become important providers—sometimes co-ordinating with the state, sometimes not. Where there are complex political emergencies—as in Afghanistan, Somalia and southern Sudan—water supply and health care are often entirely in the hands of international NGDOs.

How good are NGDOs as service providers? A number of recent impact studies permit some general, and not entirely positive, conclusions.

- ***Reaching the poorest***—Most NGDO projects do reach the poor, though not necessarily the poorest. There is still little evidence, however, that NGDOs are intrinsically better at reaching the poor than state services.
- ***Poverty reduction***—NGDO projects in health, education and water supply alleviate poverty in the communities where they operate, but generally they do not significantly reduce it.
- ***Coverage***—The scale of operations is limited and the coverage patchy. Moreover, NGDOs are often not very good at co-ordinating with each other or with the state.
- ***Quality***—There is little evidence that NGDOs provide better-quality services than the state. What seems to matter more is which of the two has more money.
- ***Technical capacity***—NGDOs perform better in sectors and sub-sectors where they have built up expertise—as in delivering local-level services. They have considerable capacity for innovation, experimentation and flexible adaptation of projects to suit local needs and conditions. They are less successful at more complex interventions such as integrated rural development.
- ***Cost-effectiveness***—There is little evidence that NGDOs are inherently more cost-effective than the state. Small projects may be more efficient than larger ones, regardless of who is running them. One comparative study in India, for example, found that the costs of NGDO and state health services were broadly similar.
- ***Policy direction***—One of the major concerns about relying on NGDOs for service provision is that they cannot provide a broader frame-

work for action. Only a government can develop clear policy and regulation in fields like health and education.

What is needed is an effective combination of state and NGDO services. Ideally, governments should be in a position to establish the overall policy framework and provide most of the funding for services, while NGDOs can bring additional creativity and strong community links. In India, for example, the government gives grants to NGDOs to provide services for indigenous peoples. In Bolivia, the government has funded NGDOs to implement its community water supply programmes.

The changing character of NGDOs

The NGDO sector is significantly different from what it was 20 years ago. The number of organizations has mushroomed to take advantage of new funding. These organizations are often established and staffed by middle-class managers. Some may bring sorely needed professional skills. At the same time, some NGDO personnel are simply seeking employment or a stepping-stone to a higher position.

Increased professionalism is apparent in the way NGDOs are working together internationally, regionally and nationally in coalitions and networks. This has enhanced their collective strength to influence policy and mobilize resources. In Latin America, for example, some 50 leading NGDOs from 20 countries are members of the Latin American Association of Promotion Organizations (ALOP). This association facilitates exchange of information, formulates development strategies, promotes integrated projects and represents NGDOs in international fora. In Cambodia, the Cooperation Committee for Cambodia has served an important role in information exchange, co-ordination of NGDO activities and ensuring that the opinions of NGDOs are heard in some government and donor decision-making processes.

Today, a much smaller proportion of organizations would describe themselves primarily as advocates for the poor or oppressed. Many NGDOs have had to step aside from campaigning, simply to survive. International donors who in the past might have supported radical organizations as a way of covertly eroding the power of repressive states are now seeking more prosaic service providers. The resulting emphasis on contract-type funding tends to decrease NGDO appetite for advocacy and campaigning—as well as their capacity for innovation. The emergence of democratic governments has also siphoned off some of the more politicized NGDO personnel. In South Africa, for example, most of the leaders from the South African NGO Coalition (SANCO) moved into government service or the private sector when the ANC took power.

This should not be cause for too much dismay. Grassroots movements obviously need to adapt to democracy. With many major political and legal objectives satisfied, they switch to more material functions. At the same time, they transform themselves from movements into organizations—with all the corresponding financial pressures and the temptation to introduce hierarchies and be less responsive to individuals and communities. This seems to have happened to some of the best-known people's movements in Latin America, such as Chile's Interregional Mapuche Council (CIM) and Brazil's Landless Rural Workers Movement (MST). Both are effective organizations, but they seem tamer than before.

NGDOs and the international aid system

Whether for service delivery or other development activities, international donors are increasingly turning to NGDOs. They believe the latter can do things that government organizations cannot. They also want the NGO ethos to pervade official aid programmes. Unfortunately, the reverse appears to be happening: NGDOs are becoming dependent on foreign donors and are tempted to mirror donor policies, thus losing much of their value and character. This tends to fragment local civil society into those groups that will simply accept contracts—and do as they are told—and the more awkward ones that want to change things to meet locally expressed needs and priorities.

Instead of developing a shared long-term vision of improvements for society as a whole, donors and NGDOs often end up with a "projectized" approach to aid. This makes the work of the latter easier to insert into the framework of international bureaucracies—and it frequently implies imposing the same uniform, logically framed approach for almost every intervention.

If progressive NGDOs are to survive and make a useful contribution to development, they will need more encouragement from donors. Donors should allocate funding less on the basis of their particular project priorities and more on the characteristics of the organizations they support. There are three questions they could ask. First, does the NGDO represent an authentic response to community needs, or is it simply adapting to funding fashions? Second, is the NGDO concerned above all with meeting the needs of disadvantaged groups, or is it just working in its own organizational or pecuniary interest? Third, does it give a voice to those who would otherwise not be heard? International funding can help exemplary organizations that meet these criteria to survive, and engage in criticism and advocacy.

Donors can also help by recognizing the strengths of NGDOs and working to reinforce them. Donors admire these organizations for their ability to work creatively and flexibly, yet may give them little opportunity to exercise those strengths. An evaluation of two projects in Nepal and Ghana, which were part of a larger World Bank-funded water and sanitation scheme, revealed, for example, that the local implementing organizations received blueprints showing how the system was to be constructed. They were prohibited from adapting the design to local conditions or exploring with community members the construction and maintenance procedures that might have encouraged them to take fuller ownership of the project.

Creativity requires independence and—just as important—permission to make mistakes and adapt. A creative learning process that would contribute new insights to development problems and solutions would thus require a network of independent organizations—adequately and non-conditionally funded—capable of self-analysis and communication. The experimental nature of such organizations might limit their immediate impact, but their cumulative impact over the longer term could be considerable.

State versus NGDO provisioning

Donors and governments should be cautious when employing NGDOs as alternative providers of public services. Their limitations have been mentioned earlier. NGDOs tend to have an uneven reach, are inconsistent in quality, and offer sporadic coverage. Just as state-run services may be susceptible to patronage politics, NGDOs too are open to accusations of favouritism—particularly when members work in their own communities.

But probably the most important issue is accountability. If NGDOs are to fill gaps left by the state, they must have clearly defined responsibilities and their work must be overseen. They must be held accountable for their activities in a clear and concrete way. Beneficiaries can play a role in this process—making demands and requiring transparency. But in the last analysis NGDOs must be accountable to the state, which has ultimate responsibility for the quality of subcontracted services.

Nevertheless, there can be advantages to employing NGDOs for service delivery. Indeed, in some cases, this may be the only way in which services can be provided to the poor. Such involvement also offers NGDOs the opportunity to steer provision in a more progressive direction. Even if they are not determining policy, the way they implement it will often determine the outcome. The paradox is that as NGDOs become increasingly institutionalized and oriented toward service delivery contracts, some are becoming less interested in taking advantage of this political space to benefit the poor.

Another danger of involving NGDOs in service provision is that of setting NGDOs against the public sector. Some donors and governments are now using NGDOs as a lever to dislodge public sector employees and to informalize their work—having it carried out instead by a "flexible" labour force that commands few benefits and no job security. Sometimes this is financially more efficient, sometimes not. In any case, immediate efficiency gains have to be set against possible long-term erosion of the standards of public service. As the government withdraws, it may reduce its capacity to formulate effective strategies or to monitor or evaluate the outcome.

Precarious partnerships

Increasingly, NGDOs and community-based organizations are providing services in collaboration with government—through "partnerships". Most governments and donor agencies now stress the role of partnerships as an essential element of good governance. But the language of partnership is often distorted. Key aspects of genuine partnership—like mutual respect, equitable sharing of benefits and balanced power relations—are often absent. This applies as much to the relations of civil society organizations with government as it does to relations with donors. It is also evident in relations between Northern and Southern NGDOs.

In many instances, partnership means giving NGDOs too much to do with too few resources. One case, which illustrates the dilemmas and trade-offs that affect NGDO-government partnerships in the health sector, is that of the Swaziland Schools HIV/AIDS and Population Programme (SHAPE). This activity was originally a government programme funded by CARE International. It was only registered as an NGDO after the Ministry of Education declined to run the project. Initiated in response to the mounting prevalence of HIV/AIDS, SHAPE performs a large array of preventive activities, mostly based in secondary schools. SHAPE has found itself caught in inter-sectoral rivalries between the Ministries of Health and Education with which it works. In practice, this relationship means that both ministries slough off responsibility for virtually all HIV/AIDS education and outreach services—and their co-ordination—onto the NGDO's shoulders. It also means that the government guards its revenues for purposes that it apparently regards as more important than sexual and reproductive health.

In addition to being overburdened, NGDOs working in partnerships may find themselves less able to criticize the government. In some cases this may be the result of co-optation; but frequently, closer personal ties prompt a change of tactics—from public criticism to quiet diplomacy.

CSO-local government partnerships

Partnerships involving local governments, NGDOs and community-based organizations proliferated in the 1990s. A number of national legislatures, including Bolivia, Colombia and India, have enacted laws to enable community-based organizations to take their place in official organs of local government. And municipal authorities themselves have been legalizing and promoting greater participation of CSOs in governance.

Despite the increase in CSO-local government partnerships, long-lasting collaboration in most developing countries appears to be rare. Studies of such partnerships in some major Third World cities have highlighted various constraints. First, this kind of collaboration faces the same difficulties that affect the wider society—trying to build new structures in an often hostile environment, affected by economic adjustment and political instability. There is also the risk of political violence, which can deter individuals who would otherwise participate in public-spirited activities. This was evident in Lima in the early 1990s, when the guerrilla group Sendero Luminoso attacked a number of community leaders.

The scope and quality of partnerships may also depend on the party in power. Some impressive results have emerged in recent years through a new variety of participatory schemes put in place by left-leaning municipal and state governments. In Rio Grande do Sul in Brazil and Kerala in India, state and city budgets have been formulated on the basis of extensive local-level consultations involving residents, community organizations, politicians and bureaucrats. These cases demonstrate the value of backing grassroots activism with strong support from political parties and trade unions.

More commonly, institutional support for community-based organizations is likely to come from NGDOs. They can serve an important intermediary role between community organizations and local or central government, acting as mediators or conduits for information. They can also support community-level organizations with training, contacts and, sometimes, funding. But the NGDOs carrying out such roles are relatively few and overstretched, and often have short time horizons. In Mumbai, for example, with four million people living below the poverty line, there are only three NGDOs that are widely recognized to provide a comprehensive range of support activities, including advocacy (box 6.2).

Successful partnerships often depend on the ability of intermediate NGDOs to enable multiple grassroots organizations to work together or to come together themselves in coalitions. Through collective strength, CSOs can exert stronger claims on the state and international donors, and muster the resources needed to

Box 6.2 – The need for intermediate organizations in Mumbai

In Mumbai there is a high demand for NGOs that can support community-based organizations. One well-known NGO, YUVA, has 11 full-time professional staff members with a small number of volunteer assistants. These people support some 50 grassroots organizations in communities that have a total population of roughly 250,000. They mentor and act as a sounding board for CBO issues and plans, provide technical inputs, and offer financial and administrative training. Roughly 60 per cent of YUVA's budget comes from abroad.

In the past, some of these functions might have been served by local trade unions. But employment in textile mills, formerly the largest employers in Bombay, has been decimated, and the unions are moribund. Most of the CBOs and other grassroots groups therefore turn for help to religious associations, neighbourhood political bosses, employers, slum lords or even criminal groups.

If CBOs were to be properly served, there should be not three but approximately 23 intermediate organizations—one for each of the city's wards.

implement projects. In Lima, this has been an important feature of community action. But here, as elsewhere, local governments are sometimes ambivalent about working with civil society groups (box 6.3). They may see them as competing for resources or political patronage that would otherwise go to the local authority.

When local authorities see the rapid proliferation of civil society groups, they may also be concerned about their representativeness, accountability and ambitions. Many local governments take an instrumental view of participation. Thus they welcome community and volunteer groups that can provide labour and material inputs. And if they see that their top-down project will go ahead only if it has a façade of democratic decision making, they will open their doors a little. But local authorities are often fearful of genuine participation—or may simply not know how to interact with community groups, or have insufficient funds to do so. A municipal official in Mumbai, for example, remarked that it would be impossible for rank-and-file municipal employees to work smoothly with CBOs—lower-level bureaucrats had too little training and had worked for too long by rules learned by rote. And even when functionaries begin to adapt, there is the problem of rapid staff turnover. Local authorities are often less stable partners than their community counterparts—regularly shaken up by changes not only in staffing but also in leadership and policy.

Community and gender tensions

Conflicts within organizations, and between men and women, threaten the success of many partnerships and CSO activities. Both NGDOs and the community organizations with which they work must struggle to live up to their democratic ideals. And like all other human groups, they are vulnerable to infighting, splits and realignments. In Mumbai, for example, the NGO Youth for Unity and Voluntary Action (YUVA) was working with a grassroots organization to resolve a long-standing dispute

Box 6.3 – Partnerships in Lima

The vigorous tradition of grassroots organizations in many of Lima's districts has spawned innovative collaboration with local authorities. Organizations with many different—and sometimes conflicting—interests have learned to work together.

In northern Lima, for example, women's CBOs and local NGOs worked with district governments to improve nutrition, sanitation and public health. In eastern Lima, neighbourhood associations, community kitchens and mothers' clubs from a set of contiguous neighbourhoods formed a committee to engage in social and economic planning with the express purpose of formulating projects that were in the best interest of the larger community—not just of specific neighbourhoods. In southern Lima, a retail merchants' association, along with community organizations, NGOs and the municipal government of Villa El Salvador, developed the infrastructure and supply links necessary to prevent hoarding, price gouging and other forms of corruption in the marketing of food.

All of these initiatives ultimately broke down or fragmented, so that far less was achieved than participants had hoped for. Although they illustrate the potential of local actors, they also show that success and sustainability depend on multiple factors, both internal and external to community organizations. The role of local government has been particularly important.

between two low-income groups of tenants on public land. YUVA eventually terminated the relationship after the grassroots organization diverted more of its energy to political activity and was also accused of fraud. In order to continue working on the tenants' case, a number of people formed another community organization that is now collaborating with YUVA.

In many informal urban settlements, the primary managers are women. In addition to their responsibilities as care-givers and income earners, they also participate in community work. Yet in many societies and cultures, men persistently undermine their position and prevent them from acquiring equal status as community members. In northern Lima, for example, women drawn from the District Organization of Self-Managed Community Kitchens managed the municipal slaughterhouse in the Comas district. Male workers continuously sabotaged their efforts until the federation lost its contract. In São Paulo, some of the most successful examples of land invasion and collective housing construction were also the causes of frequent marital disputes and even divorces. In two well-known cases—Apuanã Community and Residents Association of Vila Arco Iris—women with children were the primary contributors to community organization and building campaigns that lasted several years. Some husbands saw this as too great a sacrifice and left their spouses, only to return after the deserted spouse had received her apartment or house.

Such tensions can also split higher-level organizations. The failure of the Nairobi-based Central Organization of Trade Unions to accept the demand by its own women's wing to put reproductive issues on the labour agenda was the last of a decade's-worth of rebuffs by the male leadership of the union. The women's wing had no choice in 1993 but to form a separate union. KEWWO, the Kenya Women Workers Organization, is the result of their efforts. While successful in creating a space for advocacy of women's issues within Kenya's union movement and in the larger society, KEWWO remains outside the traditional union structure. Nevertheless, recognition by—and assistance from—the ILO may eventually change this situation.

Civil society and international advocacy

Another area in which civil society organizations have achieved greater prominence in the 1990s is international advocacy. Leaving aside specific campaigns designed to change certain activities of international business, the strategy through which CSOs have exerted most pressure is through engagement with international organizations, primarily the United Nations and the international financial institutions. Today most UN bodies and IFIs have formal consultative mechanisms to canvass CSO opinions.

CSOs and the UN

CSOs do not generally participate in formal decision making at UN meetings. The ILO (which is composed of trade unions and employers' organizations, as well as governments) and UNAIDS (which has representatives from organizations of people living with AIDS on its Governing Council) are exceptional in this regard. But CSOs do affect the terms of the debate. They have helped place a number of issues firmly on the UN agenda: gender, participation, the environment, and a broader view of rights and development. And they have amplified their influence through well-planned information and media campaigns. This is particularly evident in human rights and other areas where CSOs are free to present politically controversial information that intergovernmental agencies cannot formally handle themselves.

In the 1990s, civil society also achieved greater recognition at the apex of the UN system.

A group of some 1,500 CSOs have official accreditation to the United Nations Economic and Social Council (ECOSOC). This permits them to sit in as observers and offer comments in many UN decision-making processes—although they do not have any decision-making power, and indeed could not within this intergovernmental structure.

Since the 1972 United Nations Conference on the Human Environment, in Stockholm, most UN gatherings have had CSOs running parallel events as well as lobbying at the main conference. By the time of the Rio Earth Summit in 1992, CSOs were participating extensively in all aspects of preparation for the conference and its follow-up, and the commitments and programmes of action from most of these gatherings bear CSO fingerprints. Thus in the preparatory process for the Social Summit, CSOs debated and provided alternatives to every key phrase in the draft documents. Many of these were ultimately rejected—such as the implementation of the Tobin Tax, aspects of the 20/20 initiative, and a more rig-

Jorgen Schytte/Still Pictures

Village meeting. Bhutan

orous commitment to increasing development assistance; but these ideas reappeared anyway in an Alternative Declaration signed by more than 600 NGOs.

Should civil society organizations have more formal status in the General Assembly? This issue resurfaced during preparations for the various five-year follow-ups to the UN conferences of the 1990s—the series of "plus five" General Assembly Special Sessions. CSOs were virtually excluded from Vienna Plus Five, but there seems to be more progress in the cases of Rio, Copenhagen and Beijing.

The possibilities for a CSO role in the Security Council beyond that of invited consultation have only begun to be addressed. In 1996, the Chilean Permanent Representative to the UN noted that the Security Council increasingly deals with disputes in which the parties are not states but groups or factions. Given the growing role and presence of civil society bodies, he argued that the Council could incorporate their inputs; and he suggested that for this purpose the Security Council should

Mark Edwards, Still Pictures

Women's meeting. Burkina Faso

organize a regular "consultative window". In February 1997, he was able to convince the Security Council to hear presentations by CARE, Oxfam and Doctors Without Borders on the humanitarian aspects of the crisis in the Great Lakes Region of Africa.

Some NGOs can also claim to have achieved policy change. The international human rights movement, for example, can point to its role in the creation of the post of UN High Commissioner for Human Rights, as well as the move to establish human rights as a core issue throughout the UN.

CSOs and the World Bank

The international agency that has received the most sustained criticism from CSOs is the World Bank. From protests against individual projects to the blanket condemnation expressed by the Fifty Years Is Enough campaign, the World Bank has been subjected to closer scrutiny than any other international organization.

This is largely because of the vast scale and high profile of World Bank operations. Its role in structural adjustment lending from the 1980s onward has affected hundreds of millions of people around the world. The organization has also acquired a reputation for arrogance and secrecy.

Since much of the Bank's work has profound environmental implications, it inevitably has drawn the attention of environmental activists working with NGDOs in a number of high-profile campaigns. A combination of political lobbying, mass media campaigning, and direct grassroots action eventually hit the mark, contributing to significant changes in the environmental policy of the institution. The cancellation in 1994 of the World Bank's support for the Narmada Dam in India, followed in 1995 by withdrawal from the Arun III Dam project in Nepal, were among key moments. At the same time, the Bank has been forced to concede greater access to project information and to other means of holding the organization accountable. It has also agreed to establish an in-house review mechanism known as the Inspection Panel. Not all of this has been due to NGO pressure. Reformers inside the World Bank had been pushing in the same direction. Even so, their hand has been strengthened by vocal external criticism.

But while civil society activism has undoubtedly had an impact on certain target issues and projects, it has not yet shifted the World Bank's basic frames of reference—or its economic rationale for project decisions. Although the Bank now has over 270 staff members with environmental expertise, their department remains demoralized, fragmented and largely powerless. At best, there are now patches of green.

The women's movement has also had some impact on Bank activities. The institution now has a Gender Analysis and Policy Group and a Gender Sector Board. And it has diverted some resources to women's health and education, and to improving access to micro-credit. On the surface, the Bank appears to take gender equity concerns seriously. But many CSOs remain sceptical. They see far too few of their gender-related concerns addressed substantively in Bank policy.

The Bank's method of interacting with women's networks remains seriously flawed. This is evident even in the most feminist sector of the Bank, the Health, Nutrition and Population Division. The Bank's purpose has not been genuinely to incorporate gender-sensitive advice and analysis: instead it tries to involve CSOs on the Bank's terms. Thus while there are CSO members in Bank consultative groups (including the Gender Consultative Group), they are appointed as individuals, not as representatives of social movements or even of organizations.

Nonetheless, the Bank has offered more recent, and possibly significant, openings to CSOs. It has, for example, invited CSOs to participate in the assessment of its Country Assistance Strategies and in the Structural Adjustment Programme Review Initiative Network. Launched in 1997 in response to NGO pressure, this involves the World Bank, governments and civil society organizations in reviews of structural adjustment programmes in eight countries (box 6.4).

Some World Bank officials believe the initiative has for the first time created real openings for meaningful dialogue. But there have been problems. SAPRIN staff members complain that the lack of consistency of lower-level Bank management in implementing the commitments made to SAPRIN has caused tensions. They also want SAPRIN to include a wider range of countries, including emerging markets. From outside the Bank there are other concerns. It remains to be seen whether the changes in Bank procedures resulting from SAPRIN will be anything other than cosmetic, and whether decision making between Bank and country-level government officials will involve more democratic accountability. Such negotiations often continue to take place behind closed doors, without the elected representatives of affected groups.

Changes in the World Bank's stance on many issues represent some limited success for CSOs. But as relations between the Bank and some organizations of civil society grow closer, new issues arise. One is the familiar danger of co-optation. The more CSOs work in close consultation with, or under contract to, the World Bank, the more they risk being granted pseudo-influence.

This problem becomes more general as the Bank decentralizes and creates new offices at the national level. More than 70 NGDO specialists now work in the Bank's field offices; and national CSOs have often been happy to use the World Bank as an ally in struggles with their own governments. Indeed, the Bank can use its great power to insist that governments channel international funds toward civil society organizations. This may sometimes be useful, but it compromises the ability of those CSOs to monitor the Bank. While working as insiders may promote useful initiatives, more fundamental change in both national and

Box 6.4 – Adjusting structural adjustment

One of the most ambitious attempts to challenge the World Bank and make it reconsider its development model has been SAPRIN—the Structural Adjustment Programme Review Initiative Network, which itself is a product of NGO pressure on the World Bank. SAPRIN, which was launched by the Bank and NGOs in 1997, attempts to review the impact of structural adjustment programmes on social development. It involves participatory reviews of SAPs in 12 countries. Eight of these—Bangladesh, Ecuador, El Salvador, Ghana, Hungary, Mali, Uganda and Zimbabwe—involve the national government, the Bank and civil society organizations. In four others—Canada, Honduras, Mexico and the Philippines—similar consultative exercises are being organized by civil society organizations themselves.

One of the basic tools of SAPRIN has been the holding of national fora: five in 1998 and seven in 1999. These are to be followed by field research involving Bank and civil society participants, who will examine the "hows" and "whys" of adjustment impacts. The findings will be fed back into a second round of national meetings. As of end-1999, some 1,500 CSOs were participating in the network.

Bank policy will probably only come from persistent, objective external criticism.

CSOs and the Inter-American Development Bank

CSOs have also been interacting with the regional development banks, though not traditionally on such antagonistic terms. Here many of the initiatives have come from the banks themselves, rather than as a result of CSO pressure. A case in point is the Inter-American Development Bank (IDB). Headquartered in Washington, DC, the IDB's structure and operations parallel those of the World Bank, although its loan portfolio covers only Latin America and the Caribbean.

The IDB's declared interest in working more closely with civil society organizations emerged following a conference in 1994. Some CSOs hoped that this would lead to creation of a new fund to which they could have direct access. But the IDB, like other development banks, is composed of governments. CSOs who want to obtain support must be associated with government initiatives. Their influence must be asserted both through affecting government policy—speaking out as citizens in favour of or against certain propositions—and through forming part of specific projects requested by governments and funded through the international banks.

Therefore the IDB sought to incorporate CSOs into the mainstream of its lending to governments. In 1995–96 it held a series of consultations that brought civil society groups more systematically into discussions on national development agendas. These meetings were intended both to build greater capacity among CSOs and to foster greater consensus between CSOs and governments.

By the late 1990s, the IDB had approved loans involving CSO participation in five Latin American countries—Argentina, Brazil, Colombia, Guatemala and Venezuela (box 6.5). Their total monetary value was $138 million, less than 3 per cent of the IDB's total portfolio. But because the bank has committed itself to the goal of channelling 50 per cent of all loans to the social sector, this amount may increase quickly.

It is clear that if CSOs are to take advantage of this opening, they need to be more assertive and to weigh in more intelligently. This will mean getting to know the key people in the

Box 6.5 – Community development for peace in Guatemala

The Inter-American Development Bank (IDB) has been trying to work more closely with civil society organizations. In October 1996, the IDB met in Panajachel, Guatemala, with 100 people to examine how CSOs could participate more fully in Guatemalan government programmes. Those present included NGOs, indigenous community organizations, entrepreneurs, micro-entrepreneurs and philanthropists. One project they looked at in considerable detail was Community Development for Peace (DECOPAZ), a fund of $50 million for community projects in the Peace Zone—the northern and western departments of Guatemala that suffered most during the civil war.

This IDB loan to the government is in fact managed primarily by community-based CSOs, with technical assistance from specialized development agencies and NGOs, in collaboration with municipal governments. The affected communities control implementation of social policy and, to a lesser degree, the design of successive stages of the projects.

IDB and in the governments, and also becoming more familiar with the bank's project cycle, so they can make timely, strategic and tactical interventions.

CSOs AND THE INTERNATIONAL TREATY BODIES

The World Trade Organization (WTO), and the North American Free Trade Agreement (NAFTA) are treaties that bind signatory countries to follow a set of norms applied to international trade and investment. These have a narrow intent; and any positive or negative impacts on the environment, social development or even on growth are presumed to be incidental.

Decisions are taken by member countries. Each has one vote, although the countries with greatest economic clout have the most influence. Advocacy groups are formally excluded from debates, negotiations and decision making. But they are never far away. Transnational corporations have always circled around the meetings. CSOs, on the other hand, have largely been excluded and have protested their culture of secrecy.

In recent years the situation has been changing. In the case of the North American Free Trade Agreement, civil society organizations in the three countries concerned, Canada, Mexico and the United States, began organizing in the early 1990s to inform themselves and their constituencies of NAFTA's probable economic and social impact. One of the most influential coalitions was the Hemispheric Social Alliance. While it was ultimately unable to defeat NAFTA, its coalitions in the three countries gained recognition for their alternative approaches to the free trade agenda and for their repertoire of direct lobbying, legislative engagement and public action.

CSO organization around NAFTA also has had other repercussions—altering international alliances in the labour movement and establishing campaigns in support of unionization, worker safety and human rights, particularly in Mexico. Thus at the 1998 Santiago Summit of the Americas, there was a large assembly of trade unions and federations along with events sponsored by indigenous, women's, environmental, church, ethnic and development associations and agencies.

In terms of achieving policy change, however, one of the most significant events for international CSOs was the sinking, or at least the temporary submersion, of the Multilateral Agreement on Investment (MAI). Discussions on this treaty started at the OECD in 1995. The MAI aimed to establish ground rules for foreign direct investment—primarily to ensure fair treatment for transnationals wishing to invest anywhere in the world. NGO critics began to campaign on the issue in 1996, condemning it as a corporate charter that would allow TNCs to ride roughshod over national sovereignty—particularly over labour standards, environmental protection and public service delivery. Campaigns took off in many OECD and developing countries, uniting environmental, development and human rights CSOs—as well as consumer organizations, trade unions, church groups and even associations of local authorities.

OECD negotiators, who had expected to work quietly to finalize the treaty in 1997, found they had an increasingly unpopular mission. Changes of government in France and the UK also made their life more difficult, and the treaty was effectively set aside when France withdrew from negotiations in October 1998. At the end of 1998, the OECD officially announced that negotiations had been abandoned.

The MAI also probably signalled the coming of age of the Internet for the hundreds of pressure groups that used e-mail to communicate with each other and set up Web sites to spell out the potential costs of the MAI. OECD negotiators may have understood the MAI in

Barry Sweet, Associated Press AP

Rainforest Action Network Protest. Seattle, Washington, United States

narrow economic terms; but when it came to the social and political ramifications, they were clearly outmanoeuvred. Their ability to work in secrecy was undermined: a draft of the MAI appeared on an NGO Web site and was rapidly circulated. In future, it will be difficult not to involve CSOs and other civil society actors in any follow-up negotiations.

The experience of civil society organization against the MAI was employed to good effect in campaigns against the WTO. Trade negotiations under the GATT never attracted the glare of the global spotlight. But the third Ministerial Conference of the WTO in November 1999 in Seattle was to be very different.

A number of things had changed. First, the developing countries were less pliant. They realized they had been short-changed in the GATT rounds and demanded fairness—particularly, greater access to industrialized country markets. Second, America and Europe were already in dispute over such issues as bananas and beef hormones, and were in no mood to compromise. The long-lasting dispute over the WTO leadership also slowed down any efforts to prepare the ground for agreement.

In the public mind—as expressed by the CSOs—the more fundamental problem was that the WTO was a secretive and powerful entity whose rulings could effectively override agreements reached in other international fora—particularly on the environment. According to the WTO, it was not the organization's job to enforce environmental and labour agreements. Nevertheless, it had at its disposal trade sanctions—among the most effective international weapons short of missiles. This means that the WTO, which is not even a UN organization, is probably the second most powerful institution after the UN Security Council—and yet it makes its rulings essentially in private and with limited participation of the poorest countries.

Not surprisingly, the world's CSOs, most of which were already deeply disturbed by many aspects of globalization, seized on the WTO as a target. Prior to the meeting, nearly 1,200 CSOs from 87 countries signed a statement that called for a fundamental reform of what they saw to be a flawed and undemocratic organization. By the time of the meeting in Seattle, tens of thousands of people were jamming the streets—anarchists, trade unionists, environmentalists and human rights activists. Other large rallies were held simultaneously in cities all over the world.

These demonstrations did not themselves scupper the talks that organizers had hoped would launch a new round of international trade negotiations. The talks were already foundering long before the meeting started. But vivid news reports from the "battle of Seattle" will profoundly influence the atmosphere for all future multilateral trade negotiations.

The future for international NGO mobilization

Mobilization against the WTO was the culmination of a series of successes for international campaigns. The Jubilee 2000 coalition on debt and the campaigns against landmines, the MAI and genetically modified food—as well as campaigns against companies such as Nike, Shell or Nestlé—have raised the prospect of a new era of radical and effective protest. This may be over-optimistic. But at least there are signs of fundamental change in the ways such campaigns work.

One of the most important changes is the quality of the technical information that is available. The data and analysis on debt produced by Jubilee 2000 were strong enough to keep finance ministers on the defensive, and the same was true for the MAI and the WTO. Much of this is generated and disseminated by smaller campaigning organizations such as the Transnational Resource and Action Center, through its online magazine, *Corporate Watch;* but international CSOs like Oxfam and the WWF have skilled and respected teams of analysts, who not only develop well-argued criticisms but also have clearly worked-out alternative strategies of their own. This has now been combined with Web sites that can be used not just to transmit technical data but also to present the information in a format that can be understood by a wide audience.

The Internet has also helped activists with many different interests, scattered around the globe, to co-ordinate their activities. These alliances may melt away as rapidly as they appear. At present, it is probably safe to say that these are contingent tactical groupings that enable national organizations to establish links with those in other countries.

What happens next depends on the reaction of governments and international organizations. Probably they will start to absorb some of the key players, particularly the technical analysts, into official processes—an approach the World Bank has long used to good effect. This can be seen either as a new step toward broadening the range of views within international organizations or as a defensive tactic of co-optation.

Intelligence, energy and rights

The diversity of CSOs, and the multiplicity of levels at which they operate, make it difficult to draw general conclusions about their future prospects. CSOs have had many partial successes. In service delivery, they have often reached communities and groups hitherto neglected by state services. Project design and implementation can also benefit from their attention to participation, innovation, local needs and social relations. But there is no systematic evidence to suggest that civil society is a more effective delivery agent than the state. It should not be regarded as a substitute for basic universal services.

Internationally, CSOs have discovered effective ways to shake the foundations of the global economic order. Some have called the emergent CSO formations a global civil society. That probably overstates the case. What has emerged is a raucous and intelligent combination of research, idealism and cheap technology, now armed with human rights law. With this combination of energy, technology and development experience, they now have a voice that governments, corporations and international agencies ignore at their own peril.

Getting development right for women

Rhodri Jones, Panos Pictures

Street scene. Kunming, Yunnan, China

Women are gaining formal rights, but this has not been matched by an improvement in their quality of life. Although women's groups have become increasingly visible and vocal, their political influence remains limited. And as governments shift more social responsibilities to families and communities, most of the burden falls on women's shoulders.

The democratic openings of the past decade have offered greater opportunities for women. Women's groups have helped draft national constitutions and have developed new legislation in areas such as family law and violence against women. Women's groups have also been among the most influential NGOs. In the 1990s, feminist ideas and practices proliferated across a wide range of public arenas—in black and indigenous movements, for example, and in trade unions, universities, political parties, and international development agencies. Women also played a prominent part in the international conferences of the 1990s.

1995 was particularly significant in this respect. It was the year of the Social Summit, which established that "equality and equity between women and men is a priority for the international community". It was also the year of the landmark Fourth World Conference on Women, in Beijing.

But have formal declarations on gender equity actually had a political and social impact? Have women's lives started to change? Here the story is much less optimistic. Many of the hidden barriers and ceilings to women's meaningful participation remain stubbornly in place. Whether in UN meeting halls or in national or local governance, social conservatism continues to block the implementation of many hard-won rights. And the social dislocation that has accompanied economic liberalization has often thrown extra burdens on women's shoulders.

Women in democratization

The transitions to democracy around the world owe a great deal to pressure from women's movements. Indeed, in some respects women achieved greater prominence during periods of protest against autocratic governments than they have during subsequent democratic regimes.

Women's groups take many different forms, but they can be divided into roughly three general types:

- ***Human rights groups***—Some of the best-known of these emerged in Latin America during the 1970s and 1980s, notably the Mothers of the Plaza de Mayo in Argentina. These and similar "non-political" protest movements relied to some extent on the hope that the military was less likely to persecute women than men because of women's seemingly apolitical nature. Women also derived some of their power from the fact that they were turning against their oppressors the very symbols—motherhood and family—that the state was claiming to uphold.
- ***Popular women's groups***—These groups arose as forms of mutual support during periods of great economic hardship. Thus many women organized communal kitchens in the poorest areas of large cities. Often these groups had links with religious organizations. In Latin America, they usually emerged from Catholic community organizations; and in the Arab states and elsewhere, Islam has inspired popular women's groups. Activism by itself does not necessarily lead to a more gender-egalitarian order: in Iran, religious fervour impelled the society out of autocracy but only into theocracy (box 7.1). Even so, in the urban areas of countries such as Turkey, Islamist women have managed to provide a space in which women of

Box 7.1 – "Years of hardship, years of growth": Feminism in an Islamic Republic

In the first months and years following the Iranian Revolution of 1979, secular professional women became easy targets of "revolutionary purification and cleansing campaigns". Barely two weeks after the overthrow of the old regime, the Family Protection Act was scrapped as un-Islamic. Eventually, the veil was imposed and an elaborate "code of modesty" was put in place. Women were dismissed from the judiciary and subsequently barred from many positions and disciplines of higher education. Acts of defiance and resistance by women were instantly branded as counter-revolutionary, a label that not only made participants in these protests easy targets of repression, but also foreclosed the possibility of building alliances between secular professional women and Islamic women activists of the Revolution.

With the defeat of secularists, Islamic women activists (inside and outside the Parliament) found themselves acting as critics of the new government on women's issues. It was thanks to their efforts that universities were once again opened to women, and that a new set of laws virtually reinstated the Family Protection Act. Out of these early years of Islamic women's activism also emerged a radical re-thinking of gender in Islam—evident in a variety of women's journals published in Iran.

One of these journals, *Zanan* (Women), undertakes a direct re-interpretation of Islamic texts from a woman's perspective, founded on the principles of women's choice and autonomy—a move that has provoked the anger of more traditional Islamic advocates. *Zanan* also declares affiliation and solidarity with a variety of feminisms—both Western secular and Iranian secular—and it freely cites from them. This breaks down suspicion and hostility between the religious/traditionalist and secular/modernist tendencies, which was dominant in twentieth-century Iran.

More than two decades after the Revolution, women's issues remain central to Iran's political agenda. Indicative of the primary place "the woman question" occupies, and the broad constituency it attracts, is women's visibility in politics—both as voters and candidates. Iranian women played a big role in the 1997 election of Mohammad Khatami, the reformist president. They were also an active and visible force in the February 2000 parliamentary elections. In Tehran, six out of 30 parliamentary seats were won by women—significantly, without any quotas or "reserved seats".

Even with a predominantly reformist Parliament, women face an enormous task in asserting their rights. The extent to which gender equality can be incorporated into reforms of the legal system and the judiciary will reflect the constraints facing President Khatami, as he tries to promote human rights and the rule of law in a system where conservatives have the final say.

diverse backgrounds seek empowerment, even if their rhetoric and ideology does not always endorse gender equality.

- ***Feminist groups***—These tend to consist of middle-class and professional women. During military rule in Latin America, feminist groups often emerged from militant left-wing organizations and student groups that had been driven underground. Indeed, it was often women's subordination within such groups that planted the seeds of feminist consciousness. Other women gained new ideas from periods of exile in Europe or the United States.

One of the most crucial questions for women activists is how far they should co-operate with each other and take part in broader political processes. How closely should feminist groups ally themselves with popular women's movements? Many would argue that this is a strategic imperative. A major challenge for feminists in Morocco and Turkey, for example, is to free themselves from the tutelage of political parties without becoming isolated; this means they must extend their social base to a more diverse constituency. But as yet there are too few signs of such cross-class alliances.

In Latin America during the period of dictatorship, feminist groups often focused their attention on the material conditions of women's lives and supported the survival struggles of poor and working-class women. Many feminists feel that these ties with popular movements have now been weakened.

Indeed, one of the major concerns of feminist activists in the 1990s was the increasing "NGO-ization" of the women's movement. Women's groups have been shifting away from feminist-inspired activities such as mobilization, popular education and consciousness-raising. They have taken on more technical and advisory functions, such as the delivery of social services, advising government agencies on how to design gender-sensitive programmes, or training their staff in "gender planning".

Some argue that as feminist groups and NGOs have become more professionalized and specialized, they have severed their links with grassroots and community-based organizations. They could respond that when implementing state- or donor-funded projects for female-headed households, or evaluating the gender impacts of projects, they still come into contact with poor and working-class women's organizations. But the nature of NGO-grassroots linkages seems to have changed. Moreover, the NGOs that are selected as partners and thus receive funding are not necessarily those with the strongest links to the grassroots. To maintain their legitimacy and their claim to be representative, NGOs and their leaders require organic ties to this base. But such ties cannot be taken for granted; they must be consciously nurtured.

Women's groups may also be wary about taking part in mainstream politics. Many deliberately keep their distance from broader political processes and are ambivalent about becoming embroiled in party politics. In Uganda, for example, women's self-help groups and voluntary associations struggling for economic and social rights deliberately distance themselves from public authorities, even at the local level. They also avoid formal political activity, which they regard as sectarian, corrupt and divisive.

This is comparable in some respects to the situation in Eastern Europe and the former Soviet Union. Many women in communist countries identified feminism with state socialism and government policies of "emancipation from above", which often pressured women to work outside the home. As a reaction, many women now question the core feminist tenet that women who stay in the private sphere are being oppressed, and that they need liberating into work and public life. This radical rejection of Western feminism is thus partly a repudiation of communism. But it is clear that feminism emerging in this part of the world is more compatible with the family, motherhood and femininity. In Hungary, for example, women are very visible in public life—but are to be found outside formal party politics. Many women are working in NGOs or committees of local government. The few avowedly feminist initiatives tend to be linked with specific services, such as hostels for battered women.

Working within and against the state

States may have been weakened in recent years, but they still hold crucial influence over women's lives. In the industrialized countries, feminists have tended to adopt different positions vis-à-vis the state. At one extreme is the view that the state is immutably masculine—the ultimate vehicle of social control over women's lives. This perception is common among feminists in the United States, for example, and in the United Kingdom. The alternative view is that the state is an important vehicle for social justice—a view more likely to be heard in Canada and New Zealand, which have a strong tradition of social liberalism, and in Australia where "femocrats"—feminist bureaucrats—have used the state to the advantage of women. Scandinavian women take a similar approach: they have strong welfare states and more faith in the merits of state intervention.

The situation in developing countries provides further contrasts. Compared to their counterparts living in European welfare states, women here are less touched by the state's welfare provisioning. Their states also tend to be weaker and less able to enforce civil rights across the national territory and for all social strata. They are less likely to disseminate information about new legislation—or to enforce it—due either to political expediency or because they lack power. Women's lives are thus shaped more by the prevailing norms—often fluid but usually conservative—of their societies. In some cases, weak systems of internal regulation result in high levels of state violence and violation of civil rights. A number of women's organizations in India, for example, are rooted in their opposition to police brutality.

Nevertheless, the transition to democracy does allow some women to have a greater influence in state bureaucracies. This has been most evident in Latin America. In virtually all Latin American countries, some specialized "women's machineries" have been set up in the public administration. The reasons for this have been varied. In some cases, it has been in response to pressure exerted by foreign donors, or to funding made available for this purpose. In other cases the dominant political party may see it as a useful political resource—as a means either of demonstrating progressive national attitudes to the international community (as in Bangladesh) or as a source of political support from a hitherto neglected constituency (as in Uganda). In yet other cases, such as in Brazil, Chile, and South Africa, it has been through the persistent advocacy of certain streams within the women's movement that state machineries for women have been set up.

Strategically positioned within the state, femocrats are, in theory, well situated to identify and take advantage of political opportunities to push forward items on the women's agenda. But their position—at once within and against the state—raises questions of legitimacy in the eyes of both their colleagues in the bureaucracy and the women's movement on the outside.

In Brazil, the early years of democracy saw the emergence of Councils on the Feminine Condition, first in São Paulo and later in other states, as well as at the national level. These councils, often staffed by feminists, successfully promoted women's health and reproductive rights—and also helped introduce women's police stations specialized in cases of violence against women. In the late 1980s, the National Council helped incorporate women's demands into the new constitution. The links between these councils and the women's movement are weaker now than they used to be, but women's influence over state policy, particularly on health, is probably stronger in Brazil than in most other developing countries.

In Chile, the women's movement exerted pressure on the centre-left coalition that won the 1989 election, leading to the creation of the National Service for Women (SERNAM) within the Ministry of Planning. But SERNAM's role was unclear from the outset and it drew strong opposition from right-wing parties. It seems to have concentrated on awareness raising and implementing various pilot projects. Recently it has taken the lead in developing new legislation in family law and on violence against women, and in modifying the labour code—though it steers clear of controversial issues such as abortion.

Chile's experience also reflects broader dilemmas. While SERNAM derived its original dynamism and legitimacy from a strong women's movement, its relations with the women's movement have been ambivalent because it is seen as an arm of the government. There has been some disappointment with SERNAM's conservative approach to gender issues. Popular women's groups, in particular, feel alienated from SERNAM: many poor and working-class women fail to identify with the campaigns it runs.

Most other countries also have some specialized machinery for women. However, in many cases the relationship between women's units in public administration and women's constituencies in civil society has proved difficult to establish or exploit. Women's groups and NGOs are often reluctant to associate themselves too closely with these units. This reflects a healthy concern about retaining autonomy, but it makes strategic collaboration difficult. In Morocco, for example, the women's movement has tended to bypass the women's units in public administration and has worked primarily on the outside or through alliances with political parties.

Women in politics

Women's representation in political parties and in national legislatures is weak. As figure 7.1 indicates, the proportion of women members of the lower houses of parliament has increased only marginally over the past two to three decades, and at 12 per cent remains far below that of men. Table 7.1 shows that representation in lower houses is highest in Europe, though high proportions in the Nordic countries boost Europe's overall figure. As table 7.2 indicates, these countries have the strongest women's representation in the world. The United States comes well down the list, with a proportion of only 13 per cent.

Figure 7.1 – The proportion of women in lower houses of parliament worldwide

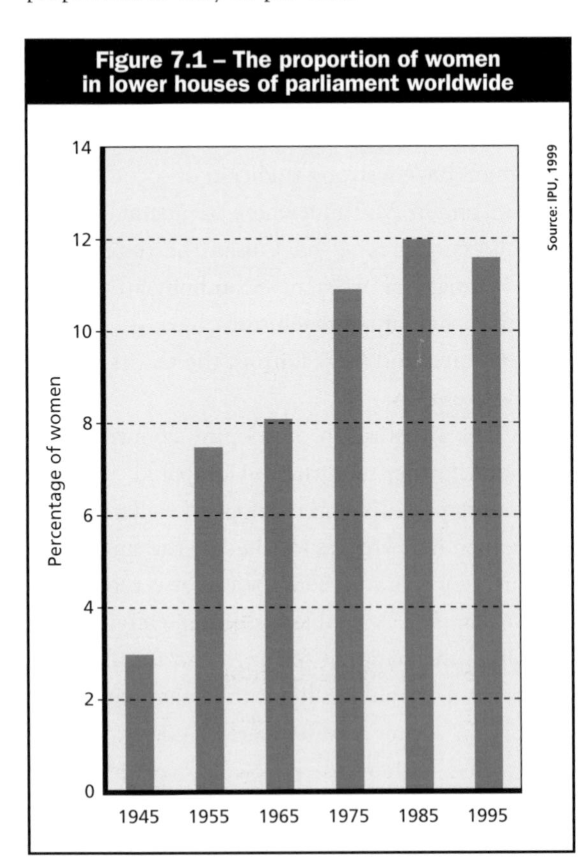

Table 7.1 – Women's representation—regional averages

	Single House or Lower House %	Upper House or Senate %	Both Houses combined %
Europe	16	10	14
Asia	15	12	15
Americas	15	15	15
Sub-Saharan Africa	11	13	11
Pacific	9	21	11
Arab states	4	3	4
World average	13	11	13

Note: Europe refers to OSCE member countries.
Source: IPU, 1999

The poor representation of women in national legislatures is astonishing. Since all versions of liberal democracy link the right to vote with the right to stand for office, the fact that the gender composition of national assemblies is so at odds with the gender composition of the population signifies that something is wrong. Echoing this sentiment, the Platform for Action agreed upon at the Fourth World Conference on Women identifies women's representation in decision-making bodies as one of its key areas of concern.

Women's invisibility in the world of institutional politics is partly a historical legacy, but it also reflects the "boys' club" prejudices of parties and electorates. Deeply entrenched barriers exclude women from meaningful participation in political parties, where they are habitually relegated to women's wings and per-

Table 7.2 – Women in lower houses of parliament in selected countries

Rank	Country	Election year	Number of women	% women
1	Sweden	1998	149	43
2	Denmark	1998	67	37
3	Finland	1999	74	37
4	Norway	1997	60	36
5	Netherlands	1998	54	36
6	Iceland	1999	22	35
7	Germany	1998	207	31
8	South Africa	1999	120	30
9	New Zealand	1996	35	29
10	Argentina	1997	71	28
24	Costa Rica	1998	11	19
26	United Kingdom	1997	121	18
28	Uganda	1996	50	18
41	United States	1998	58	13

Source: IPU, 1999

form cheer-leading roles. At the same time, the cultural construction of political office as masculine makes it extremely difficult for women to be elected without some form of electoral engineering, such as through quota systems or reserved seats. Women candidates tend to attract fewer votes than men even when they do not campaign on women's issues. And when they do stand on a feminist platform, they have even less success—often being seen as anti-men, anti-tradition or anti-family.

There have been some attempts to redress the balance. Progressive political parties determined to improve women's representation have made efforts to favour women. A number of parties in Latin America have boosted the number of women candidates by operating informal quotas. In Argentina, they include the two largest parties, the Radical Civic Union, and the Party of Justice; in Bolivia, Nation's Conscience; and in Mexico, the Revolutionary Democratic Party.

In Europe a number of centrist and left-wing parties have pursued similar policies. In Scandinavia they did so in response to pressure from women's groups. The Swedish Social Democratic Party has taken one of the most advanced positions: since 1994 it has insisted that if the first person on the list of electoral candidates is a man, the next must be a woman—and that they should alternate thereafter.

Other countries attempting positive discrimination have run into problems. In the United Kingdom for a brief period, for example, some local branches of the Labour Party were required to produce women-only short lists. This was subsequently abandoned, since it conflicted with equal opportunities legislation. But it nevertheless resulted after the 1997 election in a striking increase in the number of women Labour MPs—101, almost one-quarter of the total.

A common way for parties to boost the number of women MPs is through the party list. If elections are based on proportional representation using party lists, then parties are free to choose candidates for their lists as they see fit—and women candidates will appear on the list if gender equality is a priority for the party. To some extent this de-personalizes the vote and reduces the opportunity for electorates to discriminate against individuals on the basis of ethnic identity or gender. In South Africa the ANC has taken advantage of this to boost the number of women in the National Assembly; as table 7.2 indicates, South Africa now ranks eighth in the world, with women comprising 30 per cent of parliamentarians.

Positive discrimination may also be enshrined in legislation or in the constitution—typically by reserving a specific number of seats for women. In Uganda, for example, one parliamentary seat from each of the 39 districts is reserved for woman. In Argentina, 30 per cent of candidates for elective posts must be women. In Bangladesh, 30 seats out of 330 are reserved for women; in Eritrea, 10 out of 105; and in Tanzania, 15 seats out of 255. The same principles have also been used in the *panchayats*, or village councils, in India (box 7.2). One unfavourable outcome of reserved seats is that it risks creating an enclave for women's political participation, with the electorate assuming that the reserved seats are the only legitimate seats for women.

THE IMPACT OF WOMEN ON GOVERNMENT

Unfortunately there is no guarantee that women elected to parliament will stand up for women's interests. Many of the most successful women politicians have not been feminists. And those who have been elected to office through quotas or reserved seats may be reluctant to voice dissent, being at the mercy of the central or provincial party that compiles electoral lists.

In Uganda, many women MPs were persuaded to enter politics by male elders, and some regard their position as a favour granted by the National Resistance Movement (NRM) rather than as a right; they are therefore reluctant to voice criticism of the NRM government. In political systems where a single party is dominant and women politicians have no other realistic political option, their leverage on the party is drastically reduced, and they are less able to explore issues that may not be on the party's agenda. Nevertheless, women parliamentarians in Uganda have on several occasions come together to create a united front and to push for progressive legislation, as happened in 1997–98 over the Land Law.

Similarly in India, while the local political elite may have hoped that "suitable" women, or proxy representatives, would be elected to the *panchayats*, the outcome has been more complex. Women's participation in structures of power and decision making has itself provided opportunities for rapid growth and learning. Many women have been outstanding chairpersons and members of the *panchayats*, demonstrating initiative and leadership—and countering the idea that they are mere namesake or proxy representatives. Indeed, the term "proxy" symbolizes a complete denial of the possibility of women's agency, growth and learning.

Women MPs are more likely to represent women's interests if they maintain strong links with women's organizations. Instead of operating on their own in a political vacuum, they need working relationships with other women

Box 7.2 – Women in local government in India

In April 1993, India's Constitution was amended (the 73rd Amendment), to provide special incentives for women to be elected to local government. This amendment directed all state legislatures to amend their respective *panchayat* legislation to conform to the constitutional amendment, within one year. Henceforth one third of representatives in the village councils, the *panchayats,* as well as in the corresponding municipal bodies, would be women. This met with stiff resistance and procrastination in many states. And men sometimes tried to subvert the process by nominating their daughters or daughters-in-law to serve as proxies.

Nevertheless, the benefits are starting to be felt. Around one million women have been elected to *panchayats* and have been focusing on important local government issues, such as the Public Food Distribution System and minimum wages. And they have been pressing for improvements in health, education and water systems. Just as important, they have highlighted major social issues such as domestic violence and alcoholism.

Rajasthan has some of India's greatest gender inequities—with female infanticide, high female illiteracy, and a low ratio of women to men. So there was considerable resistance to the election of women and scepticism about their abilities. Men still heavily criticize the women members' performance—and some women *panchayat* chairs will clearly be more effective than others, depending on their experience and ability. But when questioned more closely, many people in Rajasthan, especially women, point out that the women members have actually worked harder on important matters, such as repairing water pumps, and are generally far more approachable and willing to listen. Still, real progress can only be claimed when more women contest the general seats and not just the "ladies' seats".

"on the outside". It is particularly important to maintain these links during transitions toward democracy. When the political centre of gravity shifts from informal political movements to conventional political parties, there is always a danger that women will again be marginalized.

Women's more obvious successes in government have been at the formal level—ensuring that new constitutions are grounded in gender equality. Women have also helped introduce progressive legislation in such areas as divorce, domestic violence and reproductive rights. But enforcing this legislation has often proved more difficult, not just because of social resistance, but also because of state weakness in administering justice and a political and economic environment that is hostile to social expenditure. Many women's reproductive rights services, for example, have been undermined by a general weakening of primary health care. Thus in Zimbabwe the introduction of user fees for prenatal care has dissuaded many women from attending clinics and resulted in a dramatic rise in maternal mortality.

This also reflects a more basic problem. One policy area that has consistently eluded scrutiny is decision making on public expenditure. Some have argued that part of the problem lies in women's lack of fluency and skill in economic analysis. If this is the case, then the Women's Budget Statements and Initiatives first introduced in Australia and Canada, and more recently in South Africa, which require all government departments to account for the impacts of their activities on women, can provide a useful tool for strengthening the technical capacities of women's machineries.

But the problems are more deep-seated. To some extent they reflect a more general shift in the balance of power away from social sector ministries and MPs and toward technocrats in the ministries of finance and trade. Parliamentarians of both sexes have been disempowered. Women bureaucrats well equipped with economic analytical skills may be able to contribute to what goes on inside these insulated technocracies, in ministries of finance for example. But this is no substitute for a more open public debate that enables the parliament, women's groups and networks, along with other social groups, to scrutinize economic policies and decisions that affect the well-being of their constituents. To see women's exclusion from economic policy making simply in terms of the skills that they lack (and need to be equipped with) misses the larger question of whether the emerging political arrangements enable the public as a whole to review and control the actions and decisions taken by the executive.

Women's NGOs

As indicated in chapter 3, governments have been shifting many social responsibilities from state agencies to civil society. This has important implications for women. Governments have been passing much of the burden not to organizations but to individual women—requiring that they fill the vacuum of diminished social services by spending more time caring for sick and disabled relatives and neighbours. In this way, governments are "privatizing" health care by recruiting unpaid family labour.

Donors have encouraged the NGO-ization of women's health services. Some organizations, such as the World Bank, may see this as a way of avoiding the perceived corruption and inefficiencies of existing state services. In Tajikistan, for example, the British NGO Christian Aid and the EU are funding the Khatlon Women's Health Project, which offers poor communities services that the government has neither the means nor the will to provide.

Does the willingness of women's NGOs to shoulder these burdens encourage governments to slough off their responsibilities? Even when governments claim to be improving service provision by entering into partnerships with women's NGOs, the outcomes of such partnerships can be ambiguous. As chapter 6 argued, in many instances "partnership" means giving the NGOs too many tasks with too few resources.

NGOs also run a number of risks by entering into such partnerships. In addition to being overburdened, they may find themselves less able to criticize the government. In Peru, for example, the Manuela Ramos Movement ("Manuela") administers the USAID-funded Reproductive Health in the Community Project (ReproSalud). This aims to bring innovative services to poor women, while also encouraging them to make more effective claims on government services. But these official links proved a disadvantage when the government health services were accused of coercive sterilization. Manuela had to choose between quiet diplomacy and openly criticizing public services in ways that might play into the hands of right-wing forces that wanted to shut down all public reproductive health care. In the event, after diplomacy failed Manuela came out publicly against sterilization abuses.

Women's NGOs have to make choices appropriate to their own circumstances. In many cases this must mean taking a deliberately dissident stance. In Egypt one of the most controversial issues addressed by women's groups is female genital mutilation (FGM). Egypt's FGM Task Force maintains a vigilant role of critique and advocacy. It refuses close collaboration with a government that frequently attacks NGOs, especially those involved in the promotion of human rights.

Finally, given the dependence of NGOs on external sources of funding, the priorities of funders can encourage the proliferation of specific types of NGOs and activities. In the case of Chile, for example, in order to remain economically viable many women's NGOs are letting go of projects that were closely associated with their feminist commitments—such as popular education projects on sexuality and parenting, and leadership training. Instead, they are taking up projects that are more attractive to funders—such as women's health, micro-enterprise development, and job training programmes for women heads of household.

Some NGOs manage to adapt to new funding criteria that encourage more technical-professional endeavours, while others lose out. Sadly, some of the losers are organizations that have strong links with poor and working-class women, and with community-based organizations.

At the same time, it should be emphasized that the distinction between women's NGOs and the women's movement is not clear-cut. First, the vast majority of professional NGO activists also view themselves as part of a larger women's movement. Second, women's NGOs vary tremendously in their power, resources, ideology, relations to donors and governments—and above all in the extent and quality of their connections with grassroots movements. In recent years, the crucial ties between NGOs and their grassroots constituents have begun to change, and in some contexts, they have been weakened.

To some extent this is because donors, when choosing which NGOs to fund, rarely give priority to the extent of their links to grassroots organizations and to the people they are presumed to represent and service. If donors established funding criteria that enhanced NGO linkages to these constituents, this would go some way toward reversing this trend.

Fulfilling women's rights

As a result of the social damage caused by structural adjustment, many people have begun to focus more on poverty—and specifically on women's poverty. One of the key areas of concern of the Beijing Platform of Action is poverty and women's disproportionate share of it.

This attention to women's poverty is welcome. But it has also been limited. Many organizations have targeted particular groups—notably female-headed households, which both fails to grasp the diversity within this group, and sidesteps the more difficult and politically sensitive area of intra-household poverty. They have also cordoned women off as a vulnerable group that needs to be protected by weak and frequently non-existent safety nets. More positively, given the growing phenomenon of the working poor, among whom women are present in large numbers, some organizations have tried to organize women workers and provide a space for them to articulate their demands more forcefully.

A more fundamental issue, however, is why women are poor in the first place. More light needs to be shed on the gender aspects of impoverishment—the social and economic relations and institutions that continue to send women and men into poverty along different trajectories. If one generalization can be made, it is that women's lack of power constitutes not only an important dimension of women's disadvantage in itself, but also shapes the kinds of claims and entitlements to resources that women can mobilize.

Reducing women's poverty will therefore mean fulfilling their rights—rather than simply meeting their needs. This is an important distinction. The rights approach reformulates needs as ethical and legal norms—implying a duty on the part of those in power to provide all the means necessary to ensure that needs are met. This may not appear to take matters forward: many developing country governments argue that they lack the necessary resources, so repackaging needs as rights does little more than restate those needs more vehemently.

The advantage of asserting the issues not merely in terms of needs, but of rights, is that the bearers of rights can make official claims as citizens. Women as individuals and groups become part of the decision-making process. They are also in a stronger position to defend themselves against other powerful influences—including religious and fundamentalist groups. And they can stand against those whose macroeconomic or neo-Malthusian agendas serve to perpetuate racial, ethnic, class and gender inequities.

The sections that follow examine women's rights in three crucial areas: reproductive health, education and work.

Reproductive health rights

One of the most notable developments of the 1990s was that reproductive health rights came to be viewed more comprehensively. When women's health movements in the West first introduced the concept, they were primarily concerned with women's right to control their fertility. Women's groups in the South embraced these principles but took them further, incorporating them into a much broader vision that encompassed all of women's health needs and linked them to development.

Women's groups have rightly argued that women's reproductive health should be set in a broader context. If women cannot control their fertility and be free from sexual abuse and violence, they cannot function fully as responsible, participating members of families and communities: they cannot truly exercise citizenship. At the same time, reproductive health and well-being demand such basic conditions as clean water and decent housing. Without these, women find themselves in untenable dilemmas. Thus women who are HIV-positive must choose between breastfeeding their infants and exposing them to risk of AIDS—or bottle-feeding them and exposing them to deadly bacterial infection from contaminated drinking water (box 7.3).

Women's groups in developing countries concerned with reproductive health do not, of course, form a homogeneous bloc. They have emerged in different circumstances and have different priorities. In South Asia, for example, they have been concerned primarily with such issues as sterilization and coercion, and the promotion of long-acting hormonal contraceptives—and have always had to struggle against a donor-driven preoccupation with overpopulation. Women's groups in Latin America, on the other hand, emerged as part of broader movements for democratization, in a political climate emphasizing concepts of citizenship and rights. They have put more emphasis on women's autonomy and their rights to higher quality health services. In Africa, women's health activists have been preoccupied with issues of basic survival—in the face of high maternal and infant mortality rates and the growing menace of HIV/AIDS—as well as with controversial rights issues such as female genital mutilation.

But women's organizations all over the South have insisted that reproductive rights must be set in a broader context. They argue that there is little prospect of fulfilling women's individual rights in a generally hostile economic and social climate. A number of international networks have argued this case forcefully.

Box 7.3 – The story of Futhi

The following is an imaginary profile based on fact.

Futhi is one of the 18.5 million women worldwide, and one of the nearly 11 per cent of pregnant women using urban prenatal clinics in South Africa, who are infected by HIV. The roots of Futhi's infection start with marriage—a husband who works in the mines, is away a good deal, and has unprotected sex with prostitutes. But there has never been a question of leaving him, since she is unable to earn enough on her own to support her two children.

Thanks to South Africa's progressive reproductive health policy, Futhi has access to a caring reproductive health clinic nearby. She learned about condoms from the clinic nurse, but she was afraid to suggest them to her husband for fear he would call her promiscuous and beat her. Besides, Zulu culture tells women to accommodate their husbands' desires.

Then Futhi discovered she was pregnant and HIV-positive—and faced the dilemma of what to do. In South Africa, abortion is a woman's right for any reason during the first trimester. Nurses at the prenatal clinic have warned her she cannot breastfeed the new baby without great risk of infecting it with HIV, and there is not yet safe drinking water in her township to use for bottle feeding. She has heard there are drugs that can prevent HIV transmission to the foetus, but these drugs—made by US-based pharmaceutical companies—are too expensive for the economically pressed South African government to buy on the world market.

Faced with threats of punitive sanctions under existing patent laws, the government has not authorized the local manufacture of cheaper drugs. Even if transnational drug companies lower prices in African countries, the drugs are still likely to cost too much for Futhi, and South Africa's inadequate health care system will lack the capacity to distribute them. So advanced drugs will not protect Futhi's baby or assure her a longer life to care for her children. Apparently, abortion is her only choice. Fortunately, in South Africa, at least it is a choice.

One of the most influential has been Development Alternatives with Women for a New Era (DAWN), a network of women activists from all regions of the South. DAWN has long argued that reproductive rights can only be achieved in a supportive environment that allows women adequate housing, education, employment, property rights and legal equality, as well as freedom from physical abuse, harassment, and all forms of gender-based violence.

Reproductive rights thus require legal recognition and protection in the courts, freedom from repressive religious and traditional codes that constrain choice, and freedom from domestic violence and forced pregnancy. All these are civil and political rights. But at the same time, reproductive rights also require reliable and affordable maternal and child health services, and access to safe contraception and follow-up care, not to mention adequate nutrition to avoid a wide range of risks. All these are economic or social rights.

Women all over the world have an increasing sense of entitlement—that their rights should be upheld. One seven-country survey, by the International Reproductive Rights Research Action Group (IRRRAG), found that most respondents thought they were entitled to make their own decisions about marriage, fertility, contraception, childcare and work. However, if they wanted to fulfil these rights, they often had to act in secrecy, to evade the censure of family or neighbours, or the prohibitive laws of the state. Or they had to engage in a series of trade-offs—accepting sexual demands, say, in return for greater help with childcare. What would help them to resist abusive husbands, disrespectful doctors, and religious dictates in making their reproductive and sexual decisions? One of the most important factors appeared to be membership in a community group that took them out of their isolation—enabling them to act together both on their own behalf and that of their daughters, and on behalf of future generations.

The Programme of Action (POA) that emerged from the International Conference on Population and Development in 1994 in Cairo endorsed this vision, moving on from demographic targets and a narrow preoccupation with family planning to a broader understanding of reproductive rights—insisting that population and development strategies be based on women's empowerment, and on gender equality and equity (box 7.4).

Nevertheless, the Cairo Programme of Action also endorsed market-friendly policies that, in practice, hamper the achievement of women's reproductive rights (table 7.3) In its chapter on health, the POA recognizes the devastating impacts that structural adjustment programmes and the transition to market economies have had on health, especially among the poor. But in its implementation chapters, the POA reverts to the market-oriented policies that have actually widened disparities in income, mortality and morbidity. The POA urges governments to improve the cost-effectiveness, cost-recovery and quality of services by reintroducing user fees. It also asks them to "promote the role of the private sector in service delivery and in the production and distribution...of high-quality reproductive health and family planning commodities"; and to "review legal, regulatory and import policies ...that unnecessarily prevent or restrict the greater involvement of the private sector".

More significantly, in the 1990s governments have started to implement health sector reforms designed by the World Bank and other donors, with the aim of improving the cost-effectiveness of public health systems. Efforts to address crises in the financing and delivery of health care have taken different forms, but they have a number of common elements, including the pursuit of cost-effectiveness, the introduction of user charges, decentralization,

Table 7.3 – A feminist report card on the Cairo Programme of Action

New achievements	Remaining gaps and challenges
• Shift from population control to "reproductive rights and reproductive health" paradigm; comprehensive definition of reproductive health including sexual health, integrated with primary health services for all (Paras. 7.2, 8.8).	• Access to safe, legal abortion not recognized as part of reproductive health and rights; deference to national laws; where illegal, requirement of treatment for complications only (Para. 8.25).
• Definition of "reproductive rights" as part of "already recognized international human rights"; includes "the right to attain the highest standard of reproductive and sexual health", "the *means* to do so", "informed choice" and freedom from "discrimination, coercion and violence" (an end to targets and incentives—Paras. 7.3, 7.12, 7.22).	• Reliance on private market mechanisms (cost-recovery schemes, user fees, health reform to assure cost-effectiveness); increased involvement of private sector and deregulation, rather than measures for global macroeconomic restructuring, to generate resources and assure accountability (Paras. 8.8, 13.22, 15.15, 15.18).
• Recognition of adolescent rights to all reproductive and sexual health services, including "sexual education" and full protection against unwanted pregnancy, HIV/AIDS and other STDs (Paras. 7.2, 7.37, 7.45, 7.47).	• Ambiguous language about "the rights, duties and responsibilities of parents" could compromise right to confidentiality; inadequate resource allocations; absence of multi-sectoral integration (e.g., health and education sectors).
• "Gender Equality, Equity and Empowerment of Women" as a separate chapter; recognition of "the empowerment and autonomy of women and the improvement of their political, social, economic and health status" as "a highly important end in itself" (Para. 4.1).	• No resource allocations or specified amounts for any aspect of sustainable development, primary health care, women's empowerment and improved status, poverty alleviation or environment (Ch. 13).
• Recognition of all forms of violence against women, including FGM, and measures to end them as integral to reproductive health (Paras. 4.4, 4.9, 4.22, 4.23, 7.3, 7.6, 7.17).	• Treatment of "women" as a unitary category; failure to recognize racial, ethnic and class divisions in access to resources and services, and in health risks (except HIV/AIDS).
• Shared male responsibility for childcare, housework, and reproductive and sexual health as essential to gender equality (Ch. 4-C).	• No concrete strategies for implementation, no resource allocations.
• Encouragement of governments to expand and strengthen "grassroots, community-based and activist groups for women" (Para. 4.12).	• No resource allocations or specified targets.
• Recognition of the "diversity of family forms," including female-headed households, and the need for government policies to benefit all, especially the most vulnerable (Paras. 5.1, 5.2).	• Failure to expressly recognize affirmative sexual rights along with reproductive rights, including right to diversity of sexual expression and orientation.
• Definition of reproductive health services as comprising not only family planning but also prenatal and obstetric care, infertility treatment, prevention and treatment of HIV/AIDS, STDs and gynecological cancers (Paras. 7.6, 8.8).	• Specification of precise monetary target ($17 billion) but *imbalance* in resource allocations: twice as much specified for "family planning component" as for all of "reproductive health component" put together (Paras.13.14–13.15).
• Target date of 2015 for reproductive health services, increasing life expectancy, reducing infant and child mortality and reducing maternal mortality (Paras. 7.6, 7.16, 8.5, 8.16, 8.21).	• Inadequate allocation of resources to reproductive health component; no resources directed to necessary infrastructure, poverty alleviation and enabling conditions.

Source: Petchesky, 1999

and greater participation from private companies and NGOs. Many of these reforms have been disastrous for poor women. Cost recovery schemes in particular have prevented many women from attending prenatal clinics. In Zimbabwe, NGOs claim that this has led to a fivefold increase in maternal mortality rates. In Ukraine and Bulgaria, women who cannot afford to pay market prices for contraceptives are resorting to risky abortions. And while decentralization should offer better access to services, this assumes that local centres will be given the necessary resources.

Of course, no one wants health systems that are inefficient and wasteful. On the other hand, it is surely wrong to have a narrow definition of cost-effectiveness as virtually the only criterion of success, and to apply user fees as a standard prescription. The World Bank's *World Development Reports* for 1996 and 1997 reiterated the cost-effectiveness mantra. They endorsed the goal of ensuring universal access to basic health services, but argued that the best way to achieve this was through privatization. They encouraged governments to transfer less-efficient hospitals to private markets, and to transfer other services to private subcontractors whom users would pay in cash or vouchers. Whatever "universal access" means in this context, it clearly does not mean universal rights or universal coverage. Instead, it assumes that all but the poorest will be able to pay for treatment—either from their own pockets or from private insurance.

Private providers are thus positioned to make money out of what was formerly the public social sector—and derive much of the income from public revenues. Most citizens then have to buy social services, leaving those who cannot afford to pay—the most vulnerable—to be protected by often non-existent safety nets. In other words, health care splits into a two-tier system: one part for the better-off "health consumers", for whom it becomes just another commodity; and another part for the poor, for whom it becomes either another form of public assistance, or just an unattainable luxury.

These changes have important implications for reproductive health care. In population and development strategies, the centre of gravity has moved away from crude population control and the distribution of contraceptives toward a radical restructuring of health delivery systems. Those in the driver's seat are no longer the demographers, but the health and development economists. They present women with a more complex scenario. On one hand, they seek to empower women by engaging women's NGOs as providers and monitors of services. On the other hand, they disempower women by cutting away at the state services on which they depend.

Women's NGOs can play an important role

Box 7.4 – Gender equality and gender equity

The terms equality and equity are often used interchangeably. But they are not the same. They reflect an underlying tension within feminist circles, between those who want to emphasize the importance of women having the same conditions as men, and those who prefer to emphasize—and celebrate—women's differences from men.

Gender justice demands both equality and equity. Equality means equivalence between men and women—in economic resources, legal rights, political participation and personal relations. Equity means a full recognition of women's specific needs—whether these arise from historical patterns of gender bias, biological differences or social inequality.

both as service providers and as civil society advocates who scrutinize health providers. In some cases they can function as partners of the state, providing training and advice. But they should not take over the state's responsibilities for the overall regulation and assurance of basic health care. Nor should they cede their independent critical voice. The most successful models of national-level implementation of sexual and reproductive health programmes—in Brazil and South Africa, for example—are in countries that have strong state institutions that subscribe to principles of social solidarity and justice. These countries also have strong civil society organizations that push the state forward and call it to account. In these circumstances, women's NGOs can both co-operate with and critique government policies. In many other countries, where the political conditions are different, this combination is more difficult to achieve.

Women's education rights

Everyone accepts the importance of education, and the world made enormous progress in this area during the second half of the twentieth century. Between 1950 and 1998, the global literacy rate rose from 45 to 80 per cent. Sustaining these increases remains a challenge, as many children in school in developing countries are first-generation learners, and hence their enrolment is vulnerable to changes in national or parental circumstances. Moreover, that still leaves 880 million people illiterate—of whom two thirds are women. The worst problems are in sub-Saharan Africa and South

Table 7.4 – Primary and secondary education by region

	Primary school						Secondary school	
	Gross enrolment ratio[a] 1990–97		Net enrolment ratio[b] 1990–96		Net attendance[c] (%) 1990–98		Gross enrolment ratio[a] 1990–96	
	male	female	male	female	male	female	male	female
Sub-Saharan Africa	**82**	**67**	**59**	**51**	**61**	**57**	**27**	**22**
Middle East and North Africa	**95**	**82**	**85**	**77**	**85**	**75**	**64**	**54**
South Asia	**105**	**81**	**65**	**50**	**74**	**62**	**52**	**33**
East Asia and Pacific	**117**	**115**	**99**	**99**	**93**	**93**	**67**	**61**
Latin America and Caribbean	**107**	**104**	**87**	**87**	**89**	**90**	**48**	**52**
Developing countries	***105***	***92***	***86***	***81***	***81***	***75***	***55***	***46***
CEE[d]/CIS and Baltic states	**99**	**98**	**93**	**92**	**-**	**-**	**82**	**82**
Industrialized countries	***104***	***103***	***97***	***97***	**-**	**-**	***105***	***107***
World	***104***	***94***	***88***	***84***	***81***	***75***	***61***	***54***

Notes: [a] The number of children enrolled in a level (primary or secondary), regardless of age, divided by the population of the age group that officially corresponds to the same level. [b] The number of children enrolled in primary school who belong to the age group that officially corresponds to primary schooling, divided by the total population of the same age group. [c] Percentage of children in the age group that officially corresponds to primary schooling who attend primary school. [d] Central and Eastern Europe.

Source: UNICEF, 2000

Asia, where literacy rates are below 60 per cent.

These problems are likely to persist. Table 7.4, which shows the latest data for school enrolment, reveals these considerable disparities between regions—but the figures may mask some wide disparities between countries. Thus, within sub-Saharan Africa, Botswana's net primary school enrolment ratio was 81 per cent while Ethiopia's was 28 per cent. Similarly in Latin America, although the overall primary school attendance level is above 90 per cent, in Guatemala it is only 58 per cent. Within countries there are also disparities between social groups. Thus in India the participation rate of rural children lags 20 percentage points behind that of urban children. And as table 7.4 illustrates, although gender gaps have been narrowing, significant sex disparities remain—particularly in South Asia and sub-Saharan Africa. These are two of the poorest regions of the world, and many of the difficulties that girls face in obtaining an adequate education are clearly intensified by poverty. Indeed, the closing gender gap in some countries of sub-Saharan Africa is attributed to a decline in the enrolment of boys and only a marginal increase in the participation of girls.

Why poor girls get less education

A number of reasons have been put forward to explain why girls confront difficulties in receiving adequate education in the poorest countries. Some are based on pressures within the household. Others have more to do with the kind of education on offer—which may be more accessible or useful to boys than girls.

The most crucial decisions about education take place within households—and are the result of complex bargaining between men, women and children. Negotiations will necessarily involve a mixture of cultural, economic and social factors—all of which overlap and are difficult to separate. Despite their importance, relatively little is known about these decisions: while researchers are free to enter schools, they have much less access to the intra-household arena. However, it is possible to identify some of the factors involved.

Many are linked to social attitudes and culture. In some societies, parents—judging what they see to be the best interest of their daughter—may deliberately cut short her education if they think it will undermine her future marriage prospects. A prospective husband may not want an educated wife, whom he would find less easy to control. Thus parents may see it as more advantageous for a girl to stay at home and prepare for the responsibilities of motherhood.

But more often families do not deliberately reject education; they make an implicit or explicit trade-off. Although parents might want their daughter to go to school, they have to weigh the benefits against the immediate financial costs. The costs may be those of transport, say, or clothes or books. Or they may be the opportunity cost of losing their child's labour at home. While these judgements affect both boys and girls, it is the girl who often loses out. Even at an early age, a daughter may be more valuable at home: she can perform more useful tasks than her brothers within the household, such as cooking or cleaning or caring for even younger siblings.

In urban areas, where the pressures are different, it is the boys—who are easier to employ in the informal sector—who may be kept from school. In a number of Latin American countries, this means that boys' enrolment in secondary education is lower than girls'. But there is also an interaction between work and school. In Latin American cities for example, many children work as a way of paying for school.

The economic trade-off may also be a more strategic one—judging which child will offer better long-term returns. Even when primary education is free, there are generally additional costs for books or clothing that represent significant expenditures for poor families. Again the girl may lose out, because even if education does not diminish her chances of finding a husband, it might be considered wasteful if she will soon be leaving the family home. In this case, it might be better to have an educated son who can provide for parents in their old age. Yet this may not necessarily mean educating the boy: parents may well decide that their daughter is more likely than their son to maintain closer links with them after she leaves home.

In addition to economic considerations, parents may also worry about their daughter's security—particularly after puberty. The distance between home and school may be cause for concern. And parents may also be troubled if she is being taught by male teachers, or if there are inadequate toilet facilities. Some of these doubts are grounded in fears of sexual abuse—but parents can be equally sensitive to the innuendo and rumour that might undermine their daughter's marriage prospects. All of these worries will tend to reduce a girl's chances of going to secondary school.

Decisions about whether a child should go to school become more critical during times of economic crisis. Families desperate for survival will need as many hands at work as possible. And when governments are strapped for cash, they may choose to starve schools of funds or make extra charges for tuition or books.

The factors influencing these decisions may change over time. Thus if different jobs become available that make it more worthwhile to educate girls, parents may come to different conclusions. Data from the Philippines and Thailand, for example, suggest that the expansion of employment opportunities for girls is encouraging parents to invest more in their education. But labour market changes can also be damaging. An OECD/UNESCO survey of literacy levels in seven industrialized countries revealed that, on average, over 20 per cent of adults have low literacy and numeracy skills. This reflects not just the quality of schooling, but also of the lack of "fit" between the skills developed through schooling and the skill requirements of particular work and cultural environments. The declining enrolment in formal education in the countries of Central and Eastern Europe and the Commonwealth of Independent States (CIS) is also being viewed with some alarm.

Donor-driven education reforms

The Jomtien Conference in Thailand in 1990 was a landmark for international education policy. It emphasized the need for greater attention to basic education, identifying this as one of the most important ways of promoting human rights, fighting poverty and empowering women. Basic education includes preschool, primary and adult education.

The 1980s and 1990s, however, were also years of economic crisis and structural adjustment programmes—which affected governments' and parents' abilities to improve children's educational opportunities. The majority of African governments that adopted structural adjustment programmes reduced the proportion of GNP they spent on education.

In principle, the governments of developing countries accepted the importance of educating girls, but in practice most of the impetus for change has come from donors—multilateral and bilateral. The most decisive pronouncements on education have come from the World Bank. For example, the Bank has been a major participant in a research programme measuring "rates of return on education" (ROREs)—and has drawn some policy conclusions from it that have major implications for resource allocation to and within the education sector.

The World Bank's policy directives have had two main parts. The first was a concentration on primary education, which was thought to offer the best value for money. This was partly because primary education was cheaper:

the same sum of money could cover more pupils than when spent at secondary or tertiary levels.

But the basis of the World Bank's policy conclusions has been challenged on several points. The evidence for the higher rates of return on primary education compared to secondary education in sub-Saharan Africa, for example, is ambiguous and there are many counter-examples. Moreover, the analysis has tended to be static: rates of return calculated for one period may not be valid under different economic conditions. In fact, rates of return for primary education in sub-Saharan Africa have tended to fall during periods of economic crisis. Thus an education policy based on rates of return can produce a tragic situation in which educational institutions are starved of funds because of their apparently low rates of return—as measured at a particular point in time.

Some of the benefits of primary education were economic: an educated population would boost national productivity. Others were concerned with family welfare—particularly health and fertility. Educating a girl was thought to be especially valuable, since when she became a mother she could improve her family's standards of hygiene, nutrition and health. Just as important, an educated mother was expected to have a smaller family. She would be likely to marry later and know more about contraception. And she would have a better chance of working outside the home—which would decrease the time available for looking after children. Primary education would thus result in smaller families.

Governments who accepted this analysis tried to achieve universal access to education—and to make sure that girls had the same opportunities as boys. Thus Bangladesh, for example, introduced a Food for Education Project. It gave poor households that sent their children to school 15 kilograms of wheat per student—this, not surprisingly, resulted in a sudden boost in enrolment.

The Bank's second main policy thrust in education has been concerned with efficiency and managerial reform. As in most other aspects of public sector expenditure, governments and donors have been looking for ways to make education systems more cost-effective. First, there have been efforts to decentralize education, shifting more control over schools to regional and local levels—on the grounds that local people can monitor activities more effectively. Second, there have been moves to privatize education systems, particularly at the secondary and tertiary levels. Third, within the public sector there have been attempts to introduce or increase user fees. These fees can take many forms: in Nicaragua, for example, schools charge rents on textbooks. In Zambia, parents are expected to contribute to the parent-teacher association and the school fund as well as paying for books.

These two main parts of the Bank's policy directives—maximizing access while trying to operate more cost-effectively—are to some extent contradictory. Access is usually diminished by user fees, which deter the poorest parents. So it is not surprising that the results are mixed. For the developing countries as a whole, there does seem to have been an increase in access, at least in terms of primary enrolment. But drop-out rates remain high, and there is also evidence of sharp differentiation across social and economic categories.

Moreover, as chapter 2 indicates, developing country governments wanting to prove to donors and international creditors that they are spending more on primary education—at a time when budgetary resources are not increasing—have reduced the coverage and quality of other services like secondary education and vocational training. This trend is particularly worrying given that the availability of good-quality, secondary education—that is physically and socially accessible—has been found to influence primary school participation, particularly for girls. And ironically, it has been shown that the much-publicized benefits of female education, in particular fertility decline, tend to set in at higher levels of schooling. In other words, primary schooling alone does not produce significant effects.

Quality lags behind quantity

Increased access to education is vital for girls. But there is little evidence that education on its own will improve women's situation. It may simply improve their capacity to become more efficient mothers and housewives—or even their capacity to play a subordinate role. Women in industrialized countries have long had equal educational access but, as the first section of this chapter shows, this has yet to register in terms of political power.

Part of the problem lies in schools themselves, which tend to reflect the values of the wider society. They are designed to produce another generation of citizens similar to the previous one. As a result, many girls find they are being schooled for subordination. Textbooks and lessons still bear gender stereotypes. Teachers—both male and female—often give more attention to boys and distribute responsibilities in school in gender-biased ways. Girls may routinely do housekeeping tasks that boys would regard as a punishment. In Zimbabwe, for example, one study found that teachers felt it was their duty to guide pupils toward "gender-appropriate" behaviours. And in textbooks, women are presented as housewives who cook and clean and nag; the father takes the important decisions, while the mother is just the supporter.

Women may also find that non-formal education has many of the same defects. The delegates at Jomtien committed themselves to improving standards of informal education. But this has received far less attention from donors—and minimal funding. Most of the work has been left to NGOs. Generally, they have emphasized literacy training, information on health and nutrition, and activities for income generation—often reflecting many of the same gender biases as formal education, assuming that women need to be prepared for a role as "helper". Similar biases are evident in vocational training, where women tend to be confined to such areas as sewing or cookery.

But just as education can perpetuate existing gender roles, it can also help to subvert them. A number of positive examples have emerged in South Asia. In India, the Shikshakarmi Programme of the Rajasthan government has opened up access for girls in remote areas by making schools more flexible in their timing and location—and it has also helped enhance the status of women. In Bangladesh, BRAC is one of the best-known examples of a non-formal programme that draws women into relevant and useful education. But there have been many others. The REFLECT approach to women's literacy—developed in Uganda, Bangladesh and El Salvador—not only promotes basic literacy but also enables women to reflect on their own circumstances and take individual or collective action. Nevertheless, recent education reforms driven by public austerity measures have struck at teachers, rather than supporting them as the lynchpins of efforts to improve the quality of education. Demoralized teachers and systems starved of funds can rarely make for innovative education programmes.

Women's economic rights

One of the benefits of education for women should be to enhance their economic entitlements. Women are certainly more likely to be working than ever before. Between the 1950s and the end of the 1990s, the proportion of women aged 20–59 who were in the labour force increased from around one third to one half. The current participation rates by region range from 14 per cent in North Africa to

76 per cent in East and Central Europe (figure 7.2). To some extent the increase in participation is a statistical artefact—it reflects better ways of recording seasonal, unpaid family and casual wage labour.

But it does also reflect a number of real changes. First, more women must now work to ensure family survival—in the face of declining real wages and the increased monetary cost of subsistence resulting from cutbacks in both public services and subsidies for staple foods. In an increasing proportion of two-adult households, both partners now work. Data from Latin America suggest that in at least one quarter of urban households, the female partner works—and contributes, on average, around 30

Mark Edwards, Still Pictures

Home life. Chattera village, India

per cent of the household's income. Without women's income, the poverty indices in most Latin American countries would rise by 10 to 20 per cent.

A second factor is the increase in the number of women-headed households—in which women are required to meet the monetary cost of household survival from their own labour.

A third reason is that there has been a greater demand for women workers in particular sectors of the economy that have experienced long-term growth. Many industries employing a high proportion of women have expanded rapidly in response to globalization. Much of this is low-skilled manufacturing—notably in garments, footwear and electronic products—and "non-traditional" agricultural products such as cut flowers, seasonal fruits and vegetables. At the same time, with the increasing emphasis on cost-cutting competitiveness, firms have been searching for ways to reduce their labour costs. This has often meant changes in the structure of the labour market—away from formal, full-time employment with entitlements, such as unemployment and sickness insurance, pensions and maternity benefits. Instead, people must work in more flexible ways—whether part-time, temporary or casual. And this is more likely to involve women. In most industrialized countries, women make up 70 to 80 per cent of part-time employees. Women also make up the majority of home-workers. In Argentina more than four fifths of waged home-workers in the clothing and footwear industries are women.

In many cases, women's participation has increased at the expense of men's. In half the developing countries for which data were available, over the period 1975–95 the female participation rate rose while the male rate fell. The global labour force has become more female—rising from 36 per cent in 1960 to 40 per cent by 1997. Is labour force participation translated into economic rights?

Opportunities for work and income have transformed the lives of millions of women. Increased levels of education and changing methods of production mean that women are more likely to be found in positions of greater responsibility. But there is still some way to go. Because of increasing labour market flexibility, it has been very difficult for women to translate labour market participation into economic entitlements—which can be conceived of as rights—through engaging in paid employment.

The conditions of work in sectors where women are now working are far from adequate. In export manufacturing and agribusiness, women rarely have contracts of employment that guarantee adequate job security, training opportunities, unemployment and sickness insurance, or pensions. In globalized agribusiness, for example, advances in communications, transportation and refrigeration have made it possible for corporations to supply Northern markets with fruit and vegetable

Figure 7.2 – Women's labour force participation, 1980s and 1990s

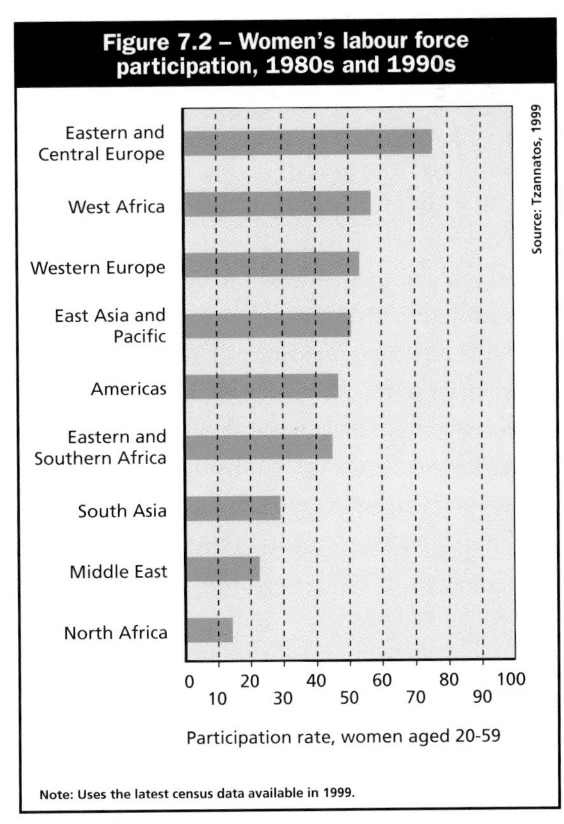

Source: Tzannatos, 1999

Note: Uses the latest census data available in 1999.

products from the South. These products range from Chilean kiwis to South African grapes and Colombian flowers. In Chile, for example, women in the export fruit sector work on temporary contracts—or no contracts at all—and so cannot accrue sufficient time in a job to have entitlement to maternity benefits, sickness leave and other social security provisions. And there is ample evidence of women suffering sexual harassment.

Women working in the feminized manufacturing sector fare little better. Many face health hazards—both physical and mental. The work is often repetitive, monotonous and fast, and it involves long working hours and exposes women workers to carcinogens. This very often leaves young workers prematurely "burned out" in the labour process. And in the case of clerical work, such as data entry, for industrialized countries there is considerable evidence of muscular-skeletal disorders, eyesight injuries, stress and fatigue, skin conditions and reproductive problems.

In recent years there has also been some controversy over the issue of gender wage gaps. Some observers claim that men's and women's earnings have converged. But such conclusions can only be regarded as tentative, given the poor quality of national statistical evidence—which does not endorse the hypothesis of general wage convergence. Moreover, where there has been some evidence of convergence—in Canada during 1990–91, for example—it has resulted from male wages dropping rather than female wages rising. In other words, men's and women's wages may have converged, but this has happened through a process of harmonizing down—hardly the ideal way to achieve gender equality.

The precarious nature of women's work also means that they are more likely to be unemployed. In the industrialized countries, unemployment rates for women can be 50 to 100 per cent higher than those for men. In developing countries the trend is less consistent. In the newly industrialized economies of Asia, for example, unemployment rates are higher for men than women, but in South Asia women fare much worse than men.

The increase in women's economic participation in the global economy has thus been paralleled by a deregulation in the conditions of work and in work-related entitlements. This relationship must challenge the view that increased participation in global markets brings those outside "economic citizenship" into a situation where their economic rights can be exercised and entitlements accessed through labour market activity.

Work and empowerment

The opportunity to work outside the home has opened up new vistas for millions of women. Even the difficult and low-paid work in the garment factories of Bangladesh has transformed the prospects of the million or so women now working there. Every morning the streets of Dhaka are crowded with confident young women striding to work.

But to what extent does this constitute empowerment? If women are bringing wages into the home, this should give them a stronger bargaining position. In some instances this does happen: women who are earning wages have been able to renegotiate the terms of their domestic relationships, and some women have been able to walk out of, or not enter into, unsatisfactory relationships. But not always. A number of other studies in South Asia have found that many women still hand their wages over to their husbands.

Moreover, even if women wage earners have increased scope for manoeuvre at home, they may be subject to different patriarchal controls in the factory. This helps keep women workers poorly paid and vastly unprotected in jobs that are sometimes dangerous.

From a gender perspective, the most persistent problem is the lack of connection between production and reproduction. Market economies assume that new workers appear costlessly at the factory gates—already healthy, nourished and educated. All the employer must do is pay for that day's labour. While in industrialized countries the state takes some of the responsibility for social reproduction, in developing countries the task remains primarily one for women. The women working in the garment factories in Dhaka have plenty to do when they get home: a survey in 1990–91 found that they were not only undertaking more hours of paid work than men—56 hours per week compared to men's 53 hours—they were also doing 31 hours per week of unpaid household work, compared with only 13 hours done by men.

STRATEGIES FOR ACHIEVING ECONOMIC RIGHTS

Men and women have very different experiences in a market economy. Fortunately, there is now much greater recognition of this—and there have been initiatives at many levels to address the related problems. Women's groups have been lobbying to ensure that gender issues are raised in national and international institutions. Women in Development in Europe is a group that has been pressing for gender issues to be raised in trade negotiations. And a number of countries, including Australia, Barbados, Canada and South Africa, now have Women's Budget Statements to review national budgets for their impact on women.

There have also been greater efforts to organize women workers. Women and men alike have been affected by the weakening of trade unions. This is partly due to the more flexible nature of employment, which is less likely to produce a stable workforce. But it has also been deliberate policy to exclude trade unions from many of the factories where women work. Women make up around 90 per cent of the workforce in the 850 or so Export Processing Zones around the world, where they are generally denied the rights to organize.

Although trade unions have had limited success, there has been support from women's NGOs. They have been active, for example, in the *maquila* factories of Mexico and Central America, which assemble final products from imported goods and parts. In Mexico, Women Group X offers women *maquila* workers education and various types of support, including protection from sexual abuse. A similar centre has been established to support young women workers in Lamphun in northern Thailand.

Women's groups have also made efforts to organize women working in the informal sector. One of the best known-models is the Self-Employed Women's Association (SEWA), in India, which is concerned with its members' productive and reproductive roles—providing services for individual traders as well as child-care and maternity services. Likewise, the Kenya Women Workers Organization brings together women outside traditional trade union structures. One of the most important developments for individual women entrepreneurs has been the extension of micro-credit services. The Grameen Bank is the highest-profile example, but a high proportion of NGOs and international development agencies are now promoting micro-credit for low-income women based on similar systems of group solidarity. These may improve women's economic situation—but very often, with their inflexible repayment schedules, they can also add to women's stress and expose them to harassment from family members (who may be using the loans) and those dispensing and recovering the loans. Still, it does appear that the collective aspects of these services—which bring women out of their narrow domestic environments—do improve women's well-being and give them greater autonomy.

It is vital to improve the opportunities and rewards for working women. But in a world where many social service duties are being assigned to communities and families, the crucial issue is still that of women's responsibility for family care. Until there is a greater recognition of the links between work and social reproduction, women's greater participation in the workforce will simply reflect and perpetuate existing gender biases. Fortunately, as more women have become regular labour force participants, there is greater recognition of the importance of the range of reproductive and caring services they provide. Loss of "economic citizenship" while absent from the labour force to fulfil the role of care-giver has therefore become more transparent. To overcome the existing bias in systems of social protection, "care" must become a dimension of citizenship—entailing rights equal to those associated with employment.

A counter-alliance for women

Women's groups and NGOs have become increasingly visible and vocal at both national and international levels. Their commitment and expertise shaped the character of the UN conferences of the 1990s. At the same time, the conferences themselves, and the UN system, have provided a vital forum and a framework through which a transnational women's movement coalesced. At the national level, democratization has meant that the state now speaks the language of gender equality and equity, and there are more opportunities for interaction between women's advocates in civil society and gender bureaucrats inside public administration.

Yet despite advances in women's formal rights, a number of persistent problems limit the degree to which these rights result in tangible gains for the vast majority of women citizens. Economic crises and market-driven policies are in ascendance everywhere and cast a shadow over these achievements. As a result, formal rights have not been matched by substantive rights or, for most women, by an improvement in their quality of life.

The restructuring of the social sectors in particular imposes a disproportionate burden on working women—especially those from the poorer social strata—who are forced to stretch their already long working days in order to compensate for public sector shortfalls.

Even the proliferation of transnational NGO activity in recent years has a sobering underside—hazards such as bureaucratism and donor dependence. Women's groups and NGOs have not escaped such dangers. If they want to maintain their legitimacy and their claim to be representative of women's interests, women's NGOs and their leaders will have to strengthen their ties to women's grassroots social movements and community-based organizations. At the same time, women's NGOs also need to work more closely with other development NGOs and movements that are attempting to change global macroeconomic policies and structures. This would improve understanding of the linkages between personal and social rights—especially for women—and also form a stronger force for social change.

CHAPTER 8

Sustaining development

Crowded streets, Dhaka, Bangladesh

Mark Edwards, Still Pictures

Development agencies and governments now claim to be pursuing people-centred sustainable development. The rhetoric may have changed; the practice seems familiar.

Two core themes came together in the 1990s to create a more ambitious development agenda. The first was sustainable development. This term was widely adopted following the Brundtland Report in 1987 and encapsulated the need to protect the environment for the current and future generations—an imperative echoed at the Earth Summit in Rio in 1992.

A second major theme of the 1990s was human development—elaborated in the UNDP's *Human Development Reports*. These reports insisted that the primary purpose of development was not to boost economic growth but to improve people's lives, and that the best way to do so was to expand the choices available to them—to ensure that they had the capacity and the opportunity to shape their own futures.

By the time of the Social Summit in 1995, these ideas had been brought together—as sustainable human development or as people-centred sustainable development, or in any number of other ways. The exact combination is probably less significant than the general intention—to argue that economic growth should not be allowed to degrade the environment; that it should be the kind of growth that benefits the world's poorest people; and that local participation should shape development programmes and projects.

Development agencies accepting these principles would have to operate in a different way. First, they would need a broader vision. They would have to set aside their narrow, sectoral fixations on population, say, or infrastructure or food production. Instead they would have to be alert to the ways in which all these issues and others form a dynamic and integrated whole. Second, they would need a different way of working. Rather than preparing top-down, central master plans, they would have to be more responsive to local needs and concerns, and co-operate closely with communities and the disadvantaged—letting them set the priorities and facilitate project implementation. All in all, they would work in a more integrated fashion—constantly aware of the complex linkages between economy, society and environment.

This proposed change of direction has yielded a fine new crop of development jargon. Most agency documentation is now peppered with such terms as empowerment, participation, integrated conservation and development, community-based resource management or sustainable livelihoods. Difficult enough to say, but even more demanding to perform. This chapter assesses progress in four areas where initiatives associated with people-centred sustainable development have been prominent: urban planning, agriculture, water management and forest conservation. It also identifies some of the main constraints that make it difficult for development agencies to practise what they preach.

Sustainable cities

Many of the most pressing social and environmental problems are to be found in cities. In the industrialized countries, three quarters of the population lives in urban areas, and developing countries are moving rapidly in the same direction—74 per cent of Latin American and Caribbean populations already live in urban areas. Africa and Asia have further to go, but one third of their populations are now urban. Globally, 60 per cent of the world's population will live in towns and cities by 2025.

Although cities in developing countries are growing from natural population increase, this is boosted by rapid immigration from rural areas. New arrivals often settle in slums and squatter settlements. Despite the squalor of slums, most people consider this to be an improvement over rural life. Their new homes may be more crowded and hazardous, but their location also offers some forms of security. In extreme circumstances, city dwellers are more likely to find food and medical care—particularly important for women and infants, who are much less likely to die in cities as a result of childbirth. People in cities also have more diverse opportunities for work, and are less likely to experience extreme poverty than those in rural areas. Beyond the advantages of today, there is also the promise of tomorrow.

In the industrialized countries a century ago, many cities grew more slowly. Some managed to create new forms of social solidarity as communities grew up around factories and workplaces, and people came together in trade unions and tenants' groups. But the mushrooming cities in the developing countries are expanding in very different circumstances. Few of the new migrants to Jakarta or Lima can expect to find formal employment when they arrive, or to live or work in stable communities. Even in modern industrial São Paulo, 43 per cent of the population earns its living in the informal sector.

These and other conditions mean that some city dwellers are difficult to organize. Usually they live in one part of the city and work in another. And they may not be permanent residents. For example, rural men come to find work during the agricultural slack season. And people may only come for short periods.

Another difference today is that the poorest communities in many mega-cities of the developing world are less likely to be found crowded in inner-city tenements. Often the poor live on the urban periphery, sometimes in vastly expanded "villages" that are effectively cities in their own right.

Local Agenda 21

The Rio conference considered ways to achieve sustainable development in cities, and spelled out the priorities in Chapter 28 of *Agenda 21*—known as Local Agenda 21. In order to promote this, a new international NGO was created, the International Council for Local Environmental Initiatives (ICLEI).

This has stimulated a wide range of activities. An ICLEI survey conducted in 1996 found that more than 1,800 local governments in 64 countries had Local Agenda 21 activities. Most of these were in industrialized countries that had specific Local Agenda 21 campaigns already under way. But campaigns had also been started, or were about to start, in a number of developing countries, including Bolivia, Brazil, China, Colombia, Malawi, Peru, the Republic of Korea and South Africa.

What has all this achieved? Not enough. One of the problems has been conceptual. Many people believe that the key to success is better urban environmental management—what has been called the "brown agenda". They have assumed that, when combined with more democratic governance, this will automatically lead to sustainable development. But this is not the case. Catalytic converters for cars, for example, may result in cleaner air but do nothing to reduce energy consumption, and may even increase it. And if communities become more adept at waste disposal than at recycling, they will make their environment more pleasant but no more sustainable.

In terms of their use of non-renewable resources, most cities in the South are already probably more sustainable than those in the North, where people consume at much higher levels. But they have done little to enhance their sustainability. Local authorities and development organizations have understandably concentrated on the most pressing issues, such as improving water supplies and managing solid waste. They cloak these programmes in contemporary green language but do little to further sustainability.

Nor has there been any consistent success in promoting wider participation. While there are many variations on what type of procedure should be followed to promote planning and management of urban sustainable development, two key points are supposed to be adhered to: the planning process should be participatory, and responsibility should be shared between public, private and community interests. In many countries there are two very different types of participatory process. First, there are initiatives dominated by middle-class citizens. In cities of Southeast Asia, for example, the middle classes have become increasingly vocal, determined to break with the autocratic past and play a stronger role in local government. But these initiatives tend to focus narrowly on the quality of life in middle-class neighbourhoods and have little if any relation to issues of poverty or the wider city context.

Second, there are community development projects in poorer neighbourhoods. This is evident in the Philippines, where communities have been concerned with water supply and sanitation and the difficulties of land tenure. Such initiatives tend to involve poor communities assisted by NGOs, and sometimes by international agencies or local government. But, unlike middle-class groups, poor communities are not usually encouraged to get involved in urban political processes.

Few of these initiatives have had much impact on local government or the private sector. In fact, in poorer countries local government itself has scarcely been in a position to plan or control the development of cities. As earlier chapters have indicated, public spending has been constrained by structural adjustment programmes and policies of state sector reform, which have tended to heighten the vulnerability of the urban poor. Participatory urban planning and management may be helped by global efforts to promote decentralization, but broad-based participation is still often blocked by local political systems based on patronage.

If cities in developing countries are to promote sustainability, they will need to overcome these divisions and the fragmented and piecemeal approaches they encourage. This will require stronger civic cultures. But fostering civic cultures takes time, longer certainly than most development agencies customarily contemplate. Local projects—such as health programmes or efforts to clean up the neighbourhood—can build confidence in the usefulness of working together. But real progress will require more assertive civic movements.

In addition to adopting horizons longer than two or three years, agencies will also need to foster a new politics of cohesion and collaboration. Poor communities have to move beyond self-help and participate more coherently and forcefully both in local government and in the wider urban political process. Until they do, problems of local government corruption, divisive patronage politics and poorly designed and executed programmes are likely to persist.

International development agencies have little experience with this kind of integrated urban development. But there are some precedents—for example, those involving USAID, Swiss and German technical co-operation, the World Bank Metropolitan Environmental Improvement Programme and the UNCHS Sustainable Cities Programme. A recent assessment of aid strategies since the 1996 City Summit shows, however, that while most donors now recognize the importance of urban development, it is generally not a priority in their aid programmes. Many have urban projects, but they often remain isolated and limited activities. There has been no sign of the anticipated increase in international aid for urban development nor of projects that promote sustainable development planning and management.

Sustainable agriculture

The world has proved remarkably successful at food production. Growing enough to feed 6 billion people is quite an achievement. But distribution is uneven and many of these people go hungry. Although data remain very approximate, the latest estimates from FAO suggest that the developing countries have around 800 million undernourished people.

As figure 8.1 indicates, the greatest numbers of undernourished are to be found in Asia and the Pacific. But more than half the countries there have managed to reduce the numbers over the last two decades. Sub-Saharan Africa, which has almost a quarter of the developing world's hungry people, has been less successful. Only 10 African countries made progress over the period 1980–96, while 28 lost ground.

Malnutrition results from a combination of factors. Often young children are not fed properly with food that is available in the household, and many suffer from parasites and ill health. In some cases there may be an absolute shortage of food in a particular country or area. But more commonly the problem is that people cannot afford to buy food. Is this situation likely to change in the future? There are various schools of thought:

- ***Business-as-usual optimists***—They argue that food supply will always expand to meet demand. Farmers will acquire more sophisticated technology and can, if necessary, bring more land under cultivation. Over the past decade there seems to have been no shortage of food, and prices have been falling—down 50 per cent for most commodities.
- ***Environmental pessimists***—They follow a neo-Malthusian line, believing that demand will inevitably outstrip supply. Degradation of land and other resources will reduce yields, while more people will be eating beef from grain-fed cattle. The only answer is to reduce the number of consumers by controlling population.
- ***Rescuers from industrialized countries***—Industrialized countries produce more food than they need, while many developing countries with weak infrastructure and fragile ecologies will never be able to feed their populations. Better to increase cereal production in the modern farms in industrialized countries and ship it to poor countries—as aid or in exchange for other commodities.
- ***New modernists***—They want to continue the science-based Green Revolution-style agriculture. Farmers in developing countries should use fertilizers, pesticides and irrigation more intensively on their best land rather than try to grow more on marginal land. There is also the promise of genetically modified food (box 8.1).
- ***Sustainable intensifiers***—They argue for greener production, saying that farmers could grow more in unimproved or degraded areas without damaging the environment. But farmers will only be able to do this if they are given the right incentives and can participate fully at all stages—choosing the best techniques for their own circumstances and exploiting their own knowledge and ingenuity.

Figure 8.1 – Millions of undernourished, 1995/97

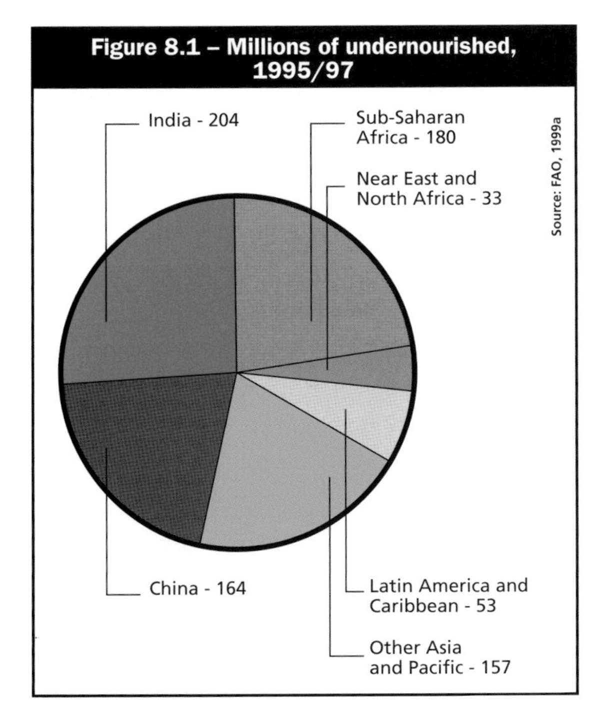

Some of these positions overlap, and each country has representatives of all points of view.

During the past decade, many NGOs and international aid agencies have been paying closer attention to sustainability and what it would entail. One notion that has gained currency is that sustainable agriculture involves conserving and expanding many different kinds of capital. These include *natural* capital—land and water, for example, and the many natural processes—along with *physical* capital in the form of roads and other infrastructure. Then there is *financial* capital, whether in stocks of money or access to credit. Also crucial are *human* capital—a healthy and skilled work-force—and *social* capital in the form of networks, relationships and institutions that bind people together.

Proponents of sustainable agriculture point to the fact that many assets are mutually reinforcing. When people are working together to meet basic food needs, they may reinforce their local culture—which may in turn feed back into a determination to protect their environment. Farmers engaged in sustainable agriculture have to ensure that as many of these assets as possible are husbanded and accumulated rather than depleted.

As with all development buzzwords, there are considerable conceptual difficulties with

Box 8.1 – Can genetically modified (GM) crops feed the world?

In the early 1990s, GM crops were not produced commercially on farms anywhere in the world. In 1997 they covered 12 million hectares; and in 1998, 29 million, mainly in Argentina, Australia, Canada, Mexico and the United States. The advocates of genetically modified foods argue that they offer an important way to feed the world's hungry. This is a doubtful proposition, especially because the world already produces enough food to feed everyone. Total annual production currently amounts to 354 kilograms of grain per person—enough to provide everyone with a nutritious and adequate diet.

Food is unavailable largely because people are too poor to buy what they need. Farmers could already grow more to feed the hungry if there were sufficient "effective demand"—demand backed up with hard cash. And poor farmers could also grow more on their farms if they were able to use some of the cheap and readily available techniques to improve their farms and livelihoods. These include techniques of nutrient cycling, soil regeneration and the use of natural pests. Interestingly, the best evidence of the success of these sustainable approaches comes from the very countries of Africa, Asia and Latin America that some say are in most need of GM technologies.

But one should not dismiss GM foods entirely. It is important to distinguish between the different types of GM technologies. Those currently on the market have mainly benefited the companies producing them—herbicide-tolerant soya, for example, which locks farmers into buying herbicide from the company marketing the GM seed. But poor farmers could benefit from crops that may appear on the market in the next few years—engineered to have tolerance to drought, say, or salt—if they can afford to buy the seeds. They are more likely to get such access if the technology is produced by public-interest bodies rather than by the transnational seed companies that will want to lock farmers into dependent and expensive relationships.

these new terms (box 8.2). Also, the emphasis on accumulating all kinds of capital and on their mutually reinforcing characteristics may overlook important trade-offs. In practice these forms of capital are interlinked, so using one will usually mean the depletion of another. Building a road means taking up land that might have been used for forest or crops; investing in motorized fishing boats may deplete fish stocks; social conflict as opposed to cohesion may be necessary to achieve more equitable land distribution.

Governments face tough choices in deciding between different development goals, and their decision as to which takes priority is often more political than technical. But the focus on sustainability and these diverse forms of capital has called attention to the need for broader agrarian development strategies that consider economic, social and environmental goals and impacts.

Most modern agriculture is based on a different model. It has undervalued natural and social capital—indeed, it often places no value on them at all. This is because they are difficult to assess in financial terms. How much is a virgin forest worth, or a clean river? What value can you put on a cohesive community? One heroic estimate of the goods and services that come from the world's ecosystems put the value in the range $16 trillion to $54 trillion per year. But it is impossible to put a price on many natural assets such as the air we breathe.

The state of many rural workers around the world—living in poor conditions and suffering ill health—also suggests that modern agriculture often erodes human capital. In the Philippines, for example, farmers using modern pesticides have higher incidences of eye, skin, lung and neurological disorders. One assessment of the benefits of boosting production

Box 8.2 – Questioning the value of capital

There are dangers in adopting the term "capital", particularly when referring to nature and social structure or society. Capital can imply substitutability. One capital asset may be exchanged for another and, provided the total asset base is not diminished, this could still be said to be sustainable. The term also implies the possibility of assigning a market price to things that, in society and in nature, are very difficult or even impossible to value. Such presumptions do not take account of the cultural, moral, ethical and spiritual aspects that may be associated with particular assets. Use of the word capital thus implies that nature and society can be turned into bundles of commodities that can be readily exchanged in an increasingly globalized market.

The term "social capital" was popularized in the 1990s, and has served to emphasize the developmental benefits that can flow from relations of trust and reciprocity, and from connectedness and networks. But it is difficult to agree on exactly what social capital is. Some have stressed the importance of collaboration to solve problems. Others emphasize the values of associational activity and organizational density. And some focus on the dark side of social capital—how cohesiveness for one group can mean exclusion for others. After all, a society may be well organized, have strong institutions and reciprocal mechanisms, but be based less on trust than on fear and coercion. Some associations can also act as obstacles to development and sustainable livelihoods, encouraging conformity and inequity.

through intensive pesticide use found they were far outweighed by the health costs.

Modern agriculture appears spectacularly successful partly because it disregards the damage to these natural, social and human assets. Thus between 1970 and 1995, wheat yields in India rose from 1.2 to 2.5 tons per hectare, and rice yields in China rose from 3 to 5 tons per hectare. But this has been at the cost of using much higher quantities of fossil fuels, whether to provide the feedstock for fertilizer production or the fuel to drive irrigation pumps. When efficiency is measured in terms of energy consumption, rather than output per hectare, the picture changes: low-input organic rice produced in Bangladesh or China is around 20 times more energy-efficient than irrigated rice produced in Japan or the United States.

Development agency initiatives associated with sustainable agriculture have attempted to integrate natural processes, such as nutrient cycling, nitrogen fixation, soil regeneration or natural enemies of pests, into food production systems (box 8.3)—and to make fuller use of the local knowledge and diverse skills of farmers. Moreover, sustainable agriculture is multifunctional—it produces food and other goods for farm families and markets, but it may also contribute to a range of public improvements, such as clean water or flood protection, and may deliver other benefits such as biodiversity and social cohesion.

In recent years, projects seeking to promote sustainable systems have become much more widespread, whether promoted by NGOs or government agencies. An analysis of 45 initiatives across 17 African countries, for example, found that 730,000 households had substantially increased their agricultural output—often increasing yields by 50 to 100 per cent.

Policies for sustainable agriculture

While there is growing awareness in most countries of the benefits of sustainable agriculture, progress in promoting this type of cultivation has been slow. A 1997 review by the Commission for Sustainable Development concluded that implementation of the agriculture and rural development objectives reached at Rio five years earlier was still far from satisfactory. Very few countries provide explicit comprehensive national policy support for sustainable agriculture. Some that do provide it are Austria, Cuba, Denmark, Finland, Sweden

Box 8.3 – Reviving land in the Sahel

Large areas of dryland in Burkina Faso and Niger have been degraded. The combined action of wind and water has sealed a thin surface layer that prevents further infiltration by water. Most drylands have been abandoned and are devoid of vegetation.

One way of using the land again is through digging holes—known as *zaï* in Burkina Faso and *tassas* in Niger. These holes, 20–30 centimetres deep, are packed with manure to provide organic matter and stimulate termite activity, and are then planted with millet or sorghum. When the rains come, the holes fill with water—especially when used in conjunction with other water retention methods such as stone bunds.

Farmers using these techniques have achieved striking increases in yields and have shifted from deficit to surplus. These methods are labour intensive, however, and are best suited to areas where there is family labour or where farm hands can be hired. In Niger the system has spawned a network of young day labourers who have mastered the techniques and who go from village to village to satisfy the farmers' growing demands.

Apichart Weerawong, Associated Press AP

Thai farmers demanding higher prices for their crops.
Bangkok, Thailand

and Switzerland. Brazil, Germany and India have such policies in place at the level of certain regions or provinces.

A much larger number of countries have reformed elements of agricultural polices through, say, new regulations, incentives or environmental taxes. In developing countries like Bolivia, Burkina Faso, India, Indonesia, Kenya, the Philippines and Sri Lanka, the economic, social and environmental benefits of certain programmes and policies to promote soil conservation, integrated pest management and irrigation management have been impressive.

But the experience is likely to remain localized unless some major constraints are overcome. One is government inertia—most innovations have had to struggle against existing national policies and conservative institutions. Another is the lack of co-operation from the suppliers of fertilizers and pesticides, which will continue to push their wares. But there are also social constraints. Modern agriculture has eroded much of our social capital, both at community and national levels—particularly our webs of trust. Farmers are often suspicious of environmentalists who, they think, are trying to restrict their freedom. Consumers are suspicious of farmers, whom they accuse of producing second-rate or dangerous food. Many communal and collective institutions have also been weakened. Migration to urban centres or abroad has often weakened rural communities. And rural co-operatives and trade unions in numerous countries have been undermined by both governments and corporations.

A key challenge is to change the policy environment, which does not reflect the long-term social and environmental costs of resource use. At present, many governments subsidize high-input agriculture. So farmers find it expensive to switch to resource-conserving or multi-functional agriculture. Some governments have made piecemeal efforts to add green tinges to modern farms, by offering incentives to improve non-crop habitats such as wetlands or hedgerows. But they have done little to ensure that policies and incentives are interlinked—and that prices reflect real costs more accurately.

Governments will also need to rethink their economic policies. Structural adjustment programmes—often associated with high interest rates, cheap food imports and weakened public sector technical assistance programmes—have devastated small farms in many countries. And many landless labourers and peasant producers even lack the most basic resource of all—land. Yet land reform seems to have disappeared from the agendas of many governments and development agencies (box 8.4).

Agencies also need to change the way they work with farmers. Instead of trying to deliver a standard package of solutions to which the farmers must adapt, they should co-operate with farmers to explore what works best under local conditions, and respond to farmers' real needs. Farmers often work best when they can make a range of improvements, none of which on its own may seem dramatic. Taken together, however, these changes do not merely accumulate—they multiply. Sustainable agriculture is not a concretely defined set of technologies, it is a process of social learning.

Sustainable water supplies

Among the most important assets for sustainable agriculture are reliable supplies of water. Attitudes to water management shifted significantly during the 1990s. Changes were reflected in both the Earth Summit and the Dublin International Conference on Water and the Environment in January 1992. The declarations from both conferences merged all the previous agendas—household water supplies, sanitation, irrigation and power generation. From then on, the emphasis in all aspects of water management would be on sustainability.

The new approach was understandable in the light of increasing pressure on global water supplies. Of the water withdrawn by human beings, about 70 per cent is used for irrigated agriculture, 20 per cent for industry and the rest is for domestic and municipal use. On average all over the world, these activities are currently using around half the 12,500 cubic kilometres of water that are readily available annually. But the resources are distributed unequally. Already, 460 million people live in countries that are highly water stressed—mostly in the Middle East, around the Mediterranean and in sub-Saharan Africa. One quarter of the world's population is moving toward a situation of high water stress.

The total availability of freshwater is, of course, only a part of the problem. More important is the question of access. Thus although the Middle East and North Africa are among the most water-stressed parts of the world, they offer better access to safe water than countries of Latin America and the Caribbean where rainfall is more abundant (figure 8.2).

In the past, it was assumed that water supply would require large-scale infrastructure, primarily the responsibility of the state. But increasingly it is argued that the private sector and communities should take greater responsibility, and that water-management schemes should be on a smaller scale and involve full participation of everyone affected. Water resources planning has therefore shared the same shift in thinking and in rhetoric as the broader field of sustainable development planning. There is, however, a considerable gap between intention and performance.

Damning the dams

Some changes in policy have affected dam construction. By 1997, there were an estimated 800,000 dams around the globe, of which approximately 45,000 were higher than a five-storey building. In recent years, dams have become increasingly contentious—primarily because of the large number of people they displace. In India in recent decades, around

4 million people have been displaced by reservoirs and irrigation schemes. In China, just one project—the Three Gorges Dam—will displace 1.3 million people. Dams also have extensive ecological implications, affecting the patterns of erosion and sedimentation downstream, as well as changing the nature of fish populations and disturbing many fragile ecosystems, particularly wetlands.

The extensive ecological and social costs of large dams became widely recognized in the 1980s. The response of international financial institutions, government ministries and construction companies was generally to lay down

Box 8.4 – Land reform, the forgotten issue

One of the most persistent causes of poverty in rural areas is the maldistribution of land. In most Latin American countries, the richest 20 per cent of farmers control around three quarters of the land. In Southern Africa as well, large farmers hold much of the best land. Even in densely populated countries in South Asia, such as Bangladesh, the richest 20 per cent of households possess more than half the land.

Millions of poor farmers would benefit from land reform, though its character would have to depend on local circumstances. Thus in Latin America, there is considerable scope for redistribution. In South Asia, on the other hand, where even the largest farms are relatively small, reforms could concentrate more on security of tenure and on improving the rights of tenant farmers.

Few countries have implemented wide-ranging land reform measures in recent years. Although there have been numerous land reform laws, there has been little effective enforcement. At the same time, there does not seem to have been much organized pressure for land reform at the national level, except in some countries like Brazil and the Philippines. Where changes in tenure have occurred, they have often come from redistribution of public land—or have been the result of land invasion, a common tactic of the rural poor in Latin America. In sub-Saharan Africa, changes in land tenure have often worked against the rural poor: privatizing what were previously communal systems has weakened security and communal solidarity.

Land reform seems to be less of a priority for international agencies now than it was in the past. Some were enthusiastic about the potential for reform in the 1960s and 1970s. Indeed, FAO held a conference on agrarian reform in 1979, but it was never seriously followed up. Today, in an era of economic liberalization, the preferred approach is market-assisted land reform—extending credit to small farmers to help them buy land from willing sellers. But this has taken place on a limited scale, and the beneficiaries have rarely had the subsequent support they needed.

Some NGOs have played an important role, notably organizations such as Brazil's Landless Rural Workers Movement and the People's Campaign for Agrarian Reform in the Philippines. But many other NGOs have withdrawn from more contentious questions of distribution and popular mobilization, and have concentrated more on achieving better rural services.

If there are going to be serious efforts to achieve people-centred sustainable development, both NGOs and official development agencies will have to look again at land reform.

improved guidelines and carry out social and environmental impact assessments. But these planning approaches can be highly flawed. Impacts often occur in areas far beyond the spatial scope of a particular project, and are thus not recognized by project developers—as occurred in the case of the Pangue and Ralco Dams in Chile. Serious impacts may also occur well after project development, but these are often not examined or anticipated.

In addition, impact assessment requires vast amounts of data that are often extremely difficult to gather. Southern countries often rely on expatriate consultants, who may lack both time and knowledge of particular regions. Their analysis may also lose some of its critical edge, given the competitive commercial environment in which consultants operate—particularly when they conform to narrow terms of reference or when their prospects for future work depend on the conclusions they reach.

A number of organizations have tried to develop more effective ways of assessing the impact of dams, engaging more directly with the people affected. But it has taken widespread public protest in both industrialized and developing countries for the issue to move to the top of the environmental agenda.

A pivotal protest concerned the Narmada Valley Project in India. This included construction of the Sardar Sarovar Dam, a further 135 medium dams and 3,000 minor dams. Construction began in 1985, with funding from the World Bank. Local communities and NGOs were outraged at the implications—the dam would displace 152,000 people in 245 villages. Their protest movement, Narmada Bachao Andolan (Struggle to Save the Narmada River), organized demonstrations and hunger strikes. International NGOs that were increasingly mobilizing against large dams weighed in—lobbying the US Congress and the World Bank.

Eventually, after a highly critical independent review in 1993, the World Bank withdrew its support. Under pressure from Friends of the Earth, the Japanese government also suspended aid for the project. The Indian government nonetheless pressed ahead until 1995, when the Supreme Court of India ordered construction of the dam wall to stop at 80 metres high (out of 136 metres), later raising the limit to 85. Meanwhile, the reservoir continued to fill and the protests and arrests persisted.

Although dam building has slowed somewhat in recent years, around 1,600 dams are currently under construction in 42 countries. The scale of international protest against large dams has, however, given international agencies pause (box 8.5). In 1998, the World Bank and the World Conservation Union (IUCN) established the World Commission on Dams—which will present its first report in June 2000. Commissioners range from the chief executives of construction companies to the founder of Narmada Bachao Andolan.

Figure 8.2 – Access to safe water by region, 1990–98

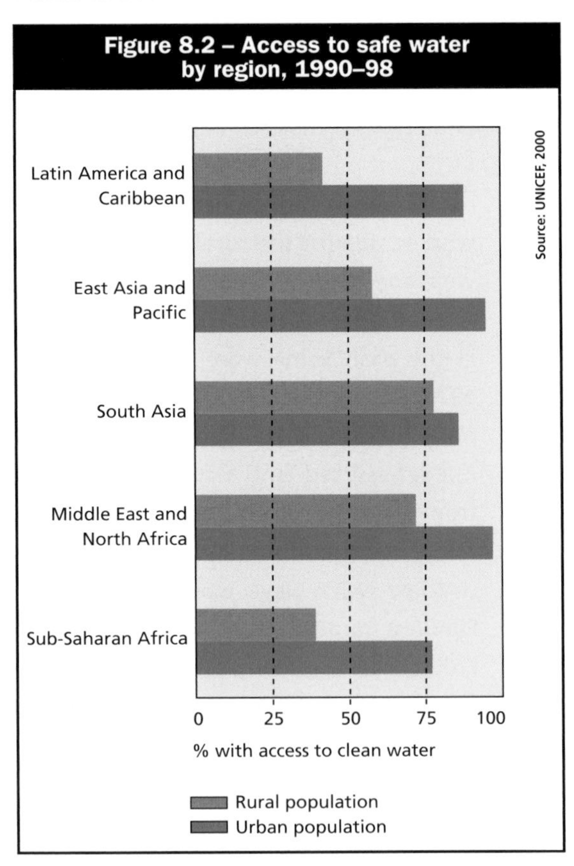

The experience with alternatives to large projects is limited but growing. Smaller scale catchment management systems have been developed, for example, in Bolivia, India, Pakistan and Peru. There have also been some attempts to link floodplain communities with dam managers, and integrate upstream dams with downstream water users, as in South Africa. Nonetheless, the dam construction framework still tends to involve remote planners and politicians weighing up costs and benefits, and taking a decision that is purportedly in the wider national interest. Participation of the communities directly affected rarely comes into it.

New channels for irrigation

More than one third of all dams are designed primarily to provide water for irrigation—and many other dams have an irrigation component. Other irrigation systems depend on diverting river water or pumping groundwater. But whatever the source of water, many large-scale schemes also have a poor social and environmental record—particularly in Africa, where they have proved difficult and expensive to implement. Schemes depending on surface water frequently have their canals blocked by sediment, and those that use pumps often suffer from poor maintenance.

Apart from technical difficulties, there can be social conflict. If the flow of water is unreliable, farmers in various parts of the system—the "topenders" and the "tailenders"—will try to take what they can, when they can. And planners have frequently ignored gender implications, generally targeting support at men, even though in much of Africa farm work is done primarily by women. Extensive irrigation systems can also create pools of standing water, which can cause health problems. In the Gezira Project in Sudan, for example, the canals provide an ideal breeding ground for snails. Around 60 per cent of adults and 80 per cent of children in this area now have bilharzia.

In the 1980s, the poor performance of large-scale irrigation systems was part of the reason

Box 8.5 – International protests against dams

Protests against dams have become increasingly internationalized. *The Ecologist,* a British magazine, began to campaign against large dams in the early 1980s; and activities in the United States over the same period eventually produced the International Rivers Network and the newsletter *World Rivers Review.* In 1988 activists met in San Francisco and demanded a moratorium on all new dam projects that failed to ensure participation by those affected. They also demanded full access to information on new undertakings—including data on their potential environmental, health and economic effects.

These demands were reiterated in 1994 in the Manibeli Declaration, named after one of the first villages to be submerged by the Sardar Sarovar Dam in India. The document, which called for a moratorium on loans for large dams until certain conditions were met, was signed by 326 groups and coalitions in 44 countries. It was presented to the World Bank on its 50th anniversary. In March 1997, the first international meeting of a group called People Affected by Dams was held in Curitiba, Brazil. The following month, there was a meeting in Gland, Switzerland, co-sponsored by the World Bank and the World Conservation Union. It was attended by senior IUCN and World Bank officials, critics of large dams, representatives from dam-building companies and agencies, and dam-affected people. It ended with agreement to found the World Commission on Dams.

for a decline in investment. The World Bank and others, on observing that more and more projects were uneconomical, searched for alternatives. Often they decided to reduce the scale of schemes, hoping that smaller ones would be better matched to local needs.

In practice, they did not achieve a great deal. First, they lost the economies of scale: many small dams cost more than one large one. Second, they did not change the nature of the schemes—they merely offered scaled-down versions of large projects, and implemented them in the same over-managed bureaucratic fashion. FAO and UNDP initiated small-scale irrigation schemes in Turkana, Kenya in 1979, for example, but found that they performed erratically, were environmentally destructive, and were also expensive—more than $20,000 per irrigating household.

By the end of the 1980s, the poor performance of many smallholder irrigation schemes caused yet another re-evaluation. One of the most common solutions was Irrigation Management Turnover (IMT)—making associations of farmers or other private entities responsible for running irrigation schemes in the hope that they would have a stronger interest than local bureaucrats in keeping systems working. This change was also congruent with the general ethos of structural adjustment and privatization.

IMT can take many different forms: in some cases, as in South Asia, farmers' associations co-operate with official irrigation agencies; in others, as in China, Indonesia, Mexico and Turkey, they replace them. This might seem an obvious direction, but it is not an easy option. First, it assumes that the system is actually working—badly designed or poorly functioning schemes are unlikely to be rescued by handing them over to farmers. Second, farmers must see some economic benefit in taking on this commitment. If their participation in running a scheme means they face greater fees and costs, they must have correspondingly greater economic returns. Third, IMT assumes that the government and its officials are sufficiently flexible to adapt to this new environment. Fourth, and most important, there must be effective user groups. In practice, many lack the necessary technical or management skills—and when they do work, they are often dominated by the richer farmers.

Another approach has been to start from existing indigenous irrigation schemes—expanding them perhaps, or making them more efficient, or introducing more formal user groups. Some traditional irrigation systems have exploited natural flooding in wetland areas; others have involved redirecting normal water flows—as in the hill-furrow irrigation systems of East Africa or the Himalayas. Others have promoted different ways of raising groundwater.

The principle of building on indigenous knowledge has a history of its own. In South Asia, for example, British colonial planners often appropriated and rehabilitated existing canal systems. While it is possible to make useful improvements, there are also dangers—technical improvements may undermine what was working already, and imposing new standard and formulaic systems of management may cause an informal system to collapse.

Informal systems generally have sets of rules about who is entitled to water, and when. But these are built on relationships that are difficult to codify. The Marakwet irrigation system in the Keiro Valley in Kenya, for example, has formal rules, but these are supplemented with many other day-to-day arrangements that include everything from borrowing to stealing.

Whatever the system, it is clear that it has to achieve sustainability and equity. Water resources planning needs to be taken out of the offices and into the villages and town squares. Only then will it address the real bottlenecks in production, and propose manageable technologies and appropriate institutions for sustainable solutions.

Forest conservation

Another key element of sustainable development is the conservation of forests and biological diversity. As the environmental movements of the past two decades have highlighted, world development has frequently been at the cost of the world's forests. And the process appears to be continuing. Between 1980 and 1995, the world's forested area shrank by 180 million hectares. Although there was a 20 million-hectare increase in the developed countries, this was far outweighed by a 200 million-hectare loss in the developing nations (figure 8.3). In much of Africa, the main direct cause seems to be an increase in subsistence agriculture, while in Latin America the process often has more to do with resettlement, logging, and the extension of commercial agriculture and infrastructure. Asia has been affected by all these phenomena.

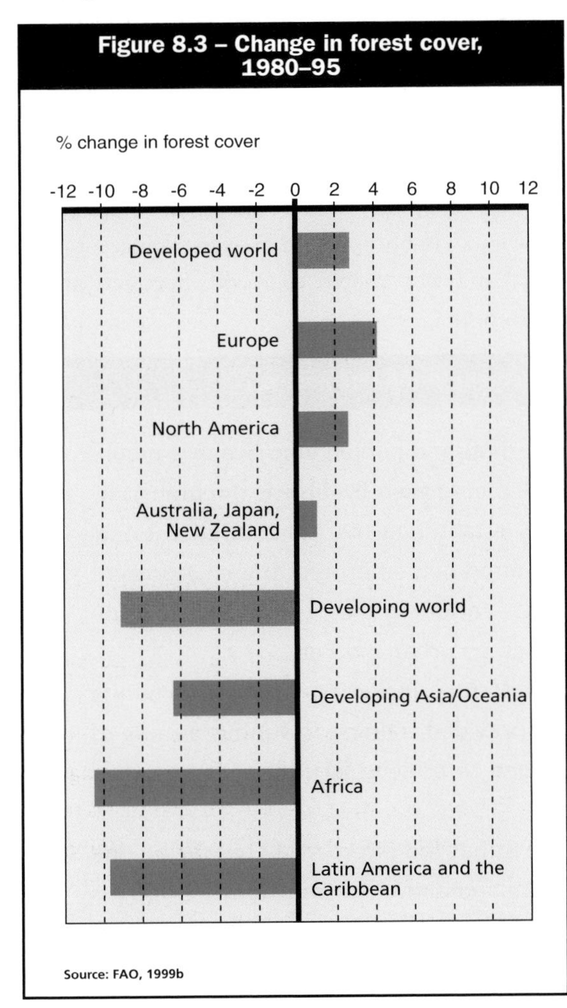

While the direct causes vary considerably by country and region, deforestation is primarily driven by market forces, government policies and institutions such as land tenure. International policies promoting trade liberalization and structural adjustment have also accelerated deforestation in some countries. In parts of Southeast Asia, for example, one of the most important factors has been export demand for palm oil, timber and pulp. In 1995 the government of Cambodia awarded 30 companies logging concessions that covered virtually all of the country's remaining forest area. According to the World Bank, Cambodia's forests could be commercially exhausted by 2003. In Brazil, problems have often been linked to resettlement. The government has encouraged the development of the Amazon and other forest regions, encouraging poor farmers or landless labourers to migrate from areas where land ownership was highly concentrated.

Many poor communities have struggled to protect their own environments, but have often been overcome by economic or climatic pressures, or have been overwhelmed by outside forces—especially large-scale resettlement programmes and the activities of logging companies.

But in the 1990s they have had increasing outside support. A number of NGOs have worked with community-based groups in defence of forests and other threatened ecosystems. In the Philippines, for example, NGOs have done a great deal to publicize environmental problems and abuses. Governments have generally been slower to react—but a number of them, along with international agencies, have been making attempts at conservation. They have been doing so in co-operation with local communities, in what has been called community-based natural resource management. This was a reaction to the failure of previous efforts, which often involved policing vulnerable areas on the assumption that local people, left to their own devices, were likely to overexploit these areas.

Governments and agencies interested in this type of participatory conservation try to take into account the rights and needs of local communities, as well as the need to protect the environment. They attempt to work more closely with community groups and NGOs—often using action-research methodologies, such as participatory rural appraisal. This approach recognizes the value of indigenous knowledge—indeed, it encourages a two-way flow between local people and technical specialists. It also promotes more diverse forms of income generation, so people can survive while sustaining their environment.

This ambitious agenda may be more realistic, but it will necessarily come up against some equally real obstacles. As always, there is a problem of resources. Some agencies that professed themselves keen on environmental protection and sustainable development in the early 1990s have subsequently switched to more fashionable issues, such as good governance, and are reassessing their funding priorities. For a country like Senegal, which has been in the forefront of attempts to design comprehensive strategies to deal with desertification, this can be particularly worrying. Having spent three years in a participatory planning process, there are concerns that the programme will not be implemented properly because of a lack of financial support from the government and donors.

There have also been real difficulties in switching priorities and methods of operation. Many agencies continue to put trees before people. But very often the success of forest protection or tree-planting schemes requires giving priority to social concerns—such as land tenure and income generation (box 8.6). The development planners' penchant for hastily implemented large-scale projects may also be difficult to overcome. In the Philippines, for example, the National Forestation Programme was implemented on such a scale and so rapidly that it inevitably operated in over-technocratic ways and was unable to work effectively in many areas.

Box 8.6 – Community forest management in the Philippines

The Ikalahan are an indigenous group of several thousand people who live in a mountainous area of Luzon, in the Philippines. In 1973, seeing their livelihood threatened by forest fires and encroachment by outsiders, they established the Kalahan Educational Foundation. Its methods of participatory conservation helped protect the environment while offering new income-earning opportunities—including the production of handicrafts, fruit, ginger and other goods destined for green urban markets.

This success has been based on a number of factors, including strong community organization and an education programme that provided training in various aspects of sustainable agriculture. The Ikalahan also managed to achieve security of tenure over their ancestral domain.

Even so, there are concerns for the future. One is that this effort relied heavily on one person, who served as a link between local people and external institutions. Another is that community solidarity could be weakened by commercialization and the expansion of market relations.

Forest and park protection programmes have to engage with complex social issues. Local people may accept a particular project, thinking that it will bring in some outside resources, but they are unlikely to give it much support if it is not compatible with their own livelihood priorities and concerns. Various park protection schemes in South Africa have been affected by these difficulties (box 8.7). Such tensions ultimately mean that many projects will not be sustainable.

Participatory conservation can be thwarted by local power structures as well. When power is in the hands of local elites, it can be extremely difficult both to democratize project design through broad-based consultation, and to ensure that project costs and benefits are distributed equally. Similarly, efforts throughout the 1990s to decentralize responsibility for natural resource management have sometimes backfired. In the Philippines and Senegal, the central government has responded to social and environmental movements, and international aid, by advocating people-centred sustainable development. But this commitment is often far weaker at the level of local authorities, who have other priorities.

Then there is the wider economic context in which these programmes have to be set—notably the chill winds of structural adjustment. Costa Rica, for example, has received worldwide recognition for its efforts to protect its forests and promote biodiversity. But the structural adjustment programmes of the 1990s reduced the capacity of the state to administer and pay for conservation programmes and policies. At the same time, the demand to boost exports of cash crops, such as bananas, has involved clearing forests and breaking up environmentally benign systems of peasant farming.

Box 8.7 – Elusive communities in South Africa

One of the central tenets of rural development in South Africa is community-based natural resource management. This seeks ways for communities to earn income from their land, forests and wildlife, while simultaneously participating in communal programmes to protect them. Once promoted only by left-leaning NGOs, these ideas now receive increasing support from both the government and the private sector. The principles underlying the effort are strongly influenced by Zimbabwe's Campfire movement, which allowed rural communities to generate income from managed hunting and invest it in schools, clinics and other local requirements.

One of the difficulties of applying this model is that officials tend to assume that everyone in a particular community has the same interests at the same time. Yet an investigation inside the Mkambati Game Reserve—to take one example—identified at least seven different clusters of people, including subsistence farmers, those relying on remittances from migrants, and those who make a living by brewing beer. In fact, only two groups made their living from wildlife.

Here, as elsewhere, the "community" can be a figment of the imagination. Project managers and donors may recognize the need to accommodate diversity and communal friction, but they continue to rely on community fora to achieve some kind of consensus. In the politically charged atmosphere of South Africa, however, these are as likely to deepen conflicts as to resolve them.

In practice, it has proved extremely difficult to implement community-based approaches to forest and park protection. They can only succeed if there are supportive institutions and social movements. In South Africa, the post-apartheid government has actively promoted community-based natural resource management in various development programmes. But in some rural areas there is considerable resistance to these initiatives—so much so that policy makers are adjusting their approach. In some areas of natural resource management, they are placing less emphasis on community participation and, instead, are strengthening the capacity of democratically elected local authorities to "deliver development". Private businesses are also being encouraged to enter into partnerships with local communities.

This situation contrasts sharply with that of rural Mexico. Here there is a long history of communal organizing for local development—and of struggle against the pattern of modernization promoted by the government and international financial institutions. Some grassroots organizations and social movements have found common cause with urban-based NGOs and international agencies promoting sustainable development, and have made use of social forestry, eco-tourism and organic farming initiatives to strengthen local livelihood systems and self-reliance.

The importance of having home-grown institutions, which have gained cohesion through struggle or long experience, is also evident in India. In Andhra Pradesh, village women's associations known as *sangams*, with support from NGOs and the state government, have improved the lives of many very poor rural women, as well as the local environment in the semi-arid Deccan plateau, through activities that included agroforestry and soil conservation. This experience—where poor women themselves are gaining control of their own institutions—contrasts sharply with another: the Joint Forest Management (JFM) programme, in which the government has attempted since 1988 to ensure that forests not only contribute to conservation but also meet the subsistence requirements of local people. Although the JFM programme set up participatory committees, its success has been undermined in many areas because there has been little transfer of power or benefits to local communities.

Enduring realities

All development agencies, whatever their intentions, come up against an enduring set of problems when they try to pursue people-centred sustainable development. These include:

- ***Community conflicts***—Communities may be idealized as harmonious, but in reality are usually heterogeneous, hierarchical and conflictive. All have dense and complex systems of social and political relations—cultural norms, property rights and other power relations—as well as cross-cutting interests, between men and women, rich and poor, and different ethnic groups. Many interventions choose to ignore this complexity and prefer to apply standard prescriptions. As a result, they frequently have unintended consequences. The commonest is that the most powerful group will manage to seize and manipulate any new resources that become available.
- ***The survival imperative***—Development projects often proclaim grand objectives that ignore people's most urgent needs. Sustainable development initiatives are particularly prone to this—sometimes restricting people's access to land, forest products or water resources. Although many projects now include income-generating activities, these often prove too limited to be of any real benefit—or collapse when the external agency supporting the initiative withdraws.
- ***Technocratic participation***—As a way of addressing local complexities, development projects are now usually predicated on local

participation. But frequently they involve little more than token consultation to legitimate a pre-designed programme. They aim to ensure acquiescence and voluntary contributions of labour and resources from beneficiaries who have no real influence over the course of events. The current terminology is that beneficiaries should "own" a project—although this may sometimes mean that donors have sold it.

There will always be a contradiction between the instincts of technocrats and the messy world with which they have to deal.

Heldur Netocny, Panos Pictures

Tree nursery, Eritrea

Box 8.8 – Institutional change?

Many international development agencies have adopted the language of sustainable development, but changing their practice is more difficult.

Food and Agriculture Organization

FAO's constitution incorporated the principal objectives of sustainable development. And FAO has indeed been one of the most vocal international organizations calling for attention to issues such as soil degradation and the loss of biodiversity.

Following the Earth Summit, FAO made some organizational changes. In 1995, for example, it declared that one of its major goals would be Sustainable Agriculture and Rural Development (SARD); and therefore it created a new Department of Sustainable Development. But this did not appear to have much impact on budgets and programmes.

In practice, most of FAO's efforts and resources have gone into agricultural modernization. This kind of development implies losers as well as winners and frequently deprives large numbers of the rural poor of access to land, jobs and livelihoods long before alternative opportunities become available. FAO sometimes acknowledges this dilemma but lacks an effective strategy for dealing with it.

United Nations Development Programme

UNDP's programme is diffuse and heterogeneous. It is tugged in different directions by funders who have different views on its priorities. In terms of policy advocacy, one of UNDP's major activities has been the production of the annual *Human Development Report* (HDR). This has performed several important functions. First, it challenges the view that development should be understood primarily in economic terms, and counterposes a more complex definition of well-being that puts people at its centre. This provides a rallying point for the more progressive development thinkers and activists, and offers the international community an alternative interpretation of basic data that competes with that of the World Bank. The Human Development Index (HDI) ranks countries not only on their ability to increase per capita income but also on their effectiveness in improving levels of living.

Critics continue to contest the value of the HDI. But the real value of the *Human Development Report* has been at the political level—arguing the case for human development (and, by extension, sustainable development) with a cogency that has attracted widespread attention and provided ammunition for advocacy groups.

The extent to which these ideas are carried through into UNDP programmes is more questionable. UNDP has to operate within constraints presented by donors. Over four fifths of UNDP's financial resources are provided by voluntary contributions from about 10 of the world's richest states. When citizens of these states read the HDR, they are reminded of the fact that present-day mass poverty and environmental degradation are linked to high-consumption lifestyles that originate in their own countries. But most of them are unlikely to support the profound structural and political reforms that these criticisms imply.

UNDP also has to operate within the constraints presented by the governments of developing countries, which may have to accept some conditions in order to qualify for aid—but tend to balk at anything that smacks of political interference, or threatens the status quo. Yet innovative efforts to promote sustainable development are likely to confront established interests.

World Bank

Given that the World Bank has to raise most of its funds in world capital markets at competitive rates, and that its voting system gives greatest weight to the richest OECD countries, it is hardly surprising that the World Bank has not granted the same priority to social and environmental issues in its lending as it has in its rhetoric. World Bank loans that are not dedicated to social purposes generally have minuscule components for environmental protection and monitoring. Otherwise they would offer unacceptable rates of return.

But the World Bank has made progress. In 1984, following some of its more socially and environmentally disastrous activities in the Amazon basin and elsewhere, it was pressured into action and introduced a policy paper that called for mandatory Environmental Impact Assessments. When ignored, the Bank issued stronger directives, though these still had numerous escape clauses and exempted structural and sectoral adjustment lending, which made up around half the total in the 1990s.

With UNEP and UNDP, the World Bank co-manages the Global Environment Facility. This was created after Rio to encourage work on global environmental problems like ozone depletion and loss of biological diversity. It has been criticized for its small budget (less than $1 billion per year) and for its rigid, top-down bureaucratic style. Also, it tends to finance discrete projects in developing countries, rather than addressing root causes of environmental degradation linked to market forces and government policies.

In the 1990s, the Bank adopted much of the pro-environment, pro-poor rhetoric of social movements and NGOs—and took on board some of their members as advisors. Nevertheless, their success in transforming the neoliberal agenda has been limited.

United Nations Environment Programme

UNEP is the agency most likely to be in tune with sustainable development. And UNEP's 1999 *Global Environment Outlook* is indeed one of the most comprehensive assessments of global environmental issues. UNEP has also been a key actor in promoting international agreements on such issues as desertification and ozone depletion. Unfortunately, UNEP has never been given enough resources to fulfil its mandate. Its core budget for 1998 was around 13 per cent that of FAO and 10 per cent that of UNDP—proportions that roughly mirror the weight of environmental ministries and agencies in UN member states.

Bilateral aid agencies

The support that bilateral agencies give to sustainable development largely depends on government policies and social forces in their home countries. It is also conditioned by each state's perceived trade and other foreign policy objectives. Some bilateral agencies have quite innovative programmes and work closely with NGOs. But like UN agencies, their aid programmes are riddled with internal contradictions. Thus in Central America, USAID and other agencies from OECD countries support a multitude of small, decentralized projects that aim to promote popular participation and sustainable livelihoods. At the same time, however, they may also be promoting massive food imports from their home countries or the expansion of capital-intensive, large-scale plantations that are far from sustainable—and may deprive many more people of their traditional livelihoods.

International NGOs

Many NGOs, though by no means all, are wholeheartedly devoted to sustainable development. But because they tend to specialize in particular issues, such as the protection of forests or the promotion of civil rights, their efforts can be very scattered. Like UN agencies, their primary responsibility is to their donors, their governing bodies and their staff. Few are systematically accountable to intended beneficiaries. NGOs are also adroit at adopting the latest development language, though again their practice may not match it. Thus WWF International has declared that its new policy of a people-oriented approach to biodiversity conservation amounts to a paradigm change. Given that this would require a significant realignment of the political, scientific and bureaucratic powers on which it depends for funds, this is a tall order.

Participation is a laudable aim, but project planners are often asked to undertake participatory activities for which they lack the skills, cultural sensitivity and political commitment.

- ***Political qualms***—Genuine participation and empowerment are likely to upset established power relations and disturb bureaucracies. Therefore communities need resolute support if they are to protect themselves against unsympathetic officialdom, or vested interests such as logging or mining companies. But most mainstream agencies find it difficult to involve themselves in the nitty-gritty of local politics—either because they have little appetite for it or because they fear a clash with the government. Programmes and projects that aim to promote participation and empowerment rarely contain an effective strategy for overcoming political resistance.
- ***Dead ends***—Technocrats prefer to work with projects and programmes that have a limited time span. This often means a substantial investment over a brief period. But when the project is finished the personnel move on, leaving behind orphaned organizations and technologies that may not survive their departure. This also makes it difficult to assess impact. What looks like a success or failure after four or five years may appear the opposite after 10 or 20 years.
- ***Macro defeats micro***—Initiatives that try to promote people-centred sustainable development often focus narrowly at the local level. They pay less attention to developments at the national or international level that could swamp their efforts and defeat their purpose. Macroeconomic polices, world commodity prices and agrarian development strategies can undermine community-based natural resource management.

Continuity or change?

Governments and international agencies have adopted sustainable development as a banner under which all can march. They were urged along this route partly by popular mobilizations against certain aspects of modernization that affect both the middle classes and grassroots organizations. The middle classes in industrialized and developing countries have been concerned about quality of life issues, while grassroots organizations and social movements have been concerned with the marginalizing effects of progress on people's lives.

The term sustainable development has been popular to some extent because it can be used in a neutral way—implying little more than a vague sense of purposeful improvement in economic, social and environmental domains. But it has served a useful purpose in reminding the international community of some fundamental issues: that development demands more than economic growth; that some features of modernization have unacceptable social and environmental costs; and that this requires different economic policies, development strategies and approaches to planning.

Governments and development agencies that accept this outlook will need to refocus their energies and resources. Some have indeed made changes, but for the most part they have merely applied new terminology to what they were already doing—with perhaps a few extra elements bolted on (box 8.8). Why are they resistant to change?

To a large extent the problem is political and ideological. People have very different views about what constitutes an environmental "problem", what sustainability is and what needs to be done to achieve it. Not long ago, for example, indigenous resource management practices—including some forms of shifting agriculture and the use of certain crop varieties in peasant farming systems—were considered backward by many scientists and development planners. It is increasingly recognized that some such practices may be relatively sustainable and efficient in the agro-ecological and socioeconomic settings where they are found.

These differences in perspective imply that certain environmental interventions must be based on a negotiated consensus involving various stakeholders. But governments, which are under pressure to meet increasing demand for food, timber, water and other natural resources, are often inclined to pursue quick fixes for reasons of economic and political expediency. They are likely to opt for a single large-scale dam rather than many smaller-scale water management schemes; for large forest concessions rather than community-based schemes; or for modernized rather than sustainable agriculture. They are even more likely to choose this route when their primary base of political support consists of groups that stand to benefit from such measures—for example, urban electorates demanding cheap food or industrialists with agribusiness or logging interests.

Many international development agencies face similar constraints. While they may be more aware of the potentially negative social and environmental costs of growth and modernization strategies, they may run into opposition from governments or those who provide their funds. Their professional profile and corporate culture may also restrict change. Experts—with well-heeled lifestyles—may resist any fundamental change in the way projects and programmes are designed and implemented, and may have difficulties identifying with local communities. They may also resist any significant restructuring of budgets that would redirect a decent proportion of funds to developing countries and poor communities.

If the problem is partly political, so is the solution. Not only do governments and international finance and trade institutions need to be far more sensitive to the social and environmental costs of the policies and projects they promote, they also need to open up the decision-making process to make it more democratic. Some agencies attempted to do this during the 1990s. But the process should not begin and end with attempts to improve dialogue with multiple stakeholders or civil society. It also needs to be translated into new policy guidelines, procedures and budgets that make a significant difference to operational practice. The popular mobilizations that helped to get sustainable development on the agenda still have much to do if they want to see it implemented.

In the last analysis, action depends on people's interpretation of what is possible and right. Thus the longer-term nature of mobilization for sustainable development depends not only on activism, but on dominant views about the where the world could—and should—be going. If those views support high-consumption lifestyles, then many hard questions about environmental sustainability will not be seriously addressed. And if they sanction unlimited individual gain, it is obvious that institutions designed to promote the common good will suffer.

Five years after Copenhagen, there is little indication that the fundamental goals and values orienting world development are moving toward greater social responsibility. Incentive structures in everything from education to investment decisions have been reoriented toward improving the options of the profit-maximizing individual. The investor has become much more important than the worker. And the consumer has gained higher status than the citizen.

Questioning extreme individualism and the unbridled power of money—reasserting the value of equity and social solidarity, and reinstating the citizen at the centre of public life—is a central challenge of our time. The "invisible hand" of the market has no capacity to imagine a decent society for all people, or to work in a consistent fashion to attain it. Only human beings with a strong sense of the public good can do that.

Bibliographical note

CHAPTER 1

This chapter is based on background papers by Bob Deacon, Thandika Mkandawire and Virginia Rodríguez, and Ajit Singh.

It has also benefited from Amsden 1985, Binder 1999, Chang 1999, Crotty, Epstein and Kelly 1998, Denny 1999, Deyo 1992, Goodman, White and Kwon 1998, Rodrik 1997, Singh 1995, Solimano forthcoming, Stalker 2000a and 2000b, G. Standing 1999a, Stewart 1994, Toynbee 2000, ul Haq et al. 1998, Wade 1991, Wolfensohn 1999, and Woo-Cumings 1999.

Other references are ECLAC 1995 and 1999, Koivusalo 1999, ILO 1995 and 1999, IMF 1995 and 1999, OECD/DAC 1996, 1998 and 1999, Social Watch 1998 and 1999, UN 1995c and 1997d, UNDP 1994, 1995, 1997, 1998a, 1998b, 1999a and 1999b, UNESCO 1998a and 1998b, UNICEF 1998, 1999 and 2000, UNICEF et al. 1998, UNRISD 1995, WHO 1996 and 1997, and World Bank 1990, 1993, 1999a, 1999b and 1999c.

Box 1.1 is based on Deacon 2000. John Maynard Keynes quote is from Moggridge 1980.

CHAPTER 2

This chapter is based on background papers by Cynthia Hewitt de Alcántara, Evelyne Huber and John Stephens, Justine Nannyonjo, Yudit Kiss, and Jorge Schvarzer.

The section on debt and debt relief draws on the following studies: EURODAD 1998, Hewitt de Alcántara 1999, Jubilee 2000 Coalition 1999, Nannyonjo 1999, Ocampo 1999, Schvarzer 1999, South Centre 1999, United Nations 1995a, 1995b, 1997a and 1999, and UNDP 1999a.

The discussion of trends in development assistance is based on Griffin and McKinley 1996, Kaul and Langmore 1996, OECD/DAC 1996 and 1999, OECD/DCD and UNICEF 1998, Randel and German 1997, Randel et al. 1998 and 2000, and World Bank 1998a. For an analysis of problems associated with conditionality, see Mosley et al. 1991, Sørensen 1993, and Stokke 1995. For a discussion of new approaches to aid, see Edwards 1999.

Sources of information on the fiscal crisis of the state and on tax reform are Clunies-Ross 1999, Grunberg 1998, Hewitt de Alcántara 1999, Kiss 1999, Rao 1999, Tanzi 1996, *The Economist* 2000b and UNDP 1999a.

The section on pension reform relies heavily on Huber and Stephens 2000. See also Orszag and Stiglitz 1999, Queisser 1998, and Singh 1996. An excellent collection of international essays on problems in social security reform is United Nations 1997b. Van Ginneken 1996 lays out some of the issues that relate to integrating the informal sector into social protection schemes.

For examples of problems encountered when trying to decentralize social services, see Di Gropello and Cominetti 1998, Glewwe and Litvack 1998, and Gupta and Gumber 1999. General problems of targeting are discussed in Vivian 1995. The study in 39 countries on the effects of imposing user fees is presented in Cornia and Stewart 1990. Experiences with micro-credit in various regions of the world are analysed in Mayoux 1998, Schneider 1997, and Sinha 1998.

Box 2.1 is based on Nannyonjo 1999, Box 2.2 on UNICEF and OXFAM 1999. The various sources for Box 2.3 are indicated in the text. Box 2.4 is adapted from Huber and Stephens 2000. Orszag and Stiglitz 1999 is the source of the quotation from the Office of the Chief Economist of the World Bank.

CHAPTER 3

This chapter is based on background papers by Yusuf Bangura, Yusuf Bangura and Toshihiro Nakamura, Björn Beckman with Emmanuel Akwetey and Lars Lindström, Edward Webster, Karl Gostner and Geoffrey Nkadimeng, and Georg Sørensen.

Other sources are Boylan 1998, Diamond 1996, Diamond et al. 1988, Dominguez 1998, Elgie 1998, Farrell 1997, Hellman 1998, Horowitz 1985 and 1990, Lijphart 1977 and 1990, Linz and Valenzuela 1994, Linz and Stepan 1996, Maxfield 1997, Mkandawire 1998, O'Donnel 1994, O'Leary 1999, Petras 1998, Przeworski 1993, Reilly and Reynolds 1999, Rose et al. 1998, Stavenhagen 1997, Stepan and Skatch 1994, Transparency International 1999, *UNESCO Courier* 1998, Warburton 1999, and Young 1999.

Box 3.1 is from Joyner 1999, and Bangura and Nakamura 1999, Box 3.2 is from Ghai 2000, and Box 3.3 is from Webster et al. 1999. Amartya Sen quote is from Sen 1997, and EBRD quote is from EBRD 1999.

CHAPTER 4

This chapter is based on background papers by Yusuf Bangura, Andrew Nickson and Ole Therkildsen. Bangura's paper draws on the following studies, commissioned for the UNRISD project on Public Sector Reform and Crisis-Ridden States: Carlson 1998, Hutchful 1999, Larbi 1999, and McCourt 1999.

Additional sources are Bartlett and Le Grand 1993, Berg 1999, Bolnick 1997, Chiwele et al. 1999, Clayton and Pontusson 1998, Esping-Andersen 1996, Ferlie et al. 1996, Goh and Sundram 1998, Halligan 1997, IMF 1988, 1996, 1998a, 1998b and 1998c, Kickert 1997, Mkandawire and Soludo 1999, Nickson 1999, Olukoshi 1999a and 1999b, Osborne and Gaebler 1992, Paul and Sekhar 1997, Stavasage and Moyo 1999, UNDP 1993, Warburton 1999, and World Bank 1988, 1995b, 1997a, 1997b, 1997c, 1998b, 1998d and 1998e.

Data on education expenditure cuts by the World Bank are from World Bank 1994. IMF's statement on low-income countries' expenditures on health and education is from Gupta 1999. Data on privatization in Russia are from Filatochev et al. 1999. Figure on resident foreign advisers in Africa is from Jaycox 1993. Output figures on the African Capacity Building Foundation are from African Capacity Building Foundation 1998.

Box 4.1 is from Nickson 1999, and Box 4.2 is from Bangura 1999.

CHAPTER 5

This chapter is based on a background paper by Peter Utting (2000).

Other references are Annan 1999, Barber 1998, Barkin 1999, Carrere, 1999, Corporate Watch 1999, Dawkins 1995, Dommen 1999, Forcese 1996, Frankel 1999, Gallin 1999a and 1999b, Gereffi et al. 1994, Goodman 2000, Greer and Bruno 1996, Hanks 1999, Hansen 1999a and 1999b, Hopkins 1997, Hurst 1999, ISO 1999, Kolk et al. 1999, Kolodner 1994, Krut and Gleckman 1998, Levy 1997, Murphy and Bendell 1999, Nelson 1996, O'Neill 1999, Porter and van der Linde 1995, Richter forthcoming, Schmidheiny 1992, Schmidheiny et al. 1997, *The Economist* 1999c, ToBI 1997, TRAC 1999, *Trade Union World* 1999, UNCTAD 1996 and 1999, UNEP 1994 and 1998, UNRISD 1995, von Moltke et al. 1998, Watts and Holme 1999, WBCSD 1999, WCED 1987, Welford 1997, West 1995, Wild 1998, and Zarrilli, Jha and Vossenaar 1997. Additional information was obtained from Corporate Watch 1999.

Boxes 5.1 and 5.2 are based on Utting 2000. Box 5.3 is from Annan 1999, Box 5.4 is from Corporate Watch 1999, and Box 5.5 is based on Barber 1998.

CHAPTER 6

This chapter is based on background papers by Asef Bayat; Andrew Clayton, Peter Oakley and Jon Taylor; John Foster; Joe Foweraker; Alan Fowler; Dan Gallin; Rosalind Petchesky; Vithal Rajan and Thimma Reddy; Charles Reilly; and David Westendorff.

Data on the number of NGOs and CSOs in the introductory section are from Porio 1997, *The Economist* 1999b, Van Rooy 1998, and Weiss 1999.

The section on civil society and service delivery draws largely on Clayton et al. 1999, and Fowler 2000. The estimate of NGO involvement in World Bank projects comes from *The Economist* 1999b, the number of professionals employed by NGDOs in Peru from Patron 1998, the example of the Cooperation Committee for Cambodia from Curtis 1998, the transfer of leadership from SANCO to the post-apartheid South African government from Everatt et al. 1998, the appraisal of the Interregional Mapuche Council and the Landless Rural Workers Movement from Foweraker 1999. The discussion of precarious partnerships draws on Petchesky 1999 for the information on SHAPE. Chavez 1999, Rajan and Reddy 1999, and Westendorff 1999 are the sources for the discussion of participatory budgets. Information on community and gender disputes is based on Lind and Farmelo 1996, Westendorff and Dey 1996, and YUVA 1999.

CSOs and the UN draws on Foster 1999, Krut 1997 and Weiss 1999. Information on CSOs and the World Bank comes from Foster 1999, Fox and Brown 1998, Petchesky 1999, Rich 1994 and *The Economist* 2000a. The discussion of CSOs and the Inter-American Development Bank is based on Reilly 1999, and of CSOs and the international treaty bodies on Foster 1999, George 2000, Krut 1997, O'Neill 1999 and *The Economist* 1999a, 1999b and 2000a. George 2000, Krut 1997, and O'Neill 1999 are the sources of information on the future for international NGO mobilization.

Box 6.2 draws on interviews with YUVA staff members. Box 6.3 combines information from Joseph 1999, and Westendorff 1999. Box 6.4 is from SAPRIN 1999, and Box 6.5 is based on Reilly 1999.

CHAPTER 7

This chapter is based on background papers by Nadje Al-Ali, Andrea Cornwall, Nikki Craske, Shail Mayaram, Ruth Pearson, Rosalind Petchesky, Shahra Razavi, and Ramya Subrahmanian.

The discussion on women in democratization draws on the following studies: Al-Ali 1999, Alvarez 1990 and 1998, Craske 1999, Goetz 1998, Gouws 1996, Jaquette and Wolchik 1998, Mayaram 1999, Miller and Razavi 1998, Molyneux 1998, Naciri 1998, Petchesky 1999, Phillips 1991 and 1992, Rai 1996, Razavi 2000, Sawer 1996, Schild 1995, Szalai 1998, Tamale 1997, Tripp 1994, and Waylen 1993.

The discussion of women's NGOs draws on Corrêa 1998, Galdos and Feringa 1998, Klugman et al. 1998, Lang 1997, Noel-De Bique 1998, Petchesky 1999, and Silliman 1999.

The discussion of gendered poverty draws on a 1999 Special Issue of *Development and Change* (30, 3). The discussion of rights and needs draws on Petchesky 1999.

The section on reproductive health rights draws heavily on Petchesky 1999. Other sources are Corrêa 1994, Corrêa and Petchesky 1994, DAWN 1999, Koivusalo 1999, Petchesky 1995, Petchesky and Judd/IRRRAG 1998, WEDO 1999, and H. Standing 1999.

The discussion on education rights draws heavily on Subrahmanian 1999. Other sources are Bennell 1996, Bouis et al. 1998, Carnoy 1995, Colclough 1994 and 1997, Bennell and Furlong 1997, Gordon 1998, Jeffery and Basu 1996, Knodel 1997, Knodel and Jones 1996, Longwe 1998, Mkandawire and Soludo 1999, Puiggros 1997, Tansel 1997, UNESCO 1998b, and UNICEF 1999.

The section on women's economic rights draws heavily on Pearson 1999. Other sources are Armstrong 1996, Barrientos et al. 1999, Chen et al. 1999, ECLAC 1995, Elson 1999, Gallin 1999a, Kabeer 1995, Pearson 1999, Razavi 1999, G. Standing 1999a and 1999b, and Tzannatos 1999.

Box 7.1 is based on Najmabadi 1999, and Khalaf 2000. Box 7.2 is based on Mayaram 1999. Box 7.3 is taken from Petchesky 1999.

CHAPTER 8

This chapter is based on background papers by Bill Adams, Adrian Atkinson, David Barkin, Solon Barraclough, Krishna Ghimire, Eddie Koch, Jules Pretty, Vithal Rajan and Thimma Reddy, and Peter Utting.

The section on sustainable cities draws primarily on Atkinson 2000, with additional information from Atkinson 1998, ICLEI 1997, Milbert 1999, Mitlin 1998, Samol 1998 and UNFPA 2000. The discussion on sustainable agriculture draws heavily on Pretty 1999 with additional information from FAO 1999a and Constanza et al. 1997. The section on sustainable water supplies is based on Adams 1999 with additional information from Houlder 1999, United Nations 1997c, and World Commission on Dams 1999. The discussion on forest conservation is based on Barkin 1999, Koch 1999, Rajan and Reddy 1999, and Utting 1999, with additional information from FAO 1999b, and Global Witness 1999. The section on enduring realities is based on Utting 1999. The discussion on continuity or change draws on Barraclough 1999.

Other sources are Barraclough and Ghimire 1995, Byron 1997, Feeny 1998, Fox and Brown 1998, Ghimire and Pimbert 1997, Goodland 1999, Holmberg 1992, Jeanrenaud 1998, Larson et al. 1998, Leach et al. 1997, Martinez 1990, McGranahan et al. 1996, Nelson and Wright 1995, Nicholls 1999, Pimbert and Pretty 1997, Pugh 1996, Scoones et al. 1996, Stiefel and Wolfe 1994, UNEP 1999, White 1996, Wood et al. 2000, and Wolfe 1994.

Boxes 8.1, 8.2 and 8.3 are based on Pretty 1999. Box 8.4 is based on Ghimire 1999. Box 8.5 is based on Adams 1999, and McKully 1997. Box 8.7 is based on Koch 1999, and Box 8.8 is adapted from Barraclough 1999.

Background papers

Adams, W.M. 1999. "Sustainable Water Management in Developing Countries".

Al-Ali, N. 1999. "Women's Movements in the Middle East: Case Studies of Egypt and Turkey".

Atkinson, A. 2000. *Promoting Sustainable Human Development in Cities of the South: A Southeast Asian Perspective*. Geneva 2000 Occasional Paper 6. Geneva: UNRISD.

Bangura, Y. 1999. "Globalization, Technocratic Policy Making and Democratization".

________. 2000. *Public Sector Restructuring: The Institutional and Social Effects of Fiscal, Managerial and Capacity-Building Reforms*. Geneva 2000 Occasional Paper 3. Geneva: UNRISD.

Bangura, Y. and T. Nakamura. 1999. "Democratization and Governance Reforms in Plural Societies".

Barkin, D. 1999. "Sustainable Development Strategies in Mexico: Grassroots Perspectives and Responses".

Barraclough, S.L. 1999. "Towards Integrated and Sustainable Development?"

Bayat, A. 1999. "Activism, Social Movements and Social Development in the Middle East".

Beckman, B., E. Akwetey and L. Lindström. 2000. "Labour Unions, Social Pacts and Democratisation".

Clayton, A., J. Taylor and P. Oakley. 1999. "Civil Society Organisations and Service Provision".

Cornwall, A. 1999. "Making a Difference? Gender and Participatory Development".

Craske, N. 1999. "The Latin American Women's Movement: Recent Developments and Challenges for the Future".

Deacon, B. 2000. *Globalization and Social Policy: The Threat to Equitable Welfare*. Geneva 2000 Occasional Paper 5. Geneva: UNRISD.

Foster, J.W. 1999. "Civil Society Engagement in International Decision Making: The Quest for an Enabling Environment".

Foweraker, J. 1999. "Grassroots Movements, Political Activism and Social Development in Latin America: A Comparison of Chile and Brazil".

Fowler, A. 2000. *Civil Society, NGDOs and Social Development: Changing the Rules of the Game*. Geneva 2000 Occasional Paper 1. Geneva: UNRISD.

Gallin, D. 1999a. "Trade Unions and NGOs in Social Development: A Necessary Partnership".

Ghai, Y. 2000. "Human Rights, Democracy and Social Development".

Ghimire, K.B. 1999. "Rural Power Structures, Land Tenure Reforms and Partnership".

Hewitt de Alcántara, C. 1999. "Financing Social Development: An Overview".

Huber, E. and J.D. Stephens. 2000. *The Political Economy of Pension Reform: Latin America in Comparative Perspective*. Geneva 2000 Occasional Paper 7. Geneva: UNRISD.

Kiss, Y. 1999. "The Political Economy of Tax System Reform in Hungary".

Koch, E. "People-Centred Development in South Africa: A Rethink of the Community-Based Approach".

Mayaram, S. 1999. "En-gendering Democratic Governance through the Panchayats in India"

Mkandawire, T. and V. Rodríguez. 2000. *Globalization and Social Development after Copenhagen: Premises, Promises and Policies*. Geneva 2000 Occasional Paper 10. Geneva: UNRISD.

Nannyonjo, J. 1999. "Uganda Debt Burden and the HIPC Debt Relief Initiative: Financing Social Development".

Nickson, A. 1999. "Public Sector Management Reform in Latin America".

Pearson, R. 1999. "Gender and Economic Rights".

Petchesky, R. 1999. "Reproductive and Sexual Rights, Social Development and Globalization: Charting the Course of Transnational Women's NGOs".

________. 2000. *Reproductive and Sexual Rights: Charting the Course of Transnational Women's NGOs*. Geneva 2000 Occasional Paper 8. Geneva: UNRISD.

Pretty, J. 1999. "Sustainable Agriculture: A Review of Recent Progress on Policies and Practice".

Rajan, V. and T. Reddy. 1999. "The Concept of People-Centred Sustainable Development: Myth and Reality in Development Experiences in India".

Razavi, S. 2000. *Women in Contemporary Democratization*. Geneva 2000 Occasional Paper 4. Geneva: UNRISD.

Reilly, C. 1999. "Weighing In: Can Citizens Bank on Bankers?"

Schvarzer, J. 1999. "External Dependency and Internal Transformation: Argentina Confronts the Long Debt Crisis".

Singh, A. 2000. *Global Economic Trends and Social Development*. Geneva 2000 Occasional Paper 9. Geneva: UNRISD.

Sørensen, G. 1999. "Democratisation and Social Development".

Subrahmanian, R. 1999. "Gender and Education: New Directions for Social Policy".

Therkildsen, O. 1999. "Efficiency and Accountability: Public Sector Reform in East and Southern Africa".

Utting, P. 1999. "Towards Participatory Conservation?"

________. 2000. *Business Responsibility for Sustainable Development*. Geneva 2000 Occasional Paper 2. Geneva: UNRISD.

Webster, E., K. Gostner and G. Nkadimeng. 1999. "NEDLAC: Labour Unions, Social Pacts and Democratization".

Westendorff, D. 1999. "Volunteer Action and Local Democracy: A Partnership for a Better Urban Future".

Selected bibliography

ACBF. 1998. *Status Report on Project Implementation*. Harare, Zimbabwe.

ADB. 1997 and 1998. *Key Indicators of Developing Asia and Pacific Countries*. Manila.

African Agenda. 1999. *The Lusaka Declaration and Areas of Action* 2, 2.

Alvarez, S. 1990. *Engendering Democracy in Brazil: Women's Movements in Transition Politics*. Princeton: Princeton University Press.

________. 1998. "Advocating Feminism: The Latin American Feminist NGO 'Boom'". Paper prepared for the Fourth Annual Schomburg-Moreno Lecture, Latin American Studies Program, Mount Holyoke College, South Hadley, Mass.

Amsden, A.H. 1985. "The State in Taiwan's Economic Development". In P.B. Evans, T. Skocpol and D. Rueschemeyer (eds.), *Bringing the State Back*. Cambridge: Cambridge University Press.

Annan, K. 1999. "A Compact for the New Century". Address to the World Economic Forum, Davos, Switzerland (31 January). <http://www.un.org/partners/business>

Armstrong, P. 1996. "The Feminization of the Labour Force: Harmonization Down in a Global Economy". In I. Bakker (ed.), *Rethinking Restructuring: Gender and Change in Canada*. Toronto: University of Toronto Press.

Atkinson, A. 1998. *Sustainability Through People's Participation in Urban Development in Selected Asian Cities: The Indonesian Experience*. Dresden: Büro für Stadtentwicklung und Umweltplanung.

Barber, J. 1998. "Responsible Action or Public Relations? NGO Perspectives on Voluntary Initiatives". *Industry and Environment* 21, 1–2 (January-June).

Barkin, D. 1999. *The Greening of Business in Mexico*. Discussion Paper 110. Geneva: UNRISD.

Barraclough, S. and K. Ghimire. 1995. *Forests and Livelihoods: The Social Dynamics of Deforestation in Developing Countries*. London: Macmillan.

Barrientos, S., A. Bee and I. Vogel. 1999. *Women and Agribusiness: Working Miracles in the Chilean Fruit Export Sector*. London: Macmillan.

Bartlett, W. and J. Le Grand. 1993. "The Theory of Quasi-Markets". In J. Le Grand and W. Bartlett (eds.), *Quasi-Markets and Social Policy*. London: Macmillan.

Bennell, P. 1996. "Rates of Return to Education: Does the Conventional Pattern Prevail in Sub-Saharan Africa?" *World Development* 24, 1.

Bennell, P. and D. Furlong. 1997. *Has Jomtiem Made Any Differences: Trends in Donor Funding for Education and Basic Education Since the Late 1980s*. Working Paper 51. Brighton: Institute of Development Studies.

Berg, E. 1999. "Aid Failure: The Case of Public Sector Reform". Revision of October Aid Conference Paper, University of Copenhagen, Denmark.

Binder, A.S. 1999. "Eight Steps to a New Financial Order". *Foreign Affairs* 785.

Bolnik, B. 1997. "Establishing Fiscal Discipline: The Cash Budget in Zambia". In M.Grindle (ed.), *Getting Good Government in the Public Sectors of Developing Countries*. Cambridge: Harvard University Press.

Bouis, H. et al. 1998. *Gender Equality and Investments in Adolescents in the Rural Philippines*. Washington, DC: International Food Policy Research Institute.

Boylan, D. 1998. "Preemptive Strike: Central Bank Reform in Chile's Transition from Authoritarian Rule". *Comparative Politics* (July).

Byron, N. 1997. "International Development Assistance in Forestry and Land Management: The Process and the Players". *Commonwealth Forestry Review* 76, 1.

Carlson, J. 1998. *Swedish Aid and State Capacity in Developing Countries*. Mimeo, UNRISD, Geneva.

Carnoy, M. 1995. "Structural Adjustment and the Changing Face of Education". *International Labour Review* 134, 6.

Carrere, R. 1999. *The Environmental and Social Effects of Corporate Environmentalism in the Brazilian Market Pulp Industry*. Mimeo, UNRISD, Geneva.

Chang, H. 1999. "The Economic Theory of the Development State". In M. Woo-Cumings (ed.), *The Developmental State*. Ithaca: Cornell University Press.

Chavez, D. 1999. "Cities for People". In Redpepper Archive. <http://www.redpepper.org.uk/xcities.html>

Chen, M., J. Sebstad and L. O'Connell. 1999 "Counting the Invisible Workforce: The Case of Homebased Workers". *World Development* 27, 3.

Chiwele, D. et al. 1999. *Private Sector Response to Agricultural Marketing Liberalisation in Zambia: A Case Study of Eastern Province Maize Markets*. Research Report 107. Uppsala: Nordiska Afrikainstitutet.

Clayton, R. and J. Pontusson. 1998. "Welfare-State Retrenchment Revisited: Entitlement Cuts, Public Sector Restructuring and Inegalitarian Trends in Advanced Capitalist Societies". *World Politics* 51, 1 (October).

Clunies-Ross, A. 1999. "Sustaining Revenue for Social Purposes in the Face of Globalization". In UN (ed.), *Experts Discuss Some Critical Social Development Issues*. New York: United Nations Department of Economic and Social Affairs, Division for Social Policy.

Colclough, C. 1994. *Under-Enrolment and Low Quality in African Primary Schooling: Towards a Gender-Sensitive Solution*. Working Paper 7. Brighton: Institute of Development Studies.

________. 1997. *Marketizing Education and Health in Developing Countries: Miracle or Mirage?* Oxford: Clarendon Press.

Constanza, R. et al. 1997. "The Value of the World's Ecosystem Services and Natural Capital". *Nature* 387.

Cornia, G.A and F. Stewart. 1990. *The Fiscal System, Adjustment and the Poor*. Occasional Paper 11. Florence: UNICEF Innocenti Research Centre.

Corporate Watch. 1999. <http://www.corpwatch.org>

Corrêa, S. 1994. *Population and Reproductive Rights: Feminist Perspectives from the South*. London: Zed Books.

________. 1998. "Reshaping the Brazilian Sexual and Reproductive Health Policy: The Role of Civil Society". Paper presented at the Rockefeller Foundation Advanced Leadership Program, Princeton University, Princeton.

Corrêa, S. and Petchesky, R. 1994. "Reproductive and Sexual Rights: A Feminist Perspective". In G. Sen, A. Germain and L.C. Chen (eds.), *Population Policies Reconsidered*. Cambridge: Harvard University Press.

Crotty, J., G. Epstein and P. Kelly. 1998. "Multinational Corporations in the Neo-Liberal Regime". In D. Baker, G. Epstein and R. Pollin (eds.), *Globalization and Progressive Economic Policy*. Cambridge: Cambridge University Press.

Curtis, G. 1998. *Cambodia Reborn? The Transition to Democracy and Development*. Washington, DC: Brookings Institution Press and UNRISD.

DAWN. 1999. *Implementing ICPD: Moving Forward in the Eye of the Storm—DAWN's Platform for ICPD+5*. Suva, Fiji.

Dawkins, K. 1995. *Ecolabelling: Consumer's Right to Know or Restrictive Business Practice?* Mimeo, Institute for Agriculture and Trade Policy, Minneapolis.

Denny, C. 1999. "From Maesteg to Dhaka, the Same Fears". *The Guardian* (29 November).

Deyo, F.C. 1992. "The Political Economy of Social Policy Formation: East Asia's Newly Industrialized Countries". In J. Henderson and R.P. Applebaum (eds.), *State and Development in the Asian Pacific Rim*. London: Sage Publications.

Diamond, L. 1996. "Is the Third Wave Over?' *Journal of Democracy* 7, 3.

Diamond, L., J. Linz and S. Lipset. 1988. *Democracy in Developing Countries*. Boulder: Lynne Rienner.

Di Gropello, E. and R. Cominetti. 1998. *La descentralización de la educación y la salud : Un análisis comparativo de la experiencia latinoamericana*. Santiago de Chile: ECLAC.

Dominguez, J. L. 1998. *Democratic Politics in Latin America and the Caribbean*. Baltimore: Johns Hopkins University Press.

Dommen, E. 1999. *Pertinence et limites des codes éthiques*. Mimeo.

EBRD. 1999. *Transition Report 1999: Executive Summary*. <http://www.ebrd.com/english/PUBLIC/transition/Exesum_281099.html>

ECLAC. 1995. *Social Panorama of Latin America*. Santiago.

________. 1997. *Economic Survey of Latin America and the Caribbean 1996/97*. Santiago.

________. 1999. *Estudio Económico de America Latina y el Caribe 1998-99*. Santiago.

The Economist. 1998. "China's Political Cage". 8 August: 14.

________. 1999a. "A Global Disaster". 11 December: 17-18.

________. 1999b. "Citizens Groups: The Non-Governmental Order". 11 December: 18-19.

________. 1999c. "Sweatshop Wars". 27 February: 66-67.

________. 2000a. "NGOs: Sins of the Secular Missionaries". 22 January: 25-27.

________. 2000b. "The Mystery of the Vanishing Taxpayer". In *Globalisation and Tax Survey*. 29 January: 1-6.

Edwards, M. 1999. *Future Positive: International Co-operation in the 21st Century*. London: Earthscan.

Elgie, R. 1998. "Democratic Accountability and Central Bank Independence: Historical and Contemporary, National and European Perspectives". *West European Politics* 21, 3 (July).

Elson, D. 1999. "Labour Markets as Gendered Institutions". *World Development* 27, 3.

Enriquez, J. 1999. "Too Many Flags?" *Foreign Policy* 116.

Esping-Andersen, G. 1996. *Welfare States in Transition: National Adaptations in Global Economies*. London: Sage Publications and UNRISD.

EURODAD. 1998. *Taking Stock of Debt: Creditor Policy in the Face of Debtor Poverty*. Brussels. <http://www.oneworld.org/eurodad/stock.htm>

Everatt D., G. Rapholo, H. Marais and S. Davies. 1998. *Civil Society and Local Governance in the Johannesburg "Megacity"*. Mimeo, UNRISD, Geneva.

FAO. 1999a. *The State of Food Insecurity in the World 1999*. Rome.

________. 1999b. *State of the World's Forests 1999*. Rome.

Farrell, D. 1997. *Comparing Electoral Systems*. London: Prentice Hall/Harvester Wheatsheaf.

Feeny, P. 1998. *Accountable Aid: Local Participation in Major Projects*. Oxford: Oxfam Publications.

Ferlie, E., A. Pettigrew, L. Ashburner and L. Fitzgerald. 1996. *The New Public Management in Action*. Oxford: Oxford University Press.

Filatochev, I., M. Wright and M. Bleeney. 1999. "Privatisation, Insider Control and Managerial Retrenchment in Russia". *Economics of Transition* 7, 2.

Forcese, C. 1996. *Commerce with Conscience?: Human Rights and Business Codes of Conduct*. Montreal: International Centre for Human Rights and Democratic Development.

Fortune. 1999. *1999 Global 5 Hundred* 140, 3 (August).

Fox, J. A and L.D. Brown. 1998. *The Struggle for Accountability: The World Bank, NGOs, and Grassroots Movements*. Cambridge: MIT Press.

Frankel, C. 1999. "One Foot in the Future". *Tomorrow* 9, 1 (January/February).

Galdos, S. and B. Feringa. 1998. "Creating Partnership at the Grassroots Level: The Reprosalud Project, Peru". In HERA (ed.), *Confounding the Critics: Cairo, Five Years On*. Conference report. Cocoyoc, Morelos, Mexico.

Gallin, D. 1999b. "Organized Labour as a Global Social Force". Paper presented at the IR2 Workshop, Washington, DC (20 February).

George, S. 2000. "Comment l'OMC fut mise en échec". *Le Monde Diplomatique* (January).

Gereffi, G., M. Korzeniewicz and R. Korzeniewicz. 1994. "Introduction: Global Commodity Chains". In G. Gereffi and M. Korzeniewicz (eds.), *Commodity Chains and Global Capitalism*. London: Greenwood Press.

Ghimire, K. and M. Pimbert. 1997. *Social Change and Conservation*. London: Earthscan.

Glewwe, P. and J. Litvack. 1998. "Provision of Health Care and Education in Transitional Asia: Key Issues and Lessons from Vietnam". Working Paper 147. Helsinki: UNU World Institute for Development Economics Research.

Global Witness. 1999. *The Untouchables: Forest Crimes and the Concessionaries—Can Cambodia Afford to Keep Them?* London (December).

Goetz, A.M. 1998. "Fiddling with Democracy: Translating Women's Participation in Politics in Uganda and South Africa into Gender-Equity in Development Practice". In G. White and M. Robinson (eds.), *Democratic Developmental State*. Oxford: Oxford University Press.

Goh, W. and J. Sundram. 1998. "Privatisation in Malaysia: A Social and Economic Paradox". In M. Hossain and J. Malbon (eds.), *Who Benefits From Privatisation?* London: Routledge

Goodland, R. 1999. *Social and Environmental Assessment to Promote Sustainability: An Informal View from the World Bank*. Mimeo, World Bank Environment Department, Washington, DC.

Goodman, A. 2000. "The Tomorrow Top 30: A New Survey of the World's Most Popular Companies Among Green Investors Throws up Some Interesting Names". *Tomorrow* 10, 1 (January/February).

Goodman, R., G. White and H. Kwon 1998. *The East Asian Welfare Model: Welfare Orientalism and the State*. London: Routledge.

Gordon, R. 1998. "'Girls Cannot Think as Boys Do?': Socialising Children through the Zimbabwean School System". *Gender and Development* 6, 2.

Gouws, A. 1996. "The Rise of the Femocrat?" *Agenda* 30.

Greer, J. and K. Bruno. 1996. *Greenwash: The Reality Behind Corporate Environmentalism*. Penang: Third World Network and Apex Press.

Griffin, K. and T. McKinley. 1996. *New Approaches to Development Co-operation*. Discussion Paper 7. New York: UNDP Office of Development Studies.

Grimes, B.F. 1996. *Ethnologue: Languages of the World*. Thirteenth edition. Summer Institute of Linguistics. <http://ww.sil.org/ethnologue/>

Grunberg, I. 1998. "Double Jeopardy: Globalization, Liberalization and the Fiscal Squeeze". *World Development* 26, 4.

Gupta, D. and A. Gumber. 1999. "Decentralisation: Some Initiatives in Health Sector". *Economic and Political Weekly* 34, 6.

Gupta, S. 1999. "Letter to the Editor". *Financial Times* (July 19).

Halligan, J. 1997. "New Public Sector Models: Reform in Australia and New Zealand". In Jan-Erik Lane (ed.), *Public Sector Reform: Rationale, Trends and Problems*. London: Sage Publications.

Hanks, J. 1999. *Promoting Corporate Environmental Responsibility: What Role for 'Self-regulatory' and 'Co-regulatory' Policy Instruments?* Mimeo, UNRISD, Geneva.

Hansen, M. 1999a. *Environmental Management in Transnational Corporations in Asia: Does Foreign Ownership Make a Difference? Preliminary Results of a Survey of Environmental Management Practices in 154 TNCs*. Occasional Paper. Copenhagen: Copenhagen Business School/UNCTAD Cross Border Environmental Management Project.

________. 1999b. *Environmental Regulation of Transnational Corporations: Needs and Prospects*. Mimeo, UNRISD, Geneva.

Hellman, J. S. 1998. "Winners Take All: The Politics of Partial Reform in Postcommunist Transitions". *World Politics* 50, 2 (January).

Holmberg, J. 1992. *Policies for a Small Planet*. London: Earthscan.

Hopkins, M. 1997. "Defining Indicators to Assess Socially Responsible Enterprises". *Futures* 29, 7.

Horowitz, D. 1985. *Ethnic Groups in Conflict*. Berkeley: University of California Press.

________. 1990. "Making Moderation Pay: The Comparative Politics of Ethnic Conflict Management". In J. Montville (ed.), *Conflict and Peacemaking in Multiethnic Societies*. New York: Lexington Books.

Houlder, V. 1999 "Hydropower Threatened by Deluge of Objections". *Financial Times* (2 November).

Hurst, P. 1999. *IUF Case Study: The Global Pesticide Industry's "Safe Use and Handling" Training Project in Guatemala*. Geneva: International Union of Food and Agricultural Workers.

Hutchful, E. 1999. *From Neo-Liberalism to Neo-Institutionalism: The World Bank, Aid Conditionality, and Public Sector Reform*. Mimeo, UNRISD, Geneva.

ICLEI. 1997. *Local Agenda 21 Survey: A Study of Responses by Local Authorities and Their National and International Associations to Agenda 21*. Toronto.

ILO. 1995. *World Labour Report*. Geneva.

________. 1999. "The International Labour Organization and the Promotion of Full, Productive and Freely Chosen Employment". In ILO (ed.), *International Consultation Concerning Follow-Up to the WSSD*. Geneva.

IMF. 1988. *International Financial Statistics Yearbook*. Washington, DC.

________. 1995. *Social Dimensions of IMF's Policy Dialogue*. Pamphlet Series No. 47. Fiscal Affairs and Policy Development and Review Departments, Washington, DC.

________. 1996. *Government Finance Statistics Yearbook*. Washington, DC.

________. 1998a. *World Economic Outlook*. Washington, DC.

________. 1998b. *Fiscal Reforms in Low-Income Countries: Experience Under IMF-Supported Programs*. Occasional Paper 160. Washington, DC.

________. 1998c. *External Evaluation of ESAF*. Report by a Group of Independent Experts. Washington, DC.

________. 1999. *World Economic Outlook*. Washington, DC.

International IDEA. 1997. *Voter Turnout from 1945 to 1997: A Global Report on Participation*. Stockholm.
<http://www.idea.int/Voter_turnout/index.html>

IPU. 1989–99 (all editions). *The Chronicle of Parliamentary Elections*. Geneva.

ISO. 1999. *The ISO Survey of ISO 9000 and ISO 14000 Certificates. The Eighth Cycle—1998*. Geneva.

Jaquette, J.S. and S.L. Wolchik. 1998. *Women and Democracy: Latin America and Central and Eastern Europe*. Baltimore: Johns Hopkins University Press.

Jaycox, E. 1993. "Capacity Building: The Missing Link in African Development". Address to the African-American Institute Conference. Reston, Virginia (20 May).

Jeanrenaud, S. 1998. *Can the Leopard Change its Spots? Exploring People-Oriented Conservation within the WWF*. Ph.D. dissertation, University of East Anglia, Norwich.

Jeffery, R. and A.M. Basu 1996. *Girls' Schooling, Women's Autonomy and Fertility Change in South Asia*. London: Sage Publications.

Joseph, J. 1999. *Lima megaciudad: Democracia, desarrollo y decentralization en sectores populares*. Lima: Alternativa with UNRISD and United Nations Volunteers.

Joyner, C. 1999. "The United Nations and Democracy". *Global Governance: A Review of Multilateralism and International Organization* 5, 3 (July-September).

Jubilee 2000 Coalition. 1999. "An International Bankruptcy Clause: A Proposal for Resolving the Current Debt Crisis and Preventing Future Ones Developing".
<http://www.jubilee2000uk.org/bankrupt0910.html>

Kabeer, N. 1995. *Necessary, Sufficient or Irrelevant? Women, Wages and Intra-Household Power Relations in Urban Bangladesh*. Working Paper 25. Brighton: Institute of Development Studies.

Kaul, I. and J. Langmore. 1996. "Potential Uses of the Revenue from a Tobin Tax". In M. ul Haq, I. Kaul and I. Grunberg (eds.), *The Tobin Tax: Coping with Financial Volatility*. New York: Oxford University Press.

Khalaf, R. 2000. "Iran's Islamic Feminists Passionate about Equality and the Koran". *Financial Times* (18 February).

Kickert, W.J.M. 1997. "Anglo-Saxon Public Management and European Governance: The Case of Dutch Administrative Reforms". In J.E Lane (ed.), *Public Sector Reform: Rational, Trends and Problems*. London: Sage Publications.

Knodel, J. 1997. "The Closing of the Gender Gap in Schooling: The Case of Thailand". *Comparative Education* 3, 1.

Knodel, J. and G.W. Jones. 1996. "Post-Cairo Population Policy: Does Promoting Girls' Schooling Miss the Mark?" *Population and Development Review* 22, 4.

Klugman, B. et al. 1998. *From Words to Action: Sexual and Reproductive Rights, Health Policies and Programming in South Africa, 1994–98*. Johannesburg: Women's Health Project.

Koivusalo, M. 1999. *World Trade Organisation and Trade Creep in Health and Social Policies*. GASPP Occasional Paper 4. Helsinki: Stakes.

Kolk, A., R. van Tulder and C. Welters. 1999. "International Codes of Conduct and Corporate Social Responsibility: Can Transnational Corporations Regulate Themselves?" *Transnational Corporations* 8, 1 (April).

Kolodner, E. 1994. *Transnational Corporations: Impediments or Catalysts of Social Development?* Occasional Paper 5. Geneva: UNRISD.

Krut, R. 1997. *Globalization and Civil Society: NGO Influence in International Decision Making*. Discussion Paper 83. Geneva: UNRISD.

Krut, R. and H. Gleckman. 1998. *ISO 14001: A Missed Opportunity for Sustainable Global Industrial Development*. London: Earthscan.

Lang, S. 1997. "The NGOization of Feminism". In J.W. Scott, C. Kaplan and D. Keates (eds.), *Transitions, Environments, Translations: Feminisms in International Politics*. London: Routledge.

Larbi, G. 1999. *The New Public Management Approach and Crisis States*. Discussion Paper 112. Geneva: UNRISD.

Larson, P., M. Freudenberger and B. Wyckoff-Baird. 1998. *WWF Integrated Conservation and Development Projects: Ten Lessons from the Field, 1986–96*. Washington, DC: World Wildlife Fund.

Leach, M., R. Mearns and I. Scoones. 1997. "Community-Based Sustainable Development: Consensus or Conflict?" *IDS Bulletin* 28, 4 (October).

Levy, D. 1997. "Environmental Management as Political Sustainability". *Organization & Environment* 10, 2 (June).

Lijphart, A. 1977. *Democracy in Plural Societies: A Comparative Exploration*. New Haven: Yale University Press.

________. 1990. "The Power Sharing Approach". In J. Montville (ed.), *Conflict and Peacemaking in Multiethnic Societies*. New York: Lexington Books.

Lind, A. and M. Farmelo. 1996. *Gender and Urban Social Movements: Women's Community Responses to Restructuring and Urban Poverty*. Discussion Paper 76. Geneva: UNRISD.

Linz, J.J. and A. Valenzuela. 1994. *The Failure of Presidential Democracy: Comparative Perspectives*, Vol. 1. Baltimore: Johns Hopkins University Press.

Linz, J.J and A. Stepan. 1996. *Problems of Democratic Transition and Consolidation: Southern Europe, South America and Post-Communist Europe*. Baltimore: Johns Hopkins University Press.

Longwe, S.H. 1998. "Education for Women's Empowerment or Schooling for Women's Subordination?" *Gender and Development* 6, 2 (July).

Martinez, A. 1990. *Ecological Economics: Energy, Environment and Society*. Oxford: Blackwell.

Maxfield, S. 1997. *Gatekeepers of Growth: The International Political Economy of Central Banking in Developing Countries*. Princeton: Princeton University Press.

Maxwell, S. and L. Hanmer. 1999. "For Richer, For Fairer. Poverty Reduction and Income Distribution". *Insights* 31. London: ODI

Mayoux, L. 1998. *Women's Empowerment and Micro-Finance Programmes: Approaches, Evidence and Ways Forward*. Working Paper 41. Milton Keynes: The Open University, Development Policy and Practice Research Group.

McCourt, W. 1999. *Pay and Employment Reform in Developing and Transition Societies*. Mimeo, UNRISD, Geneva.

McGranahan, G., J. Songsore and M. Kjellén. 1996. "Sustainability, Poverty and Urban Transitions". In C. Pugh (ed.), *Sustainability, the Environment and Urbanization*. London: Earthscan.

McKully, P. 1997. "Independent Commission to Review World's Dams". *World River Review* 12, 3 (June). <http://www.irn.org/pubs/wrr/9706/9706cover.html>

Milbert, I. 1999. *What Future for Urban Cooperation? Assessment of Post-Habitat II Strategies*. Berne: Swiss Agency for Development Cooperation.

Miller, C. and S. Razavi. 1998. *Missionaries and Mandarins: Feminist Engagement with Development Institutions*. London: Intermediate Technology Publications and UNRISD.

Mitlin, D. 1998. *Sustainability through People's Participation in Urban Development in Selected Asian Cities: The Thai Experience*. Dresden: Büro für Stadtentwicklung und Umweltplanung.

Mkandawire, T. 1998. "Crisis Management and the Making of 'Choiceless Democracies'". In R. Joseph (ed.), *State, Conflict, and Democracy in Africa*. Boulder: Lynne Rienner.

________. 1999. *Human Rights and Development*. Mimeo, UNRISD, Geneva.

Mkandawire, T. and C. Soludo. 1999. *Our Continent, Our Future: African Perspectives on Structural Adjustment*. Trenton: Africa World Press and International Development Research Centre.

Moggridge, D. 1980. *The Collected Writings of John Maynard Keynes*. Vol. XXV. Cambridge: Cambridge University Press.

Molyneux, M. 1998. *Gender, Citizenship and Democracy: Reflections on Contemporary Debates*. Mimeo, ILAS, University of London, London.

Mosley, P., J. Harrigan and J. Toye. 1991. *Aid and Power: The World Bank and Policy-Based Lending*. London: Routledge.

Murphy, D. and J. Bendell. 1999. *Partners in Time? Business, NGOs and Sustainable Development*. Discussion Paper 109. Geneva: UNRISD.

Naciri, R. 1998. "Engaging the State: The Women's Movement and Political Discourse in Morocco". In C. Miller and S. Razavi (eds.), *Missionaries and Mandarins: Feminist Engagement with Development Institutions*. London: Intermediate Technology Publications and UNRISD.

Najmabadi, A. 1999. "Feminism in an Islamic Republic—'Years of Hardship, Years of Growth'". In Y. Yazbeck Haddad and J.L. Esposito (eds.), *Islam, Gender and Social Change*. Oxford: Oxford University Press.

Nelson, J. 1996. *Business as Partners for Development: Creating Wealth for Countries, Companies and Communities*. London: The Prince of Wales Business Forum.

Nelson, N. and S. Wright. 1995. *Power and Participatory Development: Theory and Practice*. London: Intermediate Technology Publications.

Nicholls, L. 1999. "Birds of a Feather? UNDP and ActionAid Implementation of Sustainable Human Development". *Development in Practice* 9, 4 (April).

Noel-De Bique, D. 1998. "The Caribbean: NGO Partnerships for Advancing Male Responsibility in Implementing the Goals of the ICPD". In HERA (ed.), *Confounding the Critics: Cairo, Five Years On*. Conference report. Cocoyoc, Morelos, Mexico.

Ocampo, J.A. 1999. "A Broad Agenda for International Financial Reform". Speech delivered to the closing session of the 9th General Conference of the European Association of Development Research and Training Institutes. Paris (25 September).

O'Donnell, G. 1994. "Delegative Democracy". In L. Diamond and M. F. Plattner (eds.), *The Global Resurgence of Democracy*. Baltimore: Johns Hopkins University Press.

OECD/DAC. 1996. *Shaping the 21st Century: The Contribution of Development Co-operation*. Paris.

________. 1998 and 1999a. *Development Co-operation Report*. Paris.

________. 1999b. *Net ODA Flows 1950-1997*. <http://www.oecd.org/dac/htm/oda5097.HTM>

________. 1999c. *A Comparison of Management Systems for Development Co-operation in OECD/DAC Members*. <http://www.oecd.org/dac/pdf/compaida1.pdf>.

OECD/DCD and UNICEF. 1998. "Better Reporting on Donor Support to Basic Social Services: Opportunities and Constraints". Technical report prepared by Development Initiatives for the Hanoi Meeting on the 20/20 Initiative, Hanoi (27–29 October).

O'Leary, B. 1999. "The Nature of the British-Irish Agreement". *New Left Review* 233.

Olukoshi, A. 1999a. *Privatised Tax Collection and Revenue Generation in Lagos State, Nigeria*. Mimeo, UNRISD, Geneva.

________. 1999b. *The Elusive Prince of Denmark: Structural Adjustment and the Crisis of Governance in Africa*. Research Report 104. Uppsala: Nordiska Afrikainstitutet.

O'Neill, K. 1999. *Internetworking for Social Change: Keeping the Spotlight On Corporate Responsibility*. Discussion Paper 111. Geneva: UNRISD.

Orszag, P. and J. Stiglitz. 1999. "Rethinking Pension Reform: Ten Myths about Social Security Systems". Paper presented at the Conference on New Ideas about Old Age Security. World Bank, Washington, DC.

Osborne, D and T. Gaebler. 1992. *Reinventing Government: How the Entrepreneurial Spirit is Transforming the World*. Reading: Addison-Wesley.

Patron, P. 1998. "Peru: Civil Society and the Autocratic Challenge". In A.Van Rooy (ed.), *Civil Society and the Aid Industry*. London: Earthscan.

Paul, S. and S. Sekhar. 1997. "A Report Card on Public Services". *Regional Development Dialogue* 18, 2 (Autumn.)

Perraton, J. et al. 1997. "The Globalisation of the Economic Activity". *New Political Economy* 2, 2.

Petras, J. 1998. "Continuismo in Latin America: Detour in the Democratic Transition". *LASA Forum* (September).

Petchesky, R. 1995. "From Population Control to Reproductive Rights: Feminist Fault Lines". *Reproductive Health Matters*, 6.

Petchesky, R and K. Judd/IRRRAG. 1998. *Negotiating Reproductive Rights: Women's Perspectives Across Countries and Cultures*. London: Zed Books, and New York: St. Martin's Press.

Phillips, A. 1991. *Engendering Democracy*. Cambridge: Polity Press.

________. 1992. "Must Feminists Give up on Liberal Democracy?" *Political Studies*, Special Issue, Vol. XL.

Pimbert, M. and J. Pretty. 1997. *Parks, People and Professionals: Putting "Participation" into Protected Area Management*. Discussion Paper 57. Geneva: UNRISD.

Porio, E. 1997. "Urban Governance and Poverty Alleviation in Southeast Asia". In E. Porio (ed.), *Urban Governance and Poverty Alleviation in Southeast Asia: Trends and Prospects*. Toronto: Global Urban Research Initiative.

Porter, M. and C. van der Linde. 1995. "Green and Competitive: Ending the Stalemate". *Harvard Business Review* (Sept.-Oct.).

Premdas, R. 1995. *Ethnic Conflict and Development: The Case of Guyana*. Aldershot: Avebury and UNRISD.

Przeworski, A. 1993. *Democracy and the Market*. New York: Cambridge University Press.

Pugh, C. 1996. *Sustainability, the Environment and Urbanization*. London: Earthscan.

Puiggros, A. 1997. "A World Bank Education Policy: Market Liberalism Meets Ideological Conservatism". *International Journal of Health Services* 27, 2.

Queisser, M. 1998. *Pension Reform: Lessons from Latin America*. Policy Brief 15. Paris: OECD Development Centre.

Rai, S. 1996. "Women and the State in the Third World: Some Issues for Debate". In S. Rai and G. Lievesley (eds.), *Women and the State: International Perspectives*. London: Taylor and Francis, Ltd.

Randel, J. and T. German. 1997. *The Reality of Aid 1997/98: An Independent Review of Development Cooperation*. London: Earthscan and ICVA-EUROSTEP.

Randel, J., T. German and D. Ewing. 1998. *The Reality of Aid 1998/1999: An Independent Review of Poverty Reduction and Development Assistance*. London: Earthscan and EUROSTEP-ICVA.

________. 2000. *The Reality of Aid 2000: An Independent Review of Poverty Reduction and Development Assistance*. London: Earthscan.

Rao, J. 1999. "Globalization and the Fiscal Autonomy of the State". Background paper for the *Human Development Report* 1999. UNDP, New York.

Razavi, S. 1999. "Export-Oriented Employment, Poverty and Gender: Contested Accounts". *Development and Change* 30, 3 (July).

Reilly, B. and A. Reynolds. 1999. *Electoral Systems and Conflicts in Divided Societies*. Papers on International Conflict Resolution, No. 2. Committee on International Conflict Resolution, Commission on Behavioural and Social Sciences and Education, Washington, DC: National Research Council.

Rich, B. 1994. *Mortgaging the Earth*. London: Earthscan.

Richter, J. forthcoming. *The Regulation of the Infant Food Industry* (provisional title).

Rodrik, D. 1997. *Has Globalization Gone Too Far?* Washington, DC: Institute for International Economics.

Rose, R., W. Mishler and C. Haepfer. 1998. *Democracy and Its Alternatives: Understanding Post-Communist Societies*. Cambridge: Polity Press.

Samol, F. 1998. *Sustainability through People's Participation in Urban Development in Selected Asian Cities: The Philippine Experience*. Dresden: Büro für Stadtentwicklung und Umweltplanung.

SAPRIN. 1999. *Saprin Update* (November). <http://www.igc.apc.org/dgap/sparin/update_1199.html>

Sawer, M. 1996. *Femocrats and Ecorats: Women's Policy Machinery in Australia, Canada and New Zealand.* Beijing Occasional Paper 6. Geneva: UNRISD.

Schild, V. 1995. "NGOs' Feminist Politics and Neo-Liberal Latin American State Formations: Some Lessons from Chile". *Canadian Journal of Development Studies*, Special Issue: 123-147.

Schmidheiny, S. 1992. *Changing Course: A Global Business Perspective on Development and the Environment.* Cambridge: MIT Press.

Schmidheiny, S., R. Chase and L. DeSimone. 1997. *Signals of Change: Business Progress Towards Sustainable Development.* Geneva: WBCSD.

Schneider, H. 1997. *Microfinance for the Poor?* Paris: OECD Development Centre and IFAD.

Scoones, I., C. Reij and C. Toulmin. 1996. *Sustaining the Soil: Indigenous Soil and Water Conservation in Africa.* Drylands Programme Issues Paper 67. London: IIED.

Sen, A. 1997. "Human Rights and Human Values". *The New Republic* (July 14). <http://www.mtholyoke.edu/acad/intrel/sen.htm>

Silliman, J. 1999. "Expanding Civil Society, Shrinking Political Spaces: The Case of Women's Nongovermental Organizations". In Silliman and King (eds.), *Dangerous Intersections: Feminist Perspectives on Population, Environment and Development.* Boston: South End Press.

Singh, A. 1995. "The Causes of Fast Economic Growth in East Asia". *UNCTAD Review.*

________. 1996. "Pension Reform, the Stock Market, Capital Formation and Economic Growth: A Critical Commentary on the World Bank's Proposals". *International Social Security Review* 49, 3.

Sinha, S. 1998. *Micro-Credit: Impact, Targeting and Sustainability.* Special Issue of the *IDS Bulletin* 29, 4.

SIPRI. 1999. *1999 Yearbook.* Oxford: Oxford University Press.

Social Watch. 1998. *Social Watch* (No. 2). Montevideo: Instituto del Tercer Mundo.

________. 1999. *Social Watch* (No. 3). Montevideo: Instituto del Tercer Mundo.

Solimano, A. forthcoming. "Beyond Unequal Development: An Overview". In A. Solimano, E. Aninat and N. Birdsall (eds.), *Distributive Justice and Economic Development.* Ann Arbor: University of Michigan Press.

Sørensen, G. 1993. *Political Conditionality.* London: Frank Cass.

South Centre. 1999. *HIPC: The Limitations of an Initiative.* Geneva.

Stalker, P. 2000a. *The Oxford Handbook of the World.* London: Oxford University Press.

______. 2000b. *Workers Without Frontiers.* Boulder: Lynne Rienner and ILO

Standing, G. 1999a. *Global Labour Flexibility: Seeking Distributive Justice.* London: Macmillan.

________. 1999b. "Global Feminization through Flexible Labour: A Theme Revisited". *World Development* 27, 3.

Standing, H. 1999. *Framework for Understanding Gender Inequalities and Health Sector Reform: An Analysis and Review of Policy Issues.* Working Paper Series 99.06. Cambridge: Harvard Center for Population and Development Studies, Harvard University.

Stavasage, D. and D. Moyo. 1999. *Are Cash Budgets a Cure for Excess Fiscal Deficits (and at What Cost)?* WPS/99-11. Oxford: Centre for the Study of African Economies, University of Oxford.

Stavenhagen, R. 1997. *Ethnic Conflicts and the Nation State.* London: Macmillan and UNRISD.

Stiefel, M. and M. Wolfe. 1994. *A Voice for the Excluded. Popular Participation in Development: Utopia or Necessity?* London: Zed Books and UNRISD.

Stepan, A. and C. Skach. 1994. "Presidentialism and Parliamentalism in Comparative Perspective". In J.L. Linz and A. Valuenzela (eds.) *The Failure of Presidential Democracy: Comparative Perspectives*, Vol. 1. Baltimore: Johns Hopkins University Press.

Stewart, F. 1994. "Are Short-Term Policies Consistent with Long-Term Development Needs in Africa?". In G.A. Cornia and G. Helleiner (eds.), *From Adjustment to Development in Africa: Conflict, Controversy, Convergence, Consensus?* London: Macmillan.

Stokke, O. 1995. *Aid and Political Conditionality.* London: Frank Cass.

Szalai, J. 1998. "Women and Democratization: Some Notes on Recent Changes in Hungary". In J.S. Jaquette and S.L. Wolchik (eds.), *Women and Democracy: Latin America and Central and Eastern Europe.* Baltimore: Johns Hopkins University Press.

Tamale, S. 1997. "When Hens Begin to Crow: Gender and Parliamentary Politics in Contemporary Uganda". Ph.D. dissertation submitted to the faculty of the University of Minnesota.

Tansel, A. 1997. "Schooling Attainment, Parental Education, and Gender in Côte D'Ivore and Ghana". *Economic Development and Cultural Change* 445, 4.

Tanzi, V. 1996. "Globalization, Tax Competition and the Future of Tax Systems". Working Paper WP/96/141. Washington, DC: IMF.

ToBI. 1997. "NGO Perspective on Responsible Entrepreneurship". <http://ww.coopamerica.org/isf/tobi/resp-entr>

Tokman, V. 1997. "Jobs and Solidarity: Challenges and Post-Adjustment in Latin America". In L. Emmerij (ed.), *Economic and Social Development into the XXI Century.* Washington, DC: IADB.

Toynbee, P. 2000. "Drowing in Poverty". *The Guardian.* (7 January).

TRAC. 1999. *A Perilous Partnership: The United Nations Development Programme's Flirtation with Corporate Collaboration.* San Francisco.

Trade Union World. 1999. "Trade Unionists—Environmentalists: The Same Fight?", Vol. 2 (February).

Transparency International. 1999. "1999 Bribe Payers Index. 1999 Corruption Perceptions Index". <http://www.transparency.de/documents/cpi/index.html>

Tripp, A.M. 1994. "Gender, Political Participation and the Transformation of Associational Life in Uganda and Tanzania". *African Studies Review* 37, 1.

Tzannatos, Z. 1999. "Women and Labour Market Changes in the Global Economy". *World Development* 27, 3.

Ul Haq, M., I. Kaul and I. Grunberg. 1998. *The Tobin Tax: Coping with Financial Volatility*. New York: Oxford University Press.

UNCTAD. 1996. *Self-Regulation of Environmental Management: An Analysis of Guidelines Set by World Industry Associations for Their Member Firms*. Geneva.

________. 1999. *World Investment Report 1999: Foreign Direct Investment and the Challenge of Development*. Geneva.

UNDP. 1993. *Rethinking Technical Co-operation: Reforms for Capacity Building in Africa*. Regional Bureau for Africa, New York.

________. 1994. *Human Development Report*. New York: Oxford University Press.

________. 1995. *Human Development Report* . New York: Oxford University Press.

________. 1997. *Human Development Report*. New York: Oxford University Press.

________. 1998a. *Human Development Report 1998*. New York: Oxford University Press.

________. 1998b. *Overcoming Human Poverty*. New York.

________. 1999a. *Human Development Report 1999*. New York: Oxford University Press.

________. 1999b. *Human Development Report for Central and Eastern Europe and the CIS*. New York.

UNEP. 1994. *Company Environmental Reporting: A Measure of the Progress of Business and Industry towards Sustainable Development*. London and Paris: SustainAbility/ UNEP Industry and Environment.

________. 1998. "Voluntary Initiatives for Responsible Entrepreneurship: A Question and Answer Guide". *Industry and Environment* 21, 1–2(January-June).

________. 1999. *Global Environment Outlook 2000*. London: Earthscan.

UNESCO. 1998a. *World Education Report 1998*. Paris.

________. 1998b. "UNESCO Calls for New Paradigm for Literacy". UNESCO Press Release 98–182. <http://www.unesco.org/opi/eng/unescopress/98-182e.htm>

UNESCO Courier. 1998. "We Have a Multi-Party System—But It Is Not True Democracy", No. 168. Paris.

UNFPA. 2000. "Urbanization Accelerating". <http://www.unfpa.org/modules/intercenter/upshort/urbaniza.htm>

UNICEF. 1998. *The State of the World's Children 1998*. New York: Oxford University Press.

________. 1999. *The State of the World's Children 1999*. New York: Oxford University Press.

________. 2000. *The State of the World's Children 2000*. New York: Oxford University Press.

UNICEF and OXFAM. 1999. "Debt Relief and Poverty Reduction: Meeting the Challenge". International Position Paper. New York: UNICEF and Oxford: OXFAM (August).

UNICEF, UNDP, UNESCO, UNFPA and WHO. 1998. *Implementing the 20/20 Initiative: Achieving Universal Access to Basic Social Services*. New York: UNICEF.

United Nations. 1995a. *Macroeconomic Policy Questions: External Debt Crisis and Development. The Developing Country Debt Situation As Of Mid-1995*. Report of the Secretary General. Document A/50/379 (31 August).

________. 1995b. *World Summit for Social Development: The Copenhagen Declaration and Programme of Action*. Department of Public Information, New York.

________. 1995c. *World Economic and Social Survey 1995*. New York.

________. 1997a. *Debt Situation of the Developing Countries As At Mid-1997*. Report of the Secretary General. Document A/52/150 (18 August).

________. 1997b. *Sustaining Social Security*. Department for Economic and Social Information and Policy Analysis, New York.

________. 1997c. "Comprehensive Assessment of the Freshwater Resources of the World". Report of the Secretary General. <http:// www.un.org/esa/sustdev/freshwat.htm>

________. 1997d. *The Dancing Horizon: Human Development Prospects for Bangladesh*. Dhaka.

________. 1998. *World Population Prospects: The 1998 Revision*. Department for Economic and Social Information and Policy Analysis, New York.

________. 1999. *Finding Solutions to the Debt Problems of Developing Countries*. Report of the Executive Committee on Economic and Social Affairs, New York.

UNRISD. 1995. *States of Disarray: The Social Effects of Globalization*. Geneva.

Van Ginneken, W. 1996. *Social Security for the Informal Sector: Issues, Options and Tasks Ahead*. Working Paper. Geneva: Social Security Department, ILO.

Van Rooy, A. 1998. *Civil Society and the Aid Industry*. London: Earthscan.

Vivian, J. 1995. *Adjustment and Social Sector Restructuring*. London: Frank Cass and UNRISD.

Von Moltke, K. et al. 1998. "Global Product Chains: Northern Consumers, Southern Producers and Sustainability". *Environment and Trade* 15, Geneva: UNEP.

Wade, R. 1991. *Governing Markets*. London: Macmillan.

Wallensteen, P. and M. Sollenberg. 1998. "Armed Conflict and Regional Conflict Complex, 1989–97". *Journal of Peace Research* 35, 5.

Warburton, P. 1999. *Debt and Delusion: Central Bank Follies That Threaten Economic Disaster*. London: Penguin Press.

Watts, P. and Lord Holme. 1999. *Meeting Changing Expectations: Corporate Social Responsibility*. Geneva: WBCSD.

Waylen, G. 1993. "Women's Movements and Democratisation in Latin America". *Third World Quarterly* 13, 3.

WBCSD. 1999. "Why is CSR Climbing on the International Agenda?" *Tomorrow* 9, 3 (May/June).

WCED. 1987. *Our Common Future*. Oxford: Oxford University Press.

WEDO. 1999. *Risks, Rights and Reforms: A 50-Country Survey Assessing Government Actions Five Years After the International Conference on Population and Development*. New York.

Weiss, T.G. 1999. *International NGOs, Global Governance, and Social Policy in the UN System*. GASPP Occasional Paper 3. Helsinki: Stakes.

Welford, R. 1997. *Hijacking Environmentalism: Corporate Responses to Sustainable Development*. London: Earthscan.

West, K. 1995. "Ecolabels: The Industrialization of Environmental Standards". *The Ecologist* 25, 1 (January/February).

Westendorff, D. and K. Dey. 1996. *Their Choice or Yours: Global Forces or Local Voices?* Discussion Paper 79. Geneva: UNRISD.

White, S. 1996. "Depoliticising Development: The Uses and Abuses of Participation". *Development in Practice* 6, 1 (February).

WHO. 1996. *World Health Report 1996*. Geneva.

________. 1997. *World Health Report 1997*. Geneva.

Wild, A. 1998. *A Review of Corporate Citizenship and Social Initiatives: Social Citizenship—What's Going On … and Why?* Geneva: Enterprise and Cooperative Development Department, ILO.

Wilfried Derksen's Electoral Website. <http://www.agora.stm/elections/election.htm>

Wolfe, M. *Social Integration: Institutions and Actors*. Occasional Paper 4. Geneva: UNRISD.

Wolfensohn, J. 1999. *A Proposal for a Comprehensive Development Framework*. Discussion draft. Washington, DC: World Bank. <http://www.worldbank.org/html/extdr/cdf/cdf.pdf>

Woo-Cumings, M. 1999. *The Developmental State*. Ithaca: Cornell University Press.

Wood, A., P. Stedman-Edwards and J. Mang. 2000. *Root Causes of Biodiversity Loss*. London: Earthscan.

World Bank. 1988. *Education in Sub-Saharan Africa: Policies for Adjustment, Revitalisation, and Expansion*. Washington, D.C.

________. 1990. *World Development Report 1990*. New York: Oxford University Press.

________. 1993. *The East Asian Miracle: Economic Growth and Public Policy*. Washington, DC.

________. 1994. *The World Bank's Role in Human Resource Development in Sub-Saharan Africa: Education, Training and Technical Assistance*. Washington, DC.

________. 1995a. *World Development Report 1995*. New York: Oxford University Press.

________. 1995b. *Bureaucrats in Business: The Economics and Politics of Government Ownership*. New York: Oxford University Press.

________. 1997a. *World Development Report 1997: The State in a Changing World*. New York: Oxford University Press.

________. 1997b. *Fiscal Management in Adjustment Lending*. Washington, DC.

________. 1997c. *Annual Report*. Washington, DC.

________. 1998a. *Assessing Aid: What Works, What Doesn't and Why*. New York: Oxford University Press.

________. 1998b. *The Impact of Public Expenditure Reviews: An Evaluation*. Washington, DC.

________. 1998c. *Global Development Finance: Analysis and Summary Tables*. Washington, DC.

________. 1998d. *The Public Expenditure Management Handbook*. Washington, DC.

________. 1998e. *Privatisation in Africa*. Washington, DC.

________. 1998f. *African Development Indicators 1998/1999*. Washington, DC.

________. 1999a. *Poverty Trends and the Voices of the Poor*. Washington, DC.

________. 1999b. *World Development Indicators 1999* (CD-Rom). Washington, DC.

________. 1999c. *World Development Report 1999/2000*. Washington, DC.

World Commission on Dams. 1999. *Interim Report*. Cape Town.

Young, C. 1999. *Ethnic Diversity and Public Policy: A Comparative Enquiry*. London: Macmillan and UNRISD.

YUVA. 1999. *Our Home is a Slum: An Exploration of a Community and Local Government Collaboration in a Tenant's Struggle to Establish Legal Residency in Janata Squatters Colony, Mumbai, India*. Discussion Paper 107. Geneva: UNRISD.

Zarrilli, S., V. Jha and R. Vossenaar. 1997. *Eco-Labelling and International Trade*. London: Macmillan.

Acronyms

ACBF	African Capacity Building Foundation
ADB	Asian Development Bank
AIDS	acquired immunodeficiency syndrome
ALOP	Latin American Association of Promotion Organizations
ANC	African National Congress
BHF	Business Humanitarian Forum
BP	British Petroleum
BRAC	Bangladesh Rural Advancement Committee
BWI	Bretton Woods institution
CBO	community-based organization
CEE	Central and Eastern Europe
CIM	Interregional Mapuche Council
CIS	Commonwealth of Independent States
CODESRIA	Council for the Development of Social Science Research in Africa
CSO	civil society organization
DAC	Development Assistance Committee (OECD)
DAWN	Development Alternatives with Women for a New Era
DCD	Development Cooperation Directory (OECD)
DECOPAZ	Community Development for Peace
EBRD	European Bank for Reconstruction and Development
ECLAC	Economic Commission for Latin America and the Caribbean
ECOSOC	United Nations Economic and Social Council
EU	European Union
EURODAD	European Network on Debt and Development
FAO	Food and Agriculture Organization of the United Nations
FDI	foreign direct investment
FGM	female genital mutilation
G-7	Group of Seven
GATT	General Agreement on Tariffs and Trade
GDP	gross domestic product
GM	genetically modified
GNP	gross national product
HDI	Human Development Index
HDR	Human Development Report
HERA	Health, Empowerment, Rights and Accountability
HIPC	Heavily Indebted Poor Country
HIV	human immunodeficiency virus
ICLEI	International Council for Local Environmental Initiatives
IDB	Inter-American Development Bank
IDA	International Development Association
IDRC	International Development Research Centre
IDS	Institute of Development Studies
IFAD	International Fund for Agricultural Development
IFI	international financial institution
ILAS	Institute of Latin American Studies
ILO	International Labour Organization
IMF	International Monetary Fund
IMT	Irrigation Management Turnover
IDEA	Institute for Democracy and Electoral Assistance
IPS	Institute for Policy Studies
IPU	Inter-Parliamentary Union
IRN	International Rivers Network
IRRRAG	International Reproductive Rights Research Action Group
ISO	International Organization for Standardization
IUCN	World Conservation Union
JFM	Joint Forest Management

KEWWO	Kenya Women Workers Organization
MAI	Multilateral Agreement on Investment
MP	Member of Parliament
MST	Landless Rural Workers Movement
NAFTA	North American Free Trade Agreement
NEDLAC	National Economic Development and Labour Council
NGDO	non-governmental development organization
NGO	non-governmental organization
NIC	newly industrialized country
NPM	new public management
NRM	National Resistance Movement
ODA	official development assistance
ODF	other development finance
ODI	Overseas Development Institute
OECD	Organisation for Economic Cooperation and Development
OPA	old public administration
OSCE	Organization for Security and Cooperation in Europe
POA	Programme of Action
PPP	purchasing power parity
REFLECT	Regenerated Freirean Literacy through Empowering Community Techniques
ReproSalud	Reproductive Health in the Community Project
RORE	rates of return on education
SANCO	South African NGO Coalition
SAP	structural adjustment programme
SAPRIN	Structural Adjustment Programme Review Initiative Network
SARD	Sustainable Agriculture and Rural Development
SERNAM	Ministry of Planning of the National Service for Women
SEWA	Self-Employed Women's Association
SHAPE	Swaziland Schools HIV/AIDS and Population Programme
SIPRI	Stockholm International Peace Research Institute
STD	sexually transmitted disease
SUNAT	National Tax Office
TNC	transnational corporation
ToBI	Taskforce on Business and Industry
TRAC	Transnational Resource and Action Center
UK	United Kingdom
UN	United Nations
UNAIDS	Joint United Nations Programme on HIV/AIDS
UNCHS	United Nations Centre for Human Settlements (Habitat)
UNCTAD	United Nations Conference on Trade and Development
UNDP	United Nations Development Programme
UNEP	United Nations Environment Programme
UNESCO	United Nations Educational, Scientific and Cultural Organization
UNFPA	United Nations Population Fund
UNHCR	United Nations High Commissioner for Refugees
UNICEF	United Nations Children's Fund
UNRISD	United Nations Research Institute for Social Development
US	United States
USAID	United States Agency for International Development
YUVA	Youth for Unity and Voluntary Action
WBCSD	World Business Council for Sustainable Development
WDR	World Development Report
WEDO	Women's Environment and Development Organization
WHO	World Health Organization
WTO	World Trade Organization
WWF	World Wide Fund for Nature